D0909509

.⩘ **BOX** to remove this checkout from your record.
⸱ ⁚n on or before date due.

ᎯTE DUE   DATE DUE

MONEY, INFLATION AND EMPLOYMENT

Money, Inflation and Employment

Essays in Honour of James Ball

Edited by

S. Holly

University of Sheffield, UK

Edward Elgar

© S. Holly 1994

All rights reserved. No part of this publication may be reproduced, stored in a
retrieval system, or transmitted in any form or by any means, electronic, mechanical,
photocopying, recording, or otherwise without the prior permission of the publisher.

Published by
Edward Elgar Publishing Limited
Gower House
Croft Road
Aldershot
Hants GU11 3HR
England

Edward Elgar Publishing Company
Old Post Road
Brookfield
Vermont 05036
USA

British Library Cataloguing in Publication Data
Money, Inflation and Employment: Essays in
Honour of James Ball
  I. Holly, Sean
  332.4

Library of Congress Cataloguing in Publication Data
Money, inflation and employment: essays in honour of James Ball /
  edited by S. Holly.
      p.   cm.
   Includes bibliographical references and index.
     1. Great Britain—Economic conditions—1945– 2. Great Britain–
   Economic policy—1945– 3. Macroeconomics. I. Holly, Sean.
   HC256.6.M6487 1994
   338.941—dc20   93-41074
                                                                        CIP

ISBN 1 85278 711 2
Printed and Bound in Great Britain by
Hartnolls Limited, Bodmin, Cornwall.

Contents

Contributors

Jeremy Bray, Member of Parliament.

Alan Budd, HM Treasury, London, UK.

Sir Terence Burns, HM Treasury, London, UK.

Keith B. Church, ESRC Macroeconomic Modelling Bureau, University of Warwick, Coventry, UK.

Michael P. Clements, Institute of Economics and Statistics and Nuffield College, Oxford, UK.

Robert M. Coen, Department of Economics, Northwestern University, US.

David Currie, Centre for Economic Forecasting, London Business School, UK.

Stephen Hall, Centre for Economic Forecasting, London Business School, UK.

David F. Hendry, Institute of Economics and Statistics and Nuffield College, Oxford, UK.

Bert G. Hickman, Department of Economics, Stanford University, US.

Laurence R. Klein, University of Pennsylvania, US.

Bill Robinson, London Economics, UK.

Harold Rose, London Business School, UK.

Kenneth F. Wallis, ESRC Macroeconomic Modelling Bureau, University of Warwick, Coventry, UK.

Introduction

This book contains ten essays by distinguished economists to mark the 60th birthday of Sir James Ball. Jim's contribution to the development of econometric modelling in the United Kingdom has been immense. Many of the authors acknowledge the influence that Jim Ball has had on their own thinking about economic policy and the development of macroeconometric models. With Laurence Klein he constructed the first complete model[1] of the UK, using quarterly data and in 1959 published a forecast in the *Bulletin of the Oxford University Institute of Statistics*. Long gone are the days when an academic journal would regard a mere forecast as sufficiently novel to warrant publication. But in 1959 such an event was novel. Because of the scarcity of quarterly data, and the return of Klein to the United States, work on the model was abandoned. By the mid 1960s the greater availability of data and increased computational power made a further modelling effort worthwhile and Jim with Terry Burns put together a small model of the UK economy. This model was then used to produce forecasts and in 1966 they began to be published three times a year in the *Sunday Times*. Of course both the Treasury and the National Institute had been producing regular forecasts for a number of years. But the efforts of Jim and Terry at the London Business School were the first where a completely integrated and computable model was used. After initial scepticism, this practice spread in time to the National Institute, the Treasury and the Bank of England and into the City of London.

One of the features of Jim Ball's early work at the LBS in modelling the economy was that it was not enough to provide forecasts. A regular contribution to the economic policy debate using the model as underpinning was also essential. His influence in changing long held views on the conduct of economic policy is illustrated by Alan Budd in his contribution. It is also attested by the presence of ex-LBS economists at the highest levels of economic policy making. The switch in influence from Oxbridge to London can be traced to his success in building up the reputation of the LBS.

The book is divided broadly into those papers that address aspects of economic policy and those that address technical aspects of modelling and forecasting. However, this is not a hard and fast distinction. There are many overlaps. The contribution by Jeremy Bray, for example, reflects his long standing interest in the application of optimal control methods to economic policy making. As Jeremy explains in his paper, he was instrumental in getting a number of amendments to the Industry Act of 1976 that required the Treasury to, among other things, make its econometric model publicly available. He also won an agreement that the Treasury would set up a Committee to look into the applicability of optimal control methods. The Committee chaired by Jim Ball duly reported in 1978.

The contribution by Alan Budd provides a nice illustration of the influence that Jim in collaboration with Terry Burns had on the evolution of economic policy during the 1970s and 1980s after the abandonment of the Bretton Woods system and the movement towards floating exchange rates. Many of the issues that were current then still lie at the heart of more recent economic debates. Changes in the nominal exchange rate do not have a permanent effect on the balance of payments. Competitiveness, the real exchange rate, depends in the long run on real factors. A similar theme is also taken up by Bill Robinson and expanded on in the context of the effect of North Sea Oil on the British economy.

The econometric aspects of the effects of a change in the nominal exchange rate is taken up by Keith Church and Ken Wallis who look at the extent to which the price and wage systems in a number of econometric models deliver long-run homogeneity and therefore make the real exchange rate independent in the long run of changes in the nominal exchange rate.

A number of papers in this volume demonstrate the extent to which the problems facing economic modellers evolve over time. Few would have anticipated when the first models were constructed that unemployment would become such a seemingly intractable problem. Robert Coen and Bert Hickman provide a study of UK unemployment and look at the role of real wage rigidity and effective demand. Expectations have always been a key element in any model, and Jim Ball was always very conscious of the key role of expectations for understanding macroeconomic events. But the rational expectations revolution of the 1970s changed radically how they are treated. David Currie and Steven Hall provide a survey of how modellers have sought to endogenize forward looking expectations in order to bring empirical macroeconomic models closer to what microeconomic theorizing implied about behaviour. However, it is difficult to treat expectations without also addressing the nature of uncertainty. Laurence Klein takes up this theme and examines the effect of uncertainty on decision-making and how uncertainty can be handled with econometric models. When forecasting with macroeconometric models it has been the practice to produce the actual forecast by combining the outcome from the model with other auxiliary information as well as judgement. This practice of intercept adjustment is examined from a theoretical perspective in the contribution by David Hendry and Michael Clements as part of an effort to provide a theory of economic forecasting and to understand clearly the conditions under which intercept adjustments will improve a forecast.

Jim still remains an active teacher and researcher while also acting as Chairman of Legal and General and a director of numerous companies. May he continue to do so for many more years.

Note

1. The claim for constructing the first macro-model of the UK economy goes to Radice (1939). However, his model was very rudimentary and amounted to only four behavioural equations and two identities.

References

Klein, L.R., Ball R.J. and Hazelwood, A (1959), 'Econometric Forecasts for 1959', *Bulletin of the Oxford University Institute of Statistics*, **21** (1), February.

Radice, E.A. (1939), 'A Dynamic Scheme for the British Trade Cycle, 1929–1937', *Econometrica*, **7** (1), January, pp. 47–56.

PART I

QUESTIONS OF
ECONOMIC POLICY

1   The game of managing the economy

Jeremy Bray

The Ball Committee on Policy Optimization

The origins of the Ball Committee on Policy Optimization are not well documented. 'Yes, Mrs Butler' were the only words spoken in the House of Commons on my amendment to the Industry Bill 1975, which opened the way. They were my reply to the Chairman of the Committee, when asked if I wished to move formally a new Schedule to the Bill. The Schedule required the publication of Treasury forecasts and access to the Treasury model, and the statement of policy priorities by the Treasury.

The Industry Bill provided the statutory basis for the industrial policy of the 1974–79 Labour Government, with its apparatus of planning agreements between the Government and individual firms. I felt that if firms were to be encouraged to set out the basis of their plans, government should do likewise – a sentiment which commended itself as much to the Conservative Party in opposition as it did to all back-bench Labour members of the Committee on the Bill, as recorded in the votes of the Committee. The Committee stage of the Bill ended in some confusion with Prime Minister Harold Wilson switching Trade and Industry Minister, Tony Benn (the prime architect of the policy) with Energy Minister, Eric Varley, who was put in to emasculate the policy. My Schedule slipped through undebated, as it did in the Report stage on the floor of the House. Here, the Government attempt to remove the amendment was defeated, with a large back-bench Labour revolt supported by the Conservative opposition. Had I been able to explain policy optimization to the House of Commons at that time, I doubt if it would have reduced the time Britain has taken painfully to move towards viable principles of economic policy.

The House of Lords did at least have a debate (28 July 1975). Roy Kahn said he thought my amendment was a Conservative initiative to discredit the Bill or to expose the Treasury to public ridicule. That was mild compared with Thomas Balogh's characteristic reaction in the lobby after the debate: fortunately he was gagged in the debate itself because he was a Government adviser at the time.

Years later I asked Nicholas Kaldor (out of the hearing of others) why, to elucidate a point he had been arguing, he did not use control theory, which had become a part of the tool kit of any bright economics graduate student. He replied simply, 'You cannot teach an old dog new tricks'.

Since old dogs are nearly as good at old tricks as young dogs (Rabbitt *et al.*, 1992), the lesson is to learn new tricks young. That Professor Ball did. Klein and Ball, Hazelwood and Vandome (1961), published when Ball was 28 years old, was for me as for many others my introduction to the empirical macro-economic modelling of the British economy.

The clauses on the Disclosure of Information in the final Industry Act were drafted one afternoon by Harold Wilson himself, as he told some of us with glee at dinner in the House that evening. His intention was so to hedge about the requirements on firms to disclose information as to make them inoperable. All Part IV of the Industry Act 1975 on the Disclosure of Information has since been repealed except for my amendment which governments of both parties have allowed to stand, like the smile on the face of Lewis Carroll's Cheshire cat.

My original New Schedule required the Treasury to maintain and provide access to a macroeconomic model; and to publish forecasts on alternative assumptions, an ex-post analysis of forecast errors, and estimated standard errors both of current forecasts and of the effects of changes in policy instruments. The intention of this part of the Schedule has more or less been maintained by the Treasury, but without a full model base forecast, and with such operational difficulties in running the model as to deter all but the most determined outside users. Access to the model cannot be said yet to have played any major part in debates on public policy, although it appears to have had an effect on the quality of the Treasury model.

The publication of the Treasury forecast has become a regular part of the Chancellor of the Exchequer's Autumn and Budget Statements, but it is published only in outline, with no consistent full model solution. In this respect the Treasury has not fulfilled my intention in the original Industry Bill amendment, and my understanding of what I agreed with Paymaster General, Edmund Dell, at the time. But the Treasury has offered a stiffer stick with which people can beat its back than I intended, by publishing only one forecast instead of forecasts on different assumptions.

My original version of the Schedule also contained the following paragraph:

3. The Treasury shall state on behalf of all Ministers of the Crown, the priorities in quantitative terms which the Government attaches to a marginal improvement in each macroeconomic variable, indicating thereby the trade-offs the Government will in future seek to make in adjusting the level of policy instruments.

This instruction to the Treasury to specify priorities that could be used in policy optimization was more than Treasury ministers could stomach, and Edmund Dell was deputed to do a deal with me. Had I refused, Treasury ministers would have dug in and thrown out the amendment altogether. I agreed to the omission of paragraph 3 from the revised text of the Schedule moved by the Government in the Lords, in return for the setting up of a Committee on Policy Optimization under the Chairmanship of Professor R.J. Ball. The Committee may have been justified in its view that, 'rather than setting up *ad hoc* Committees on technical questions it would be better if the Treasury contained within itself, but open to the outside world, a capability to assess new ideas such as optimal control as they are produced' (Ball Committee, para. 43). But to be fair to the Treasury, Parliament had not left it that option.

Ball was a natural choice for Chairman, when Edmund Dell put it to me. Following his early work with Klein, he had initiated the London Business School (LBS) model as the first macroeconomic model to produce regular forecasts of the UK economy.

I had first encountered Treasury forecasting when John Boreham, whom I had met in 1961 at Richard Stone's first presentation of the Growth Model at Cambridge, invited me as a new MP in 1962 to have lunch with the core of the interdepartmental forecasting team. (It is difficult to imagine that happening today in these days of open government.) The core consisted at that time of Wynn Godley and Patricia Brown from the Treasury, and John Boreham from the Central Statistical Office. The methods seemed to me capable of improvement.

Later, after the 1966 general election when I became a junior minister in the Ministry of Power, I asked for and got the papers of the Official Cabinet Committee which produced the forecast, of which only a bowdlerized version went on to ministers. In the wake of the discovery of gas and the prospects of oil in the North Sea, I urged a full fuel policy review, despite the superficial job published by the Ministry of Power just before the election. The idea of a fresh review won the enthusiastic support of Robert Nield and John Hunt from the Treasury. So the Treasury may have been more ready to listen when I suggested that they should follow up the modelling lines opened up by Ball in the UK. Ball was invited to sit in on a Treasury round estimating the effect of a tax change, and to model the process. This led to the Treasury decision to build its own model, developed from the LBS approach.

Ball had been following the work on the use of control theory methods in empirical macroeconomics by the misnamed Programme of Research on Econometric Methods, which I had proposed and helped to launch in 1971 at Queen Mary College with Maurice Peston and John Westcott. The project moved to Imperial College as the Programme for Research in Optimal Policy Evaluation, and continued for 20 years. Its optimization methods or similar methods were adopted by all the main UK modelling teams. (See, for example, Rustem *et al.*, 1978; Holly *et al.*, 1979; Rustem and Zarrop, 1979; Zarrop *et al.*, 1979; Rustem, 1981; Artis and Karakitsos, 1983; Holly and Zarrop, 1983; Karakitsos and Rustem, 1984; Becker *et al.*, 1986; Rustem, 1986; Paraskevopoulos, *et al.*, 1991.)

I urged that the Committee on Policy Optimization should include economists and control theorists with actual knowledge and experience of policy optimization on economic models, and recommended specifically Gregory Chow, David Kendrick and Karl Astrom. But the Treasury was too chauvinist to consider foreigners. Of the Committee appointed, only David Livesey had any experience of policy optimization on an empirical macroeconomic model, the other members being Tony Bispham, Gwylim Jenkins, James Mirrlees, Michael Posner, Denis Sargan and David Worswick. Gwylim Jenkins, with George Box, had made a major contribution to empirical time-series analysis rather than control, but this was in fields other than economics and before the days of vector autoregressive analysis, so Jenkins was suspected by economists. Denis Sargan was an accomplished econometrician.

The Committee conscientiously sought evidence, and Ball and Livesey met most of those working in the field on a visit to the United States. But it did not grasp where the problem lay.

Given a description of the problems addressed by policy optimization, politicians can see themselves as born policy optimizers. As the policy optimizer might say: 'We live in an uncertain and changing world. We do not know where we are or what awaits us around the next corner. We cannot ask the world to stop while we work things out. There is much that we would like to achieve, though priorities have to change with circumstances. Our task is to use our insight, knowledge and experience of the world to decide the direction, size and timing of the next steps. Whatever we do has many effects, some good, some bad. We have always to keep in mind how others will react, but we cannot make ourselves the servant of any particular interest.'

'That sounds right,' says the politician, 'I'll buy it.' 'Well then,' says the policy optimizer, 'this is my stochastic model, this my way of updating it to take account of your experience and your problems. Now what's your objective function? All right then, your priorities? Well, all right then, it doesn't make very much difference what you say. If you want to survive, this is what you'll have to do.'

'Where will that get us then?'. 'It's impossible to be sure. This is the most likely outturn, but one thing is for sure, and that is that it won't happen just like that. It may be better, or it may be worse. I'll tell you what to do next when we get there.'

'Well stuff that,' says the politician. 'Fred here tells me it's all right to do this. I cannot please everyone, and I will just have to make up my own mind.'

'Sorry, then,' says the policy optimizer, 'when we try to climb out of the ditch you are about to land us in, your priorities will have to be rather more brutish.'

It is the considerations that make policy optimization difficult to apply that also make it essential.

The final conclusion of the Ball Committee (1978, para. 44) was that: 'an optimal control framework would push in the direction of encouraging a more coherent approach to economic policy making and its public presentation'.

The Ball Report anticipated that the technical problems of policy optimization would not be difficult to overcome, and so it proved. Given the technology of the time, to install such a framework would have required perhaps a doubling of the size of the economic modelling teams, and strong leadership. Since then there has been a formidable development of economic and econometric theory and methods, in policy design and analysis, and in available computing power: the work needed could now be done with no additional resources.

The Committee, however, missed an opportunity to establish economic policy-making methods at a political and technical level which could have saved Britain from major economic policy mistakes in the 14 years which followed.

The Committee was justified in the diffuseness of its recommendations by the general tenor of the evidence it received. But it is not by the general tenor of the evidence that such a Committee has to work. It can work by rational argument, insight and analysis.

The next major economic Report on which I had more influence, the Treasury and Civil Service Committee (1981) Report on Monetary Policy, had more impact on economic policy, pointing to the inadequacy of money supply targets and the necessity of taking into account the exchange rate. It may have been less easy for a professional committee like the Committee on Policy Optimization to have been as specific as a select committee. Many individual economists, however, including Ball and Burns (1976), were quite specific at the time.

On the face of it the failure of the Committee on Policy Optimization to anticipate the fashions and avert the policy mishaps of later years lay in the methodological conservatism and narrowness of experience of the economists of the day, and the philistinism of Chancellors of the Exchequer. However the real cause may lie in the kind of policy game that economists and politicians are able to play, given their capabilities and interests.

Ensuing diversions
Old fashioned Keynesians, who had never dreamed that they were policy optimizing, were like the Bourgeois Gentilhomme, somewhat bemused when they were told by Lucas (1976), that they had been policy optimizing all their lives. Their alleged error was that they thought it a game against nature, not against rational agents who would change their game in response to whatever government did. The monetarists sought to tie up politicians with simple rules so that economic agents could be free to play their own games uninterrupted. But that did not work. Structural changes bedevilled the money supply equations when monetary targetry was pursued seriously in the UK in the early 1980s.

There were also more fundamental considerations. In the heady atmosphere of the rational expectations revolution, Kydland and Prescott (1977) proclaimed: 'We conclude that there is no way control theory can be made applicable to economic planning when expectations are rational'. But as Lucas and Sargent (1981, Introduction p. xxxvii) soon pointed out, to obtain time-consistent plans, Kydland and Prescott in effect computed a Nash equilibrium of a differential game. Far from being able to consign Riccati equations to some bonfire of control theory, they have to be solved for each agent, not just for the Chancellor of the Exchequer! Lucas and Sargent acknowledged that time inconsistency arose from the nature of the game being played. Play a different game, and nobody worries about requiring time consistency. There is no time consistency in bridge.

The fault of the Lucas critique, if there was any, was that it did not go far enough. It did not concentrate attention on the games being played.

The nature of the game

Politicians prefer bridge. You may not know all the facts, but at least you know the cards in your own hand, how to bid and how to read the other bids. The bidding is soon over. Play begins with more evidence, with possibilities of mis-understanding, but moves are soon made, and tricks won or lost. Then round again.

What are the features of bridge that politicians can cope with, and of economic policy-making that they cannot? First, bridge is explicitly a game with recognizably conflicting objectives, in which each player is equally informed about different sets of information.

Within the game, the bridge player can be far sighted, of broad vision, committed and firm. If the economic management game is constructed correctly, can the politician be so too?

A decent game depends on finding partners of the same size and skill. In the game-playing of economic agents in modern microeconomics, the agents are at least of commensurate size in oligopolistic markets, with the individual agents able to affect each other. This has been treated in a wide range of situations (Tirole, 1988). Economic management in a multi-party democracy, and between countries, is likewise a game between agents of commensurate size, and able to affect each other.

In a game between Celtic and Rangers, the supporter in the crowd, with his own personal game, is every bit as engaged in the big game as the economic agent is in his national economy.

Is it possible that we would do better to see economic management as the multi-level game that it is?

The nature of games is that they are man made, with man-made rules. Football did not have to wait until the elasticity, ballistics and aerodynamics of spherical or ellipsoidal balls had been adequately described, the speed and weight of players adequately measured, and inter-communal disputes contained within a football pitch. Nor were the rules of football frozen for all time.

Perhaps we should see economic management as a developing game, contributed to by politician-players, economist-coaches and lawyer-referees, not to mention the voter-punters.

Within the present concept of the economic management game, the process of setting the objective function to embody policy makers' priorities has been too trivial to attract the interest of economists and modellers, yet beyond certainly *my* capacity to explain to any other minister or journalist. This is not because the literature abounds with more practicable formulations of objectives and strategies by economists. Nor does the concept of priorities fail to address the needs of politicians.

Economists have concerned themselves with many more trivial matters. And many politicians have handled more complex logic and mathematics.

Nor can it simply be resistance by politicians to an idea because it comes from a colleague, and from economists because it does not come from a colleague – the right idea in the wrong place. As computers have penetrated every nook and cranny of business, science and the professions, the typical delay in applications because of such restrictive practices is perhaps ten years – not 20 years.

My submission is that it is not a problem of presentation, nor of content, nor relevance. The problem is that we think of economics and policy in the wrong way, as the wrong sort of game.

Economists – particularly academic economists – think of themselves as some sort of scientists, objectively exploring the world, pursuing positive economics. They are also prepared to admit the normative, distinguishing between what is and what ought to be. The Committee on Policy Optimization itself felt that:

> Understanding the behaviour of the economy proves in many respects more difficult than understanding the behaviour of, for example, physical systems, though the study and modelling of biological, business and other organisational systems can present problems of equal complexity and difficulty (para. 119).

In saying this, the Committee was still assimilating economics to science, or would-be science. The economy was seen as something that has to be *understood* rather than something that has to be *done*, acted in. There is no harm in understanding football or bridge. It may even help you to be a good player or coach. But it does not *make* you a good player or coach. It is the game that matters.

It has been said of one of the lawyers who has dominated what has passed for economic debate in the House of Commons in recent years, that he is never concerned with the truth – with whether or not the accused is guilty – but solely with how he can persuade the jury that the accused is innocent. Is he perhaps right?

It is not to trivialize a great concern of mankind that can bring great blessing or cursing to liken it to a game. The aim is to get it right.

Can we construct the game of economic policy in such a way that it works better? It is not a matter of throwing out the great intellectual achievements of economics, of pretending that we could do half as well if we threw out the tools that we use today. It is a matter of how we see and use those tools, and how we set about developing them.

The purely technical use of game theory is a useful development both in micro-economics and macroeconomics. However, such technical uses of game theory on their own make economics still less accessible to the policy-maker, and still more a fascinating puzzle than a game itself.

As it is seen today, the framework of economics is a positive study of objec-tively observed behaviour from which will emerge policy proposals which can be passed on to the policy-makers.

The Chancellor of the Exchequer and his Shadow are happy enough with the economic management game as it is played today. It is that that has got them where they are. The rougher the ride and the hairier the shirt, the greater the scope for their forensic skills and for abusing economists in general. Their Cabinet and Shadow Cabinet colleagues and supporters are not quite so happy.

The target is not the Treasury. In the Treasury's game the other players are other departments, foreign finance ministries and central banks. It would suit the Treasury as well if other departments were prepared to enter more fully into the economic game. As for other finance ministries and central banks, they each have their own problems, and the Treasury could reckon not to lose out if the game got faster. A badly performing economy is good for the development of economics: it generates a lot of information. The economics profession has left the British Treasury with potential intellectual strength at least equal to its foreign partners.

The micro-games, too, should be brought out more into the open. As they develop at company and sector level, they will offer a different kind of face to the macro-game. In macroeconomics today, agents are seen at best as represented by a typical agent, and more typically as dismembered contributors to national economy aggregates with the economy viewed as if it were a single agent. The macroeconomy should be seen less as a mass, and more as a mess. Moves in the macroeconomic game should instead be seen as interacting with specific, actual micro-games in a way that cannot be dismissed as market intervention.

The limitations of positive macroeconomics
The conclusion of Britton and Pain (1992), and many other similar exercises assessing the accuracy of forecasts, is that there is information in the models which has been significant for prediction. However, developments in econo-metric and measurement methods have not resulted in a secular improvement in the accuracy of economic forecasts.

There have been major structural changes in the economy with the floating of exchange rates in the early 1970s and financial deregulation in the 1980s. There is the prospect of further change with the movement towards EMU in the 1990s. There have been exogenous shocks such as the oil price increases of the 1970s, and changes in economic strategy such as monetary targetry in the 1980s. There have also been major changes in technology and the composition of output. Coupled with those considerations, modern microeconomics and perceptions of strategic behaviour by economic agents encourage doubts as to the existence of stable macroeconomic behavioural relations.

So there is no lack of possible explanations for having to run hard to stay in the same place in the accuracy of forecasts. It is a reasonable assumption that:

A.   Further improvements in methods will not increase the accuracy of forecasts, although improvements and constant vigilance will continue to be needed to track structural change.

A stronger statement is:

B.   Empirical macroeconomic models do not offer a reliable means of discriminating between rival economic theories even in cases where different theories lead to significantly different forecasts, with different implications for policy.

Put another way, it is in the no-man's land between rival non-falsified theories that the substantial debate on economic policy takes place. There have been and there will continue to be particular refutations of theories at the time when those theories are made the basis of policy. But that is different from an overwhelming consensus on the evidence. Plainly it helps if the policy community makes, and pays attention to, tests of policy against the evidence.

Another statement stronger than A. is:

C.   Models do not give sufficiently reliable forecasts to make it sensible to adopt the policy which merely gives the most acceptable or least unacceptable forecast at that point in time.

Believing statements B. and C. monetarists and others advocated simple policy rules. A conclusion from both analysis and experience of the policy rules that have been proposed leads to the statement:

D.   No operable and robust simple policy rules have been proposed, and none are likely.

The practice of macroeconomics is divided between those who implicitly accept B. and C. but reject D. and those who implicitly reject B. and C. but accept D.

The wise course seems to be to accept the limitations B. C. and D. The choice then is between the seat of the Chancellor of the Exchequer's pants, and giving more attention to the design of economic policy, using the significant information that is achievable by macroeconomic analysis, but recognizing the limitations of the evidence. It calls for new developments in econometric method, different emphases in the balance of modelling work, and different presentations of results. But more generally, it calls for a different perception of the economic policy game, in which the information is seen primarily as evidence for, and a way of defining, the next move, not simply as a positive statement about supposedly objective behaviour.

With this perspective, attention is concentrated on what matters. There may be differences in economic theory. These will lead to models with different structures. The priorities or objective function needed to represent the same broad approach to policy will then differ for different models. But the actual policy instrument adjustments called for may not differ very much. The implication, then, is that the differences in theory and models do not matter very much. The essential requirement is to carry the analysis through to the actual design of policy.

On the other hand, there may be real differences between the policy instrument adjustments called for from different theories or models. There is then the opportunity to track down the reasons for the difference, and eventually to test the performance against other theories or models in ex-post policy comparisons, which will test the whole chain of argument from theory to policy advice.

This points to the intelligent use of the increasingly powerful armoury of policy optimization, with the developments opened up by game theory. A useful step may be to demystify it by showing how far it is possible to go with quite manageable and understandable arguments.

Policy optimization results on the Treasury model

Since 1987, when it became practicable for a Member of Parliament with a desk-top computer to run non-linear policy optimization algorithms with consistent expectations on large data-based macroeconomic models, I have carried out, sent to the Chancellor of the Exchequer, the Treasury and others, and published, policy optimization exercises on the Treasury model. These have produced policy recommendations which, in retrospect, look as if they would have been less destabilizing than the policies pursued (Bray, 1987a, 1987b; Bray and Nana, 1989a, 1989b; Bray, 1990, 1992). These can now be compared both with the record and with the Chancellor's own very readable account of the considerations behind economic policy-making during this period (Lawson, 1992).

Lawson (1992) is preoccupied to the point of obsession with the fallibility of forecasts, econometrics, models and all their uses, sometimes with some justification. Straight after the 1979 election he tried to persuade Geoffrey Howe, then Chancellor of the Exchequer, to repeal my 1975 Industry Act amendment requiring the Treasury to maintain a model and publish forecasts (p. 49). He describes changes that were made in the 1980 Budget forecasts of GDP and inflation, after representations he made to Howe. The original official forecasts were 'unbelievably gloomy', and the changes brought the forecasts near to the outturn (p. 50).

When it comes to 1986–88, Lawson acknowledges; 'I cannot, however, claim to have foreseen the full extent of the boom that began to develop. Moreover, I was not helped by the Treasury's economic forecasts, which despite being regularly castigated by Labour as ludicrously optimistic, in fact seriously and consistently underestimated the strength of the outturn' (p. 643).

However, the Treasury model, reasonably used, was warning at the time about balance-of-payments difficulties and the need for corrective action, long before the 'staggering ... 1988 August trade figures and the consequent rise in base rates marked the turning point in my Chancellorship' (Lawson, 1992, p. 845). I had sent the studies described below to the Chancellor at the time and he had acknowledged them. Something in the Treasury went wrong between the model itself and the Chancellor's perception of the state of the economy.

Even with the wisdom of hindsight it is not possible to demonstrate without at least an implicit economic model that had a different policy been pursued better results would have been achieved. A different policy would have made economic agents behave differently: for a comparison, a model is needed of how agents would have changed their behaviour. There is also the question of whether the comparison of events should be with the succession of first year counter-factual departures of policy. A more valid comparison is longer trajectories of policy and cumulatively counter-factual histories, from successive points in the past. A new such ex-post trajectory could be initiated each year, and sustained for a few years.

Such a systematic comparison on, say, an annual basis, requires a counter-factual history of policy settings, built up over successive past years with the assumption that the recommended optimal policy, derived with the then available versions of the model, had been pursued at the time. No such history has been maintained for the Treasury model, and it has been beyond my resources to prepare it myself.

What is presented in Table 1.1 is, therefore, a simple comparison of the optimal policy recommendations and associated forecasts put forward in past years, compared with the outturn. Even such a comparison as this does not seem to have been put forward for any other models of the UK or any other country.

Table 1.1   Policy optimization studies on the Treasury model

	Short-term interest rate (%)	Basic rate of income tax from Q2 (%)	Real govt. expend. on cons. and investm. (%p.a.)	Retail price index (%p.a.)	Real GDP at factor cost (%p.a.)	Current balance (%GDP)	Effective exchange rate index (1985=100)	PSBR (%GDP)	Unemployment (% workforce)	Real personal disposable income (%p.a.)

27 September 1987: just before the stock market exchange crash, and modified little after it, warning of balance-of-payments problems (Bray, 1987a)

1987	10.6	27.0	2.3	3.9	3.9	−0.2	89.1	1.7	10.8	3.8
1988	9.9	27.9	1.4	6.6	3.5	−0.4	82.1	1.1	10.8	1.9
1989	7.7	28.3	1.4	5.8	4.1	−0.1	77.6	0.5	10.2	2.4
1990	10.3	27.7	1.4	8.0	3.0	−0.0	75.0	0.9	9.6	5.2
1991	10.8	27.6	1.4	8.9	2.8	−0.2	69.3	0.7	9.0	3.3
1992	9.2	27.2	1.4	7.2	3.1	0.0	65.5	0.8	8.4	1.8

5 July 1988: seeking a rationale for the Chancellor's fiscal and monetary policies (Bray, 1990)

1988	9.5	25.0	0.0	4.6	2.7	−1.7	95.1	−0.6	9.6	4.1
1989	9.8	23.8	0.4	5.8	1.1	−1.5	85.9	−0.1	9.7	2.5
1990	8.1	21.6	2.5	5.4	3.1	−1.0	80.7	0.7	9.0	3.6
1991	9.1	23.4	1.1	3.7	2.6	−0.8	80.4	−0.4	8.1	4.3
1992	8.5	23.4	0.5	5.1	1.8	−0.5	78.5	−0.8	7.7	2.8

27 June 1989: postponing poor prospects, with risk in foreign exchange markets (Bray and Nana, 1989a)

1988	10.3	25.0	−0.2	6.5	4.1	−3.1	95.5	−2.5	8.3	2.7
1989	11.1	25.0	0.0	4.7	2.7	−3.9	95.6	−2.6	6.8	3.1
1990	8.9	25.0	−0.1	3.4	1.8	−4.1	93.4	−3.3	6.7	4.3
1991	8.6	25.0	−0.3	3.3	2.3	−4.5	94.1	−3.7	6.8	3.7
1992	10.5	25.0	−0.7	4.2	1.5	−4.6	94.3	−4.1	7.0	1.7
1993	12.6	25.0	−1.2	3.3	0.6	−4.0	93.1	−4.2	8.0	0.4
1994	13.7	25.0	−1.5	2.7	1.0	−2.9	90.9	−4.2	9.1	−0.1
1995	13.8	25.0	−0.3	3.0	2.5	−1.9	86.6	−4.2	9.7	0.6
1996	13.5	25.0	1.5	5.1	4.1	−1.2	80.2	−4.5	9.4	1.8

	Short-term interest rate (%)	Basic rate of income tax from Q2 (%)	Real govt. expend. on cons. and investm. (%p.a.)	Retail price index (%p.a.)	Real GDP at factor cost (%p.a.)	Current balance (%GDP)	Effective exchange rate index (1985=100)	PSBR (%GDP)	Unemployment (% workforce)	Real personal disposable income (%p.a.)
16 February 1992: meeting the Maastricht conditions only with large sustained improvements in non-price competitiveness (Bray, 1992)										
1990	14.8	25.0	0.1	9.5	0.5	–2.6	91.3	–0.3	5.8	3.2
1991	11.6	25.0	3.5	5.7	–2.2	–1.1	91.5	1.3	8.0	1.2
1992	9.0	25.0	2.3	2.3	1.7	–1.8	91.2	2.9	9.9	1.6
1993	9.0	25.0	1.8	1.8	3.0	–2.0	91.2	3.0	10.1	3.3
1994	9.0	25.0	1.2	1.5	3.9	–2.1	91.2	2.2	9.7	3.8
1995	9.0	25.0	1.2	1.9	3.3	–2.2	91.2	1.8	8.9	3.0
1996	9.0	25.0	1.6	2.0	2.6	–2.0	91.2	1.0	8.1	2.2
1997	8.5	25.0	1.6	1.7	2.5	–1.5	91.2	1.0	7.7	1.8
1998	8.5	25.0	2.1	2.2	2.7	–0.8	91.2	1.0	7.2	1.8
1999	8.5	25.0	2.1	2.7	2.9	–0.3	91.2	1.1	6.7	2.3
2000	8.5	25.0	2.1	3.3	2.9	–0.2	91.2	1.6	6.2	2.3
Outturn estimates available on 17 November 1992										
1987	9.7	27.0	–0.0	4.1	4.8	–1.1	90.1	–0.3	10.0	3.5
1988	10.3	25.0	–0.5	4.9	4.5	–3.4	95.5	–2.5	8.1	5.7
1989	13.9	25.0	3.0	7.8	2.1	–4.2	92.6	–1.8	6.3	4.5
1990	14.8	25.0	3.7	9.5	0.6	–3.1	91.3	–0.4	5.8	2.5
1991	11.6	25.0	1.3	5.7	–2.2	–1.1	91.7	1.3	8.1	–0.5
1992	—	25.0	—	—	—	—	—	—	—	—

The appropriate standpoint in judging these studies ex post is to ask whether the policy adjustments they recommended in the first year would have been better than those actually pursued. An updating of optimal policies within the annual cycle of economic policy makes it a feedback system. The forecasts given in Table 1.1 are dependent on the optimal policies recommended having been pursued. In general the policies were not pursued, even in the first year. And as is explained below, the policy priorities or objective function in these studies were sometimes chosen to expose the consequences and risks in the declared priorities of the Chancellor rather than to recommend policies.

What secures these policy optimization results is not better short-term forecasts than anyone else's, important though accuracy is, but the balancing of short- and longer-term responses against the constraints, systematically secured by judicious use of policy optimization on the model.

All the studies sought to reduce inflation, interest rates and income tax, in line with the Government's declared priorities. A consistent expectations treatment of the exchange rate required the current balance to reach zero or some other target by the end of the period. No treatment of the exchange rate has given reliable short-term forecasts, and the general current practice in forecasting is for the forecaster to fix the path of the exchange rate. In these policy optimization studies, however, the exchange rate is determined by consistent expectations in a method provided in the Treasury model programme, in what is essentially a game between the Chancellor and foreign exchange speculators. This produces a path which is consistent with the fundamentals in the long run, and short-term interest rates consistent with exchange rate expectations in the short run, thus providing a reasonable guide to medium-term strategy, which is what economic policy requires.

The first study (Bray, 1987a) covering 1987 Q4 to 1992 Q4, was despatched on 27 September 1987 shortly before the stock market crash on 19 October. It called for an immediate increase of short-term interest rates from the current 10 per cent to 11 per cent, before falling back to 10 per cent during 1988, and for an increase in the basic rate of tax from 27 to 28 per cent in the 1988 Budget. The Chancellor had already been increasing interest rates to reduce overheating, the latest increase to 10 per cent being on 7 August.

I examined the effect of the stock market crash on 19 October immediately after the crash in a variant (Bray, 1987b) of this study, despatched on 21 October. It examined the appropriate policy response to various anticipated and unanticipated falls in the FT All Share Index, which was allowed wealth and cost of capital effects in the then current version of the Treasury model. The closest case to the outturn assumed a fall of the Index from the pre-October level of 1174 to 800 (outturn 909) in 1988, and taking over five years (outturn four years) to recover to its pre-October level. None of the variants called for a reduction in interest rates relative to the base of more than 0.7, not even reversing the direction of the increase from 10 to 11 per cent required in the base; and in the standard rate of tax of more than 0.1, scarcely touching the increase from 27 to 28 per cent required in the base.

In the event, interest rates were reduced in steps eventually to 7.5 per cent on 8 May, and the standard rate of tax was reduced from 27 to 25 per cent in the 1988 Budget, thus contributing to the boom of the late 1980s. Another consideration behind the reduction in interest rates was the attempt to shadow the Deutschmark at an exchange rate of 3.0. Lawson (1992, p. 991) himself attributes a greater part of the blame for the credit boom to the sharp fall in the sterling exchange rate in 1986. That was undoubtedly a factor, but it, too, was fully taken into account in these policy optimization studies before and after the stock exchange crash.

The study (Bray, 1990) presented on 5 July 1988, for policy for 1988 Q3 to 1992 Q4, sought to find a rational basis for these fiscal and monetary actions, and for the Chancellor's declared aim of further reducing the standard rate of income tax to 20 per cent. To justify these actions, the study reduced the weight on the balance of payments in line with the Chancellor's arguments at the time (Lawson, 1992, p.854). The terminal current balance required in 1992 Q4 was reduced from zero to a deficit at an annual rate of £3 billion. This softening of objectives allowed income tax to be reduced to 24 per cent in 1989 and 23 per cent in 1990. However, the effective exchange rate index (1985=100) would fall from 96.6 in 1988 Q2 to around 80 in 1990–92 (on 17 November 1992 it had fallen to 78.1), with inflation averaging 5 per cent in 1988–92. A variant which kept the exchange rate around 94 required an increase in income tax to above 30 per cent for one year in 1989 (although a preferable longer forecast horizon would spread the pain out more thinly). It was difficult to give a persuasive rationale for the Chancellor's actions, given the evidence of the Treasury model at the time.

The next study (Bray and Nana, 1989a) published on 27 June 1989 extended the period of study from 1989 Q2 to 1996 Q4, beyond the date of the election which would have to take place not later than 1992. By mid 1989, the balance of payments had deteriorated sharply, inflation was up, the standard rate of income tax had been held at 25 per cent, and interest rates were up to 14 per cent, with the exchange rate off the top but still above the 1986 low. The first scenario presented reflected the obvious wish of the Chancellor not to increase income tax. A terminal condition bringing the deficit on the current account to 1 per cent of GDP in 1996 Q4, however, allowed the cumulative deficits until then to turn UK net external assets from +20 per cent of GDP at end 1987 to –12 per cent of GDP at end 1996. The study suggests that the exchange rate could be held, and the poor prospects for real personal disposable incomes, interest rates and unemployment could be postponed, until after a 1992 election. Clearly there would be major risks in the foreign exchange market. Other scenarios, allowing income tax to be increased, had interest rates ending up some 2 to 3 per cent lower from 1993, but an increase in the weight on the current balance had little effect.

The 1992 study (Bray, 1992) for 1992 Q1 to 2000 Q4, was published on 16 February 1992. Nigel Lawson had resigned as Chancellor on 26 October 1989. His successor, John Major, took Britain into the Exchange Rate Mechanism on 5 October 1990. Margaret Thatcher was succeeded as Prime Minister by John Major on 27 November 1990. The Treaty of Maastricht, mapping out a course to European economic and monetary union and a single European currency, was agreed on 10 December 1991.

The 1992 study was my Treasury model contribution to a medium-term inter-model comparison with the LBS, National Institute of Economic and Social Research (NIESR) and Oxford Economic Forecasting models (Whitley *et al.,* 1992). The purpose of the comparison was to check the long-run sustainability of the current policy regime, particularly as regards the balance of payments, and to examine the ability of the UK to meet the economic conditions for convergence to EMU as laid down at Maastricht.

To get a Treasury model forecast of the current balance consistent with current policies, it had become necessary to make very large extrapolations of a recent improvement in the volume of exports of manufactures. The comparison showed that forecasters with all the models were increasing exports above the levels reflecting world trade and UK price competitiveness, although the adjustments were largest for the Treasury model.

Without the large adjustments to forecasts of the exports of manufactures on the Treasury model, I could find no consistent expectations path for the exchange rate, with or without allowing fiscal and monetary policy adjustments, given the priorities expressed in the objective function. Without policy adjustments, successive iterations progressively increased the fall in the effective exchange rate until it jumped from 91.2 in 1991 Q4 to 71.5 in 1992 Q1, ending up at 59.6 in 2000 Q4, but even that did not meet the consistent expectations conditions.

The adjustments to manufactured export volume forecasts, required to establish the sustainability of then current policies, was an improvement at a rate of at least 2 per cent p.a. (or £2billion p.a.) above the rate of increase which the Treasury model indicated would otherwise be achieved, given world trade and relative prices. It would have to be achieved by sustaining improvements in technological or non-price competitiveness from 1992 to 2000 at the rate that had been achieved in 1988–89, for just two years, when other factors may have intervened.

With these exports of manufactures adjustments, an attractive scenario is presented, with GDP growth in 1992–96 averaging 2.9 per cent, unemployment falling, inflation below 2 per cent, the current balance averaging –2 per cent of GDP, and the PSBR falling back to 1.0 per cent of GDP in 1996, after peaking at 3 per cent in 1993.

Foreign exchange markets did not find such expectations credible. Sterling fell out of the Exchange Rate Mechanism on 16 September 1992, but not before the Conservatives had won the election on 9 April 1992.

Qualitatively, the effect of such systematically derived optimal policies would have been to cause policy to respond to prospective imbalances, particularly the current balance and public sector borrowing, earlier than it did in the event.

The over-reaction to the fall in the stock market in October 1987 would have been avoided: there was little difference in the optimal policy immediately before and after the fall. The high level of interest rates in 1990–92 would have been avoided, but at the cost of forfeiting the cut in the basic rate of tax in 1988. The pound could have entered the Exchange Rate Mechanism at a more competitive level.

The challenge to make the structural changes in the economy needed to join economic and monetary union within the Maastricht timetable would still have been there, but would have been less severe.

These optimal policy studies did not call consistently for soft options, nor were they consistently pessimistic. They warned about the risks to the exchange rate, but they were not alarmist over the fall in the stock market. They were consistently better balanced and more timely than the policy pursued.

The medium-term inter-model comparison made just before the 1992 general election (Whitley *et al.*, 1992) was undertaken as an independent and impartial exercise, and published as such. It was monitored, but not influenced, by the Labour Party Economic Secretariat. Labour economic spokesmen felt it was too gloomy to offer campaign material favourable to the Labour Party: emphasis on it would not increase the credibility of the Labour Party in the campaign. The election post-mortems established that Labour's tax proposals for tax increases for higher rate taxpayers were damaging as they stood, and that Labour was less trusted by the electorate on economic policy than in other fields.

It is too early at the time of writing in November 1992 to judge the medium term assessment we made, but developments in short-term prospects have created as gloomy medium-term expectations as those projected. A political conclusion must be that reputations for economic competence have to be built up over longer periods than an election campaign.

Expressing policy-makers' priorities in an objective function

The Treasury model has been consistently eclectic in its structure, evolving in response to many sources of research (as is appropriate for such an institution) rather than drawing from a single school. This makes the Treasury model less innovative than some, but probably more robust. In recent years it appears to have been slower in taking up new research results, as policy appears to have departed further from its precepts, perhaps indicating a lack of interest from ministers and a consequent lack of resources for the construction and use of the model.

In specifying the objective function, I have followed the same method each year, as specified in para. 3 of my original Schedule to the Industry Bill 1975. It takes account of:

- the economic research expressed in the structure and coefficients of the model;
- theoretical and empirical economic research not necessarily expressed in the model;

- political realities and the explicit and implicit preferences expressed by policy-makers.

There is no one-to-one correspondence between an objective function and an economic policy or strategy, because the objective variables are not independent and some redundancy is useful in insuring against structural change. The objective function I have used has varied from year, but it has started from the previous year's specification, and tends to be rather similar.

The objectives therefore include:

- final objectives (stable prices, growth and the entailed low unemployment);
- intermediate objectives (stable exchange rate, current balance);
- policy instruments themselves (tax, interest rates, government spending);
- damping on policy instruments to prevent them from being destabilized through attempts at spurious fine-tuning.

The starting point in specifying the objective function is the set of multipliers giving the effect of each instrument on each objective. Typically this is a distributed lag, tending to a final effect, to zero, or trending up or down indefinitely. The average effect from around the third to around the fifth years – the period of critical importance in bringing the economy to equilibrium – is noted. For each instrument, the sum of the effect on each objective, multiplied by its priority, is zero at the optimum. The priority, P_i, reflects what a politician would mean by priority. The priority is related to the weight, q_i, and desired value, x_{id}, of the objective variable, x_i, in a quadratic objective function by $P_i = q_i(x_i - x_{id})$.

Table 1.2 shows how the priorities, weights and desired values can be judgementally adjusted to produce an approximately calculable medium-term optimum. With experience, an objective function specified in this way will produce a reasonable dynamic optimal policy solution at the first shot. This can then be tuned up, particularly with regard to the preferred dynamics, by trial and error policy optimizations, varying the weights and desired values in the objective function.

Thus equipped, the government has a recommended short-term policy, consistent with medium-term objectives and constraints, and a way of indicating how that policy will be adapted in pursuit of the same objectives as circumstances depart from the expected course, as inevitably they will.

Without such a declared position, governments are by turns rigid and irresolute, late in avoiding disaster and over-reacting when it comes. They appear to be deceitful when they are merely avoiding pessimism, and they cloak deceit in the appearance of confidence.

Table 1.2 Setting policy priorities for policy optimization on the Treasury model (as used by Bray in Whitley et al. (1992))

Variable units i	Level x_i	Zero priority (desired) level x_{id}	Equal priority change R_i	Priority $P_i = 1/R_i$	Weight $q_i = \dfrac{P_i}{(x_i - x_{id})}$	Effect of RS		Effect of TPBRZ (%)		Effect of DPG	
						on var. x_i	on Q_i	on var. x_i	on Q_i	on var. x_i	on Q_i
Instruments											
RS (%p.a.)	10	3	0.667	1.5	0.214	1	1.5	0	0	0	0
TPBRZ% (%)	25	24	2.667	0.375	0.375	0	0	1	0.375	0	0
DPG (%p.a.)	2.5	4	-0.667	-1.5	1	0	0	0	0	1	-1.5
Targets											
DPPR (%p.a.)	5	0	1	1	0.2	-0.5	-0.5	0.1	0.1	2	2
DPGDP (%p.a.)	2.5	4	-0.333	-3	2	-0.2	0.6	-0.06	0.18	0	0
CB%GDP (%)	-1.5	0	-0.333	-3	2	0.3	-0.9	0.1	-0.3	-0.3	0.9
GE%GDP (%)	24	25	-0.667	-1.5	1.5	0.2	-0.3	0.08	-0.12	1	-1.5
RX (%)	90.8	91	-5	-0.2	1	0.5	-0.1	0.1	-0.02	-0.2	0.04
RXERR (%)	-0.005	0	-1.429	-0.7	140	0.5	-0.35	0.1	-0.07	-0.2	0.14
Damping terms											
DRS	1	0	0.467	2.14	2.14	0	0	0	0	0	0
DTPBRZ	5	0	0.667	1.5	0.3	0	0	0	0	0	0
DDPG	5	0	0.6	1.667	0.333	0	0	0	0	0	0
Effect of change in instrument x_i on objective function Q					Effect on Q		-0.05		0.145		0.08
Objective function $Q = \Sigma Q_i = \Sigma(0.5 * q_i(x_i - x_{id})^2)$											

Definition of variables:

RS — Three month inter-bank rate
TPBRZ% — Basic rate of income tax
DPG — Rate of increase of government expenditure
DPPR — Rate of increase of retail price index
DPGDP — Rate of increase of average measure of GDP at constant factor cost
CB%GDP — Current balance of payments as per cent of GDP at current market prices

GE%GDP — Government expenditure as per cent of GDP at current market prices
RX — Sterling effective exchange rate index (1985=100)
RXERR — Difference of RX from value predicted last quarter
DRS — Change in RS from last quarter
DTPBRZ — Change in TPBRZ% from last quarter
DDPG — Change in DPG from last quarter

Note

The spreadsheet is used in setting priorities, weights and desired values in the optimization criterion and estimating their effects by reference to average medium-term effects of policy instruments.

There is little information used in the preparation and conduct of a coherent strategy that is not already in the public domain. It is therefore open to challenge by the opposition. And the government is unable to dismiss as carping criticism the views of the opposition if it has its own strategy to put forward as an alternative. There is a game here that matters, that can be seen to be affecting the lives and interests of the citizen. It can be the stuff of democratic politics.

The process of expressing policy-makers' priorities is sufficiently robust and practical to come up with reasonable characterizations of the policy and problems of each of the G7 countries in a G7 Nash game, using the IMF model MULTIMOD (Bray and Nana, 1989b). As demonstrated, it is quite practicable to solve that eight-player dynamic game (one player representing financial markets) on a desk-top computer. It is absurd to claim that the process is too difficult, too technical, too demanding of resources, too incommunicable, when it can be conducted by a single Member of Parliament.

The development of the game
The game will only develop if the players, the Chancellor of the Exchequer and his Shadow, can be brought to compete, as distinct from indulging in parliamentary shadow-boxing which, however enjoyable and effective in parliamentary terms, does not seem to convince people in the country.

In both the Government and the Opposition there is now a dangerous vacuum where there should be an operable economic strategy.

'Garbage in, garbage out' is as true of Chancellors of the Exchequer as it is of computers. There is not a lot that can be done about their palates and their discrimination. But care can be taken by those who offer sustenance. Nor can much be done from outside about advice within the Treasury. Generally, if government has a good argument, it will be used. If it is not used, it is unlikely to be as good as arguments going on outside. Good work outside will shame the Treasury into following suit.

As Britton and Pain (1992) observe, there is a demand for simple unconditional forecasts from the modellers that they at the NIESR are expected to meet. But the contribution they rightly say they are expected to make to the policy debate, a forecast conditional on a policy stance, is no longer sufficient. Each of the model teams should produce a rationale (or alternative rationales) for economic policy and for its updating, and maintain a full counter-factual ex-post analysis of how that policy rationale performs. It is up to the modellers to choose whether they put forward a more or less simple rule, some form of game or policy optimization, some simulation of what they imagine to be the Chancellor's thought processes, or any other approach they favour. The ex-post tests will sort them out. A comparative policy optimization on four UK models was carried out in 1993 (Bray *et al.*, 1993).

Television gurus, economic correspondents and city economists cannot be relied upon to report and interpret technical material. They are likely to rubbish it if it does not support their current presentational line. So the prime researchers who aspire to contribute to the policy debate must write up material in such a way that the argument can get through to the policy-maker directly.

A key area is international economics, the convergence to European economic and monetary union, and the Maastricht conditions in particular. It may be argued that it is running before you can walk to solve the resulting Nash game, which as Bray and Nana (1989b) demonstrated is technically quite feasible. The separate finance ministers have not even reached the stage of realizing that they are policy optimizing, let alone that they are playing a dynamic game. But it must also be recognized that there is a tendency for economists, like other professionals, to turn out the same arguments, keeping their intellectual capital going for as long as possible. There are certainly conditions which are likely to occur in the convergence to EMU which can only be elucidated by exploring the game.

The micro-to-macro field is already being explored in order to explain the recent anomalous behaviour of aggregate consumers' and companies' behaviour. This and the micro-behaviour field itself would be facilitated and stimulated if, in pursuit of a more competitive economy, a different approach were taken by Government to the availability and collection of the prime data. There must of course be absolute guarantees about the confidentiality of information relating to persons. But for companies and for classes of consumers, workers, patients, asset holders, individuals and households, information should be collectable and more readily available, at a price if necessary. Such an information system will probably be achieved by the convergence of the Government statistical and company reporting systems for enterprises into an open, distributed, self-reporting system. The primary purpose of the micro-information is of course to serve micro-games. But it would make possible many fresh approaches in the macro-field.

The concept of 'bounded rationality' (Simon, 1957), does not endow model agents with a knowledge of the economic system greater than that available to real agents and economists who observe the system. It is now opening up related lines of research in microeconomic theory (Bray, 1982), macroeconomic theory (Sargent, 1992) and applied economics, and in the design of operable strategies in micro- and macro-games.

At the national, international, micro-to-macro and micro levels it is the development of the game that should be the guiding light, not a misconceived attempt merely to describe an objective world that is not there. The world of which we are part must be taken very seriously: we need all the sophistication of the economist, econometrician, statistician, control theorist and game theorist. But we are part of the world, and players in the game.

References

Artis, M. and Karakitsos, E. (1983), 'Intermediate target variables. Their role in policy formulation with special reference to money supply and the exchange rate', *International Monetary Arrangements*, Fourth Report, HC 21-III, HMSO.

Ball Committee on Policy Optimization (1978), *Report of the Committee on Policy Optimisation*, Cmnd 7148, HMSO.

Ball, R.J. and Burns, T. (1976), 'The inflationary mechanism in the UK economy', *American Economic Review*, **66**(4), September.

Becker, R.G., Dwolatzky, B. Karakitsos, E. and Rustem, B. (1986), 'The simultaneous use of rival models in policy optimisation', *Economic Journal*, **96**, 89–101.

Bray, J (1987a), *The Economic Strategy of the Government*. Paper submitted to the House of Commons Treasury Committee and others, 27 September.

Bray, J. (1987b) *The Appropriate Response to the Fall in the Stock Market*. Paper submitted to the House of Commons Treasury and Civil Service Committee and others, 21 October.

Bray, J. (1990), 'Policies for exchange rate stabilisation on the UK Treasury model', *Econ. Modelling*, January. Paper given at the ESRC Macroeconomic Modelling Seminar, University of Warwick, 5 July 1988.

Bray, J. (1992), 'Evidence from the Treasury model', Appendix A in Whitley *et al.* (1992).

Bray, J. and Nana, G. (1989a), 'Policy optimisation in democratic political processes', *Proceedings of the 6th IFAC/SEDC Symposium on Dynamic Modelling and Control of National Economies*, London, IFAC.

Bray, J. and Nana, G. (1989b), 'International economic coordination in the G7 as a dynamic Nash game', *Proceedings of the 6th IFAC/SEDC Symposium on Dynamic Modelling and Control of National Economies*, London, IFAC.

Bray, J., Kuleshov, A., Uysal, A.E. and Walker, P. (1993), 'Balance-achieving policies: a comparative policy-optimization study on four UK models', *Oxford Review of Economic Policy*, **9**, 3, 69–82.

Bray, M. M. (1982), 'Learning, estimation and stability of rational expectations', *Journal of Economic Theory*, **26**, 318–39.

Britton, A. and Pain, N. (1992), *The Recent Experience of Economic Forecasting in Britain*. Paper given at the ESRC Macroeconomic Modelling Seminar, University of Warwick, 7 July.

Holly, S. and Zarrop, M. (1983), 'On optimality and time consistency when expectations are rational', *European Economic Review*, **20**, 23–40.

Holly, S., Rustem, B. and Zarrop, M. (eds) (1979), *Optimal Control for Econometric Models: An Approach to Economic Policy Formulation*, London: Macmillan.

Karakitsos, E. and Rustem, B. (1984), 'Optimally derived fixed rules and indicators', *Journal of Economic Dynamics and Control*, **8**, 33–64.

Klein, L.R. and Ball, R.A., Hazelwood, A. and Vandome, P. (1961), *An Econometric Model of the United Kingdom*, Oxford: Blackwell.

Kydland, F.E. and Prescott, E.C. (1977), 'Rules rather than discretion: the inconsistency of optimal plans', *Journal of Political Economy*, **85**(3).

Lawson, N. (1992), *The View From No. 11*, London: Bantam.

Lucas, R.E. (1976), 'Econometric policy evaluation: a critique', in Brunner, K. and Meltzer, A.H. (eds), *The Phillips Curve and Labor Markets*, Amsterdam: North Holland.

Lucas, R.E. and Sargent, T.J. (eds) (1981), *Rational Expectations and Econometric Practice*, London: Allen and Unwin.

Paraskevopoulos, D., Karakitsos, E. and Rustem, B. (1991), 'Robust capacity planning under uncertainty', *Management Science*, **37**, July, 787–800.

Rabbitt, P., Forshaw, M. and Qian, Y. (1992), 'Old dogs and old tricks: how well are mental skills retained in old age?' Exhibit at Royal Society Soiree, 17 June 1992.

Rustem, B. (1981), *Projection Methods in Constrained Optimisation and Applications to Optimal Policy Decisions*, Berlin: Springer-Verlag.

Rustem, B. (1986), 'Convergent step sizes for constrained optimisation algorithms', *Journal of Optimisation Theory and Applications*, **49**, 135–60.

Rustem, B. and Zarrop, M. (1979), 'A Newton-type method for the optimisation and control of nonlinear econometric models', *Journal of Economic Dynamics and Control*, **1**, 288–300.

Rustem, B., Velupillai, K. and Westcott, J. (1978), 'Respecifying the weighting matrix of a quadratic objective function', *Automatika*, **14**, 567–82.

Sargent, Th.J. (1992), *Bounded Rationality in Macroeconomics*, unpublished typescript, November.

Simon, H.A. (1957), *Models of Man: Social and Rational; Mathematical Essays on Rational Human Behaviour in Society Setting*, New York: Wiley.

Tirole, J. (1988), *The Theory of Industrial Organisation*, Boston: MIT.

Treasury and Civil Service Committee (1981), *Monetary Policy*, Third Report, HC 163, HMSO.

Whitley, J., Bray, J., Hall, S., Westaway, P. and Meen, G. (1992), *UK Policies. Non-Price Competitiveness, and Convergence to an EMU – An Inter-Model Comparison*. Discussion paper 28, ESRC Macroeconomic Modelling Bureau, University of Warwick.

Zarrop, M. Holly, S. Rustem, B. and Westcott, J. (1979), 'The design of economic stabilisation policies with large non-linear econometric models: two possible approaches', in Ormerod, P. *Economic Modelling*, London: Heinemann.

Note

The author's correspondence and working papers over the period covered in this paper are on deposit and available for reading in the Churchill Archive, Churchill College, Cambridge.

2 Exchange rate policy in the United Kingdom: a case of paradigm shift

*Alan Budd**

Introduction

On 18 November 1967 the pound was devalued in order to restore the competitiveness of UK industry. Almost exactly ten years later, on 28 October 1977, the pound was allowed to appreciate in order to control inflation. This paper is concerned with the process which brought about this change in ideas, and the part played in it by Professor Sir James Ball.

In retrospect we can recognize that there are two central questions:

1. What determines the rate of inflation under fixed and flexible exchange rates?
2. What determines the equilibrium level of output?

Prior to 1967 it can be said that the consensus answers to those questions were as follows. Under fixed exchange rates, inflation is primarily determined by domestic forces. The equilibrium level of output is primarily determined by aggregate demand, subject perhaps to some upper supply constraint. Formally, the model could be written as follows:

1. $Y = D + X - M$
2. $X = f(WT, P_{uk}ER/P_w)$
3. $M = f(Y, P_{uk}ER/P_w)$
4. $D = f(Y, F)$

Where:

Y = Output
D = Domestic demand
X = Exports
M = Imports
WT = World trade

* The views expressed in this paper are those of the author; they are not necessarily those of the Treasury.

P_{uk} = Price level of UK goods and services
P_w = Price level of world goods and services (in world prices)
ER = Exchange rate
F = The stance of fiscal policy.

Output, domestic demand, exports and imports are endogenous. All other variables are exogenous. This is a deliberate over-simplification, but it captures the essential ideas. The story ran as follows. The UK had a tendency to have higher inflation than its competitors. That was either because it had more rapid wage increases and the same growth of productivity as the rest of the world, or the same wage increases and slower growth of productivity. This loss of competitiveness caused the balance of trade to deteriorate for a given level of GDP and world trade. Let us also assume (as most commentators did) that both the balance of trade and the balance of payments (in current prices) tended to deteriorate as competitiveness was lost. Under fixed exchange rates (so it was assumed) there was an effective balance-of-payments constraint. Thus attempts to expand domestic demand to offset the demand effect of the deteriorating trade balance were ruled out because of the balance-of-payments constraint. The result was that the UK was forced to operate at an ever-lower level of capacity. As evidence, unemployment, though cyclical, tended to rise secularly. An ever-higher level of unemployment was necessary to maintain an adequate balance of payments.

The cause of the difficulty was the loss of competitiveness. The solution was obvious; the exchange rate should be cut. That would allow competitiveness to be restored, and a higher level of GDP would be consistent with balance-of-payments equilibrium.

Britain's relatively poor economic performance in the 1950s and 1960s could be explained by its attempts to maintain an uncompetitive exchange rate. Freed from that constraint it could join its more rapidly growing partners.

Even within that consensus there were refinements. For example it was recognized that an improvement in the balance of payments following a devaluation required the Marshall–Lerner conditions to hold. It was also recognized that if the economy were already at 'full employment', domestic demand would have to be cut to offset the expansionary effect of devaluation on the trade balance. Finally, it was recognized that domestic prices could be influenced by import prices. Thus a devaluation might temporarily raise the price level (and the rate of inflation). But those refinements did not contradict the majority view that devaluation would help to solve the UK's economic problems.

As evidence of reservations even before 1967 we can quote Ball (1964). In his discussion of the problem of restoring balance-of-payments equilibrium, Ball wrote:

Devaluation has considerable intellectual appeal, and a great deal of effort has been expended in producing analyses of the effects of devaluation on an economy's trade balance. One of the difficulties here, however, is that most of the analyses are pre-occupied with the impact effects of devaluation and are essentially static in character, whereas the longer run or dynamic effects are really crucial.[1]

He referred to the argument by the Council on Prices, Productivity and Incomes that it would be impossible for the Government to offset the effect on inflation of a rise in import prices. He commented:

A major devaluation would produce similar effects, and in the absence of any effective control of costs and prices would simply provide at best a short run breathing space rather than a long term solution ... .There are, however, grave dangers involved in speculating about devaluation before a solution to the problems of costs and prices is in sight, for this involves putting the cart very much before the horse. A devalua-tion that is eroded by subsequent costs and price increases serves only to debase the weapon and to bring it into disrepute.[2]

Thus, before the devaluation of 1967, Ball was warning that the beneficial effects of a devaluation might only be temporary.

The 1967 devaluation and its aftermath
A change in world view is likely to come about as a consequence of two types of development. The first consists of events which are difficult to reconcile with the previous view. The second consists of theoretical developments which offer better explanatory and predictive power. We can start by providing a brief sketch of the events which followed the 1967 devaluation.

After some delay, the devaluation had a favourable effect on the trade balance and the UK economy enjoyed export-led growth in 1968. The Labour Government recognized the need to reduce domestic demand to offset the improvement in the trade balance and introduced restrictive Budgets in 1969 and 1970. The Con-servatives won the election in June 1970. In response to slower growth and rising unemployment in 1971, an expansionary Budget was introduced in 1972. (There were further tax cuts in 1973.) On the world scene, the Bretton Woods System came to grief in 1971. The UK took part in the Smithsonian realignment in December 1971 (its exchange rate against the dollar was fixed at 2.60).

Sterling was floated in June 1972 and fell sharply. The UK economy grew in 1973 by 7.4 per cent. However by 1975 inflation reached 27 per cent and unemployment was at a post-war peak. It certainly appeared that the devalua-tion of 1967 and the depreciation of 1972 had only produced temporary benefits. Furthermore, the simultaneous experience of rapid inflation and high unem-ployment seemed to cast doubt on one of the accepted stylized facts of the post-war consensus, namely the downward-sloping Phillips curve. At the time the most striking phenomenon was the high rate of inflation, and it was this phenomenon which produced the most heated debate.

Explaining inflation

In 'The Inflationary Mechanism in the UK Economy', Ball and Burns sought to explain inflation in the UK over the previous 20 years. They argued that neither the monetary nor the Keynesian framework could provide a complete explanation of its own.

They distinguished between the inflationary process under fixed and flexible exchange rate regimes. In their discussion of demand effects they argued that in an open economy with a fixed exchange rate, 'demand pressure will not necessarily exert a great deal of direct pressure on prices, but will manifest itself in a material deterioration in the balance of payments'.[3]

That idea was becoming familiar through the propagation of the monetary theory of the balance of payments. In the simplest version of that theory, domestic prices are equal to world prices (in a common currency) and GDP is maintained at its equilibrium level. It follows that the level of GDP in current prices is given. If there is also a simple, stable demand for money it also follows that the quantity of money will depend on the (predetermined) level of nominal GDP. If domestic credit expansion is greater than the demand for money, the result will be a loss of reserves. Again, in the simplest version, the loss of reserves will equal the current account deficit. As Ball and Burns commented:

> … with a fixed exchange rate system, the key monetary variable becomes the rate of domestic credit expansion and its major role is the determination of the balance of payments and the split of the increase in the money supply between domestic and overseas money.[4]

If the monetary theory of the balance of payments is correct under a fixed exchange rate regime, the explanation of UK inflation up to 1967 would appear to be simple. As a small, open economy, the UK's rate of inflation would be set by that of its trading partners. It should be noted that, as mentioned earlier, Ball and Burns were not prepared to accept the simple monetary approach. In their study of the 1954–67 period they drew attention to the developments shown in Table 2.1.

Table 2.1   Average price increases: 1954–67

	% per annum
World prices of manufactures	1.1
UK export prices of manufactures	2.2
UK wholesale prices of manufactures	2.2
UK retail prices	3.2
UK consumer prices	3.0

Ball and Burns also pointed out that the UK had experienced more rapid consumer price inflation than the United States and Germany during this period (1.7 and 2.3 per cent per annum, respectively). But inflation had been higher in Japan (3.7 per cent per annum) and France (4.25 per cent per annum).

On the face of it, the above history is consistent with the story presented at the beginning of this paper. The UK did appear to have more rapid inflation than its competitors. Such a development could account for the increasing problem of maintaining balance-of-payments equilibrium. The question was, what caused the discrepancy? Ball and Burns examined two possible explanations. The first was that competition in the market for manufactured goods is imperfect, and export prices are affected by domestic costs, which tended to rise more rapidly than those in the rest of the world. The second was that it is possible for a country's currency to be over- or undervalued as a result of large exchange rate changes and that this discrepancy only disappears gradually. During the period of adjustment, a country that starts with an undervalued currency will experience relatively high inflation.

Ball and Burns argued that in 1954 sterling was probably still undervalued following the devaluation of 1949, and that a substantial part of the UK's relatively high inflation was caused by the response to that undervaluation.

Ball and Burns also used the analysis of Balassa (1964) to explain equilibrium variations in consumer price inflation between countries. In brief, under fixed exchange rates, all countries will experience similar rates of inflation for traded goods. Traded goods are predominantly manufactured. The countries enjoying the most rapid growth of labour productivity will tend to have the most rapid growth of nominal wages in the traded goods sector. With labour mobility between the traded and non-traded sectors, wage increases will tend to be the same everywhere. If the growth of productivity is lower in the non-traded goods sector (and is similar in all countries), then the country with the most rapid growth of productivity in the traded goods sector will tend to have the highest rate of inflation of consumer prices (which include the prices of non-traded goods and services). That explanation is now commonplace, though it is worth recalling how counter-intuitive it seemed at the time.

The undervaluation hypothesis also explains why the UK was apparently finding it increasingly difficult to combine a satisfactory balance of payments with low unemployment. As Ball and Burns commented:

One of the features of the undervaluation of sterling in the early 1950s was the low unemployment rate that followed. The major problem was that this brought with it exaggerated views of the target level of unemployment, leading to the expectation that balance-of-payments equilibrium would be consistent in the longer run with such low rates.[5]

The attempt to maintain these low unemployment levels led to accelerating inflation and to a false diagnosis of the UK's economic problem:

> Sterling was devalued in November of that year [1967] in the mistaken belief that the inability to combine the target unemployment rate with an adequate current account performance was due entirely to an incorrect exchange rate rather than a mistaken unemployment target.[6]

An account of Ball's contributions to the macroeconomic policy debate would be incomplete if one did not recognize that he had been a supporter of incomes policies as part of counter-inflationary policy. At his most optimistic he argued that an incomes policy could be used to bring about an adjustment of real wages. A footnote to the previous quote commented as follows:

> This should be qualified by saying that the belief might not necessarily have been mistaken if the subsequent incomes policy pursued by the Labour Government had been sustained. In the event, the 'real income frustration' described by Ball (1971) persuaded the Government to abandon the policy, finally allowing the real income adjustment in the face of the exchange rate change to be blown away. It was a mistaken belief to the extent that the devaluation was undertaken without a realisation of the subsequent need to make the community accept the reduction in the rate of growth of real incomes.[7]

The paper dealt more briefly with inflation during the periods 1967–72 and 1972–75. By 1972, and following the breakdown of the incomes policy in 1969, UK prices and wages had responded to the 1967 devaluation. Thus an adjustment which had taken about 15 years after the 1949 devaluation, seemed to take only about five years after the 1967 devaluation.

After 1972 there was the experience of a floating exchange rate and the rapid rise in world prices. World prices of manufactured exports rose by 45 per cent between 1972 and 1975 in world currency terms, and sterling fell by 20 per cent. Thus the sterling price of world exports rose by about 85 per cent. UK manufactured prices rose over the same period by between 65 and 75 per cent.

What had caused the decline in the exchange rate? Ball and Burns showed that the decline in the exchange rate closely matched the excess growth of the UK money supply relative to the share of UK GDP in world GDP:

> The implication of this is that the United Kingdom was directly responsible for having a higher rate of inflation than the rest of the world due to inadequate control of the money supply and that, during 1974 and 1975, the internal price level was adjusting to the movement of the exchange rate in 1972 and 1973.[8]

We may note that this paper produced significant differences from the previous consensus view. In particular, Ball and Burns argued:

- under a fixed exchange rate regime, domestic prices depend largely on prices in the rest of the world;
- under a flexible exchange rate, domestic prices respond to monetary developments;
- attempts to hold unemployment below its equilibrium level cannot succeed permanently and will lead to some combination of accelerating inflation and balance-of-payments deterioration;
- changes in the nominal exchange rate will not have a permanent effect on competitiveness.

Exchange rate changes and balance-of-payments adjustment
The idea that the real effects of nominal exchange rate changes are only temporary was addressed in greater detail in 'The Role of Exchange Rate Changes in Balance of Payments Adjustment: The United Kingdom Case' by Ball, Burns and Laury. This paper was written before Ball and Burns (1976) but was published later (1977).

Ball, Burns and Laury used the London Business School (LBS) model to explore the effects of a devaluation and concluded that with free collective bargaining, wages and prices were likely to rise by the full extent of the devaluation in the long run. They argued that the result would hold in the following types of model:

- where, in the long run, changes in consumer prices enter the function for wage changes with a coefficient of unity, and prices themselves are a weighted average of changes in unit labour costs and import prices;
- where, in the long run, changes in the GDP deflator enter the wage function with a coefficient of unity and the deflator is itself a weighted average of changes in unit labour costs and world prices;
- where the prices of traded goods adjust to the level of world prices, and wages in *both* traded and non-traded sectors adjust to the traded-goods price level with no further impact for the pressure of demand.

The third case is generally known as the Scandinavian model of inflation.

The paper examined four simulations which showed that, according to the LBS model, the effect of devaluations on the real exchange rate was completely offset after six years. The only way in which a devaluation could have a persistent effect on the balance of payments was in cases in which Government spending (and the tax system) was not fully adjusted to take account of the resulting higher domestic prices.

The authors concluded that it was not possible to pursue a simple policy rule of directing fiscal policy towards determining full employment while allowing the exchange rate to adjust the balance of payments. Such an attempt would fail unless the community was prepared to bear, or the Government was prepared to inflict, the necessary real adjustment following an exchange rate depreciation. They drew two unpalatable conclusions from their analysis. The first was that, under a fixed exchange rate system, it was impossible for the UK authorities to control either the rate of inflation in the long run or the level of employment. The second was that the exchange rate could only be used as an instrument of economic policy to the extent that use could be made of its transitory effects.

> With a floating rate, our conclusion would be similar to that of the monetarists in that floating the rate provides an extra degree of freedom to pursue a rate of inflation in the long run different from that of our competitors.[9]

In the light of subsequent discussion it is worth considering the first unpalatable conclusion further. The first part of the conclusion, namely that under a fixed exchange rate regime the authorities cannot control the rate of inflation is (by now) familiar enough. The second part, namely that they cannot control the level of employment, was derived as follows. For any given rate of growth of world activity, there exists a level of domestic activity that is consistent with balance-of-payments current account 'equilibrium'. Attempts to sustain economic activity above that level will result in a weakening of the balance of payments, a declining exchange rate and, eventually, accelerating inflation. They suggested that the unemployment rate associated with this level of activity might be called the 'balance-of-payments' rate. If the pressure of demand in the labour market affected real wages the balance-of-payments rate would correspond to the natural rate:

> On the other hand, if there is no pressure of demand effect upon wage changes over the range of unemployment in question the concept of the 'natural' unemployment rate disappears and the 'balance of payments' rate becomes the operational constraint. The higher the real wage rate that wage-earners are attempting to maintain the higher will be the 'balance of payments' unemployment rate. Attempts to achieve an unemployment rate below this by fiscal and monetary expansion can only be achieved in the long run by repeated bouts of inflation.[10]

It may be noted that this is a particularly gloomy conclusion. It is not possible to alter the real wage by altering the exchange rate. Nor do real wages respond to high levels of unemployment. Thus a shock which caused a deterioration in the balance of payments relative to GDP (for example, a fall in world activity or a rise in the propensity to import) would inevitably cause unemployment to rise.

We may take stock of the argument about exchange rate adjustment after Ball, Burns and Laury. That paper showed that the ineffectiveness of exchange rate policy was consistent with an empirical model, the properties of which were mainly Keynesian. The effects of a nominal depreciation disappeared within six years, leaving the domestic price level correspondingly higher. If, in addition, real wages did not respond to the level of unemployment, the level of activity (and employment) was beyond the control of the authorities and depended on the level of world activity.

The long-run behaviour of the economy

Ball, Burns and Laury (1977) discussed the medium-term effects of exchange rate changes using a model that had originally been designed for short-term forecasts. Ball and Burns (1979) explicitly considered the long-run properties of econometric models. In particular they considered the problems involved in integrating financial and real flows and the adjustment of financial stocks.

From the point of view of this survey, the important element of this paper was the emphasis on the financial implications of the Government's fiscal actions. One conclusion was that, in the long run, with unchanged reserves, a fiscal expansion would only result in higher prices. That conclusion was based on a fairly simple model of an open economy. Ball, Burns and Warburton (1980) discussed the implications of that approach when it was incorporated into the full LBS model. Although that paper was published after the events of 1977, many of the properties described in the paper were recognized and discussed earlier.

The account of the model started with a description of its long-term properties, which were said to be related to the international monetarist tradition. The main properties of the model were:

- a stable demand for real money balances as a function of income;
- a similar function for world real money balances;
- equality of wages in the traded and non-traded goods sectors;
- equality of domestic and foreign prices of traded goods (in a common currency).

These properties can be united to provide the result that the exchange rate varied inversely with the ratio of the UK money supply to that of the world money supply. It followed that for a given level of domestic real income and for given values of the external variables, an exogenous increase in the supply of money would lower the exchange rate which, in turn, would cause prices to rise. Prices would rise until real balances adjusted to the (unchanged) level of real income.

In Ball, Burns and Warburton the supply of money was endogenous and was determined by the interaction of fiscal policy, net lending to the private sector and intervention in the foreign exchange market.

Finally, a key element of the model was the specification of wealth effects on the level of consumers' expenditure. It was assumed that there was a long-run desired liquid assets–income ratio. Since inflation could erode the real value of liquid assets, a rise in inflation could raise the savings ratio. (This idea had been developed in Davidson *et al.* 1978.)

With flexible exchange rates, a fiscal expansion produced an acceleration of monetary growth which in turn produced a fall in the exchange rate and a rise in inflation. The rise in inflation caused a rise in the savings ratio. Thus the effects of a fiscal expansion were rapidly crowded out.

The development of exchange rate policy

These developments have brought us some way from the simplified view presented at the start of this paper. The most significant changes have related to the process of inflation. Under a fixed exchange rate, the emphasis was on international price levels. Under a flexible exchange rate, the emphasis was on monetary and fiscal developments. The papers presented by Ball and his colleagues were consistent with the earlier view of Keynes that a country could control the internal or the external value of its currency but not both.

The question of the determination of the level of output was less clear. It was not easy to identify anything that corresponded to the natural rate of unemployment in the LBS model of that vintage. Fiscal policy was ineffective because it caused inflation, which in turn caused savings to rise. The exchange rate was the mechanism by which this happened. As was pointed out at the time, the model had an international but not a domestic version of monetarism. If the economy had been closed, a fiscal expansion would, apparently, have been effective since there was no mechanism by which inflation could have risen.

That comment is largely beside the point since the objective was to explain the process of inflation in an open economy with flexible exchange rates. The model appeared to capture the main means by which a fiscal or monetary expansion caused higher inflation. In a closed economy the process would have been different, and the model would need to be respecified accordingly, but the end result would have been the same.

How did these developments impinge on the policy debate? We have to move the narrative forward from 1975. Between February and October of 1976 sterling fell by 19 per cent against the dollar. The UK applied for a stand-by arrangement from the IMF in order to defend the currency. The terms of the arrangement were set out in a Letter of Intent signed by the Chancellor of the Exchequer on 15 December.[11] They included cuts in public expenditure for 1977–78 and restrictive targets for domestic credit expansion in 1977–78 and 1978–79.

In the course of 1977, the Government succeeded in cutting the PSBR significantly. The successful implementation of the terms of the IMF loan (and, no doubt, the loan itself) helped to restore confidence in sterling. However, for most of 1977 the Government chose to intervene to prevent sterling from appreciating. This was presumably being done to preserve the competitive advantage provided by sterling's low exchange rate. As a result, short-term interest rates were cut progressively from a peak of 15 per cent in October 1976 to 5 per cent in October 1977.

In terms of the analysis developed by Ball and his colleagues, this policy was mistaken. An 'international monetarist' interpretation of events would run as follows. The fiscal and monetary policies in place up to 1976 were consistent with continuing high inflation. The exchange rate had fallen in anticipation of higher prices. It would have continued to fall to preserve (approximate) equality between the prices of UK and world traded goods in a common currency. The UK was using a flexible exchange rate to maintain its independent rate of inflation.

The policies were changed as a condition for IMF help. The cuts in the PSBR and domestic credit expansion were consistent with lower inflation in the medium term. With a freely floating currency, sterling would have appreciated in anticipation of the lower inflation. By its refusal to allow the currency to appreciate, the Government was blocking the channel through which its tighter fiscal policy would lead to lower inflation. By the same token its actions would eventually produce the inflation that was consistent with the low exchange rate. The actual mechanism would be the monetary expansion associated with exchange rate intervention.[12]

The counter-argument was that the appreciation of sterling would be harmful for the trade balance. However, the LBS analysis suggested: (1) that the benefits of a low exchange rate would only be temporary, and (2) that lower inflation associated with a rise in the exchange rate would produce a fall in the savings ratio and a more rapid growth of consumer spending.

We cannot know what debates were conducted within the Treasury, though some hints have been provided by Lord Healey (1989). He described the conflicts in Whitehall between unreconstructed Keynesians and unbelieving monetarists:

> Each theory had its partisans in both the Treasury and the Bank of England; institutional interest led the Bank to want a high pound so as to keep inflation down, while the Treasury often wanted a lower pound to make British industry more competitive, and to reduce the balance of payments deficit through the 'automatic adjustment process' – though floating had made such adjustment far from 'automatic'.[13]

In the end, Lord Healey stopped the intervention and the pound was allowed to appreciate. He commented:

> In the event, I think I was proved right. Though the pound was about twelve cents higher in 1978, and rose above $2 once or twice, the balance of payments remained

in surplus and I achieved what was then a record; for most of my last year in office unemployment and inflation were falling at the same time.[14]

One could perhaps comment that inflation might have fallen further if intervention had ended earlier.

Conclusions

It is not the purpose of this paper to suggest that Jim Ball was uniquely responsible for the change in ideas which led to the 1977 change in policy. However, one cannot deny the prominent part played by Ball and his colleagues in shifting the public debate.

The years 1967 to 1977 were ones of great confusion for the economics profession. The overwhelming majority of economists had supported the devaluation of 1967 on the ground that an overvalued currency was inhibiting the growth of GDP. This paper suggests that that view was based on a fairly naive model in which inflation was a domestic phenomenon and output was primarily set by the level of demand. The events after 1967, and particularly the events after 1972, led to a reappraisal of the inflationary process under fixed and flexible exchange rates.

A skilled applied economist is not necessarily the one that produces innovations, but the one that sees the relevance of particular innovations to the problems of the time. Ball always acknowledged the work of other economists, particularly those who discovered (or rediscovered) the necessary theoretical ideas. The failure of the naive 'Keynesian' approach allowed attention to turn to those who had continued to emphasize the role of money.

In the simplest version of monetarist models, in a fixed exchange rate regime, the rate of inflation would be given by inflation in the rest of the world and excess domestic credit expansion would produce a balance-of-payments deficit. In a flexible exchange rate regime, inflation would be determined by monetary growth and the exchange rate would adjust to preserve purchasing power parity.

The simplest monetarist models did not, of course, include the whole truth. However, they clearly provided insights into UK economic history and produced an important test of the longer-run properties of the Keynesian models. The challenge was to incorporate the monetarist ideas into an empirical model of the UK economy. That is what Ball and his colleagues were able to do and that is why they played a major part in reshaping ideas and were able to contribute to a significant change in policy.

Notes
1. Ball (1964) p. 304.
2. *ibid.* p. 305.
3. Ball and Burns (1976) p. 469.
4. *ibid.* p. 470.

5.   *ibid*. p. 477.
6.   *ibid*. p. 477
7.   *ibid*. p. 477.
8.   *ibid*. p. 482.
9.   Ball, Burns and Laury (1977) p. 23.
10.   *ibid*. p. 23.
11.   A full account of this episode is set out in Burk and Cairncross (1992).
12.   The arguments were set out in Burns and Budd (1977). It may be noted that those arguments were not about the merits of flexible versus fixed exchange rates. The point was that the Government was attempting to hold the exchange rate at a level which was inconsistent with its objectives for controlling inflation.
13.   Healey (1989) p. 434.
14.   *ibid*. p. 435.

References

Balassa, B. (1964), 'The purchasing power parity doctrine: a reappraisal', *Journal of Political Economy*, **72**, December.

Ball, R.J. (1964), *Inflation and the Theory of Money*, London: George Allen & Unwin.

Ball, R.J. (1971), 'Inflation and the London Business School model', in Johnson, H.G. and Nobay, A.R. (eds.), *The Current Inflation*, London: The Macmillan Press.

Ball, R.J. and Burns, T. (1976), 'The inflationary mechanism in the UK economy', *American Economic Review*, **66**, September.

Ball, R.J. and Burns, T. (1979), 'Long-run portfolio equilibrium and balance of payments adjustment in econometric models', in Sawyer, J.A. (ed.), *Modelling the International Transmission Mechanism*, North Holland Publishing Company.

Ball, R.J. Burns, T. and Laury, J.S.E. (1977), 'The role of exchange rate changes in balance of payments adjustment: The United Kingdom case', *Economic Journal*, **87**, March.

Ball, R.J., Burns, T. and Warburton, P.J. (1980), 'The London Business School model of the UK Economy: an exercise in international monetarism', in Ormerod, P. (ed.), *Economic Modelling*, London: Heinemann.

Budd, A.P. and Burns, T. (1977), 'Why the exchange rate must be set free', *Economic Outlook*, London Business School, April.

Burk, K. and Cairncross, A. (1992), *'Goodbye, Great Britain': The 1976 IMF Crisis*, New Haven and London: Yale University Press.

Davidson, J.E.H., Hendry, D.F., Srba, F., and Yeo, S. (1978), 'Econometric modelling of the aggregate time–series relationship between consumers' expenditure and income in the United Kingdom', *Economic Journal*, **88**, December.

Healey, D. (1989), *The Time of My Life*, London: Michael Joseph.

3 Some reflections on the Treasury
Sir Terence Burns

Introduction

Jim Ball has played a central role in my career over many years. He taught me macroeconomics and econometrics as an undergraduate. He introduced me to macroeconomic model building and forecasting, and for many years supervised my research work. He was the senior author of our forecasts for the *Sunday Times* over a period of almost ten years. During that period we continually debated economic policy and strategy. Finally, he was the Principal of the London Business School (LBS) during my years on the academic staff.

His insight and approach to problem-solving made a lasting impression on me. It is difficult to summarize the cumulative impact of more than 15 years of close collaboration. But I would emphasize the following:

1. The benefit to be derived from *examining ideas within a wider system.* This has obvious relevance for economics and is the reason for seeking to examine economic behaviour within the framework of a model of the whole economy. The implications of a collection of interrelated ideas are often difficult to see in an intuitive way. It is an approach that can be applied to other issues with great effect, even where there is no formal model available.
2. The requirement to *test ideas against the available evidence* and a wide range of considerations. Following the development of econometrics this is more widespread in economics, although it is still often ignored. What is less intuitively obvious, but just as important, is the inconvenient reality that even if the data are consistent with your hypothesis they do not prove it; other hypotheses might also be consistent with the data. This is particularly important in looking at ideas for change, where all the ramifications need to be addressed.
3. The importance of team-work and the value of being able to *exchange and share ideas.* Few of us can fail to benefit from continuously testing our ideas with sympathetic but critical colleagues. But not all organizations are set up to encourage this constructive process.
4. The benefits from *specifying at the outset the results* that might be expected to follow from an event or proposed course of action, and then subsequently to test the results against plans and predictions. This is obviously important for anyone making regular predictions – although it is surprising how often

commentators and analysts do not subject themselves to this discipline. It is remarkable how efficient the human mind is at recalling successes and how inefficient it is at recalling failures. This approach is also of much broader relevance and is now widely used in management and administrative systems.

Since leaving the LBS at the end of 1979 I often had cause to reflect on these lessons. Between being appointed Chief Economic Adviser to the Treasury and taking up my post I benefited from reading the Ball report on 'Policy Optimization' for the insight it gave into how the Treasury worked. On the occasion of this volume, I return to the institutional framework for conducting economic policy.

The fact that the Treasury is at the centre of the formulation and execution of economic policy lays it open to considerable criticism from time to time. This becomes particularly insistent during periods of poor overall economic performance. In today's circumstances we have seen an interesting debate emerge about the responsibilities and style of the Treasury.

As a contribution to the debate I propose to examine two issues of particular contemporary concern, to do with the Treasury's main responsibilities and the way it carries them out:

1. The Treasury's role in policy design and execution, including its relationship with other Whitehall departments. Here, the criticism is that it has too much power, interferes too much and is engaged in too many issues (but not necessarily the right ones).
2. The Treasury's style of doing business, including the relationship between ministers and officials. Here the criticism is that it is secretive, insufficiently accountable and unresponsive.

On the way I hope to separate myths from reality and put the issues in context.

Responsibilities and relationships

The question has been raised whether all the Treasury's functions and responsibilities hang together. *Inter alia*, it has some, although not in every case sole, responsibility for:

- public spending;
- tax;
- management of the civil service;
- monetary policy;
- the exchange rate and the reserves;
- financial supervision;
- international financial relations;
- funding of the deficit;

- forecasting and economic analysis;
- the supply side of the economy.

In addition, the Chancellor has responsibility for the Central Statistical Office. In most other countries one or more of these functions is allocated elsewhere. It is not surprising, therefore, that some people complain that the Treasury gets involved in too many issues where others have the operational responsibility, and that it interferes too much, mistaking power for control.

A different strand is the suggestion that the Treasury concentrates on the wrong issues. Because of the resources going into public expenditure control and finance, insufficient attention is given to longer-term questions of economic strategy. It is suggested that the Treasury does not understand wealth creation, it does not concentrate sufficiently on supply-side issues, and devotes too little attention to those activities that would naturally be thought of as the province of a Ministry of Economics.

Responsibilities

In evaluating these criticisms and possible responses, it may help to start from a brief description of what the Treasury does.

People talking of 'the Treasury' normally mean the department of state as headed by its ministers. That, too, is what I normally mean by it. But the phrase is also sometimes used to refer to the official institution in distinction to its ministers, and sometimes I have used that sense. Constitutionally, it refers to the Lord Commissioners of Her Majesty's Treasury, as headed by the First Lord of the Treasury (the Prime Minister).

Macroeconomic policy   Something under one-fifth of the Treasury's resources go into the design and execution of macroeconomic policy. This is probably the best known role, and what commentators like to call 'managing the economy'. It is also the part of the Treasury's work of which I have had the most direct experience, as it is the main focus of the Chief Economic Adviser's responsibilities.

As I will argue later, policies are ultimately the responsibility of ministers. The official side of the Treasury is primarily responsible for the process of policy design and implementation. By their nature these processes require some privacy, although I will describe later some of the steps that have been taken to bring to them a greater degree of openness. At this stage, however, I will simply try to let a little light into these processes as a basis for the later discussion.

The main instruments of macroeconomic control continue to be the setting of interest rates and fiscal policy, although from time to time there is some shift in balance and in their relative importance.

Interest rates can be changed frequently in response to changes in conditions. Since the mid-1970s interest rates have been the main weapon used to control the level of aggregate nominal demand in the economy. Decisions are taken by the Chancellor after advice from the Treasury and the Bank of England and after consulting the Prime Minister. Under the discretionary regime we are now operating, this judgement is based on a general assessment of monetary conditions; at other times the maintenance of a particular exchange rate has been the primary consideration.

The assessment process follows a regular monthly pattern. Each month the Treasury produces an assessment of the various indictors that are given some weight in this judgement. This is considered initially at a meeting of officials from the Treasury and the Bank of England and subsequently by the Chancellor and Governor of the Bank of England.

By contrast, Budgetary changes are normally only made on one fixed occasion each year (except 1993, when there were two occasions). Of course, the Budget is a very elaborate public ritual which begins with a surprising amount of publicity associated with the weekend at Chevening. This meeting sets the context for decisions on tax and considers substantial papers on both the macro-economic strategy and tax strategy. The process culminates with the Chancellor leaving No. 11 waving the Gladstone Budget box.

In between are many months of intensive work in close co-operation with the Inland Revenue and Customs and Excise. The mechanics are centred around a succession of scorecards, timetables and other documentation for weekly Budget overviews, which keep track of tax options and try to ensure that all the issues are properly and systematically considered. There is also a comprehensive approach to considering 'Budget representations' from the lobby groups and processing a detailed list of 'Budget starters' in an attempt to try to make sure that nothing is lost.

To the headline writers the Budget is mainly an issue of how much tax has been increased on beer, cigarettes, whisky and motor cars. To the wider commercial world it is more a question of the success or otherwise of lobbying pressure in favour of particular industries and services. To the tax specialists the focus of attention is on the detail of the Finance Bill and various technical anomalies. And for the economists, when they are not debating the implications of the Treasury forecast, it is about the balance between spending, taxation and borrowing, even though there is little agreement about the effects of changes in any of these sectors.

Until now the macro consideration of public expenditure has taken place in the Spring and early Summer, when the Public Expenditure Survey has set the discipline for decisions on the total amount the Government will spend, and its allocation to particular programmes. From 1993 onwards this will coincide with the discussion of tax proposals.

These discussions all have as a background a regularly updated assessment of where the economy is going. This responsibility mainly falls to the Treasury's team of economists, which produces two or three forecasts a year as the main part of this assessment.

As Chief Economic Adviser I had to spend a lot of time co-ordinating and discussing forecasts. But I have been amazed at the importance accorded to this by others, almost as if forecasting is the Treasury's main activity. By its nature forecasting the economy is extremely difficult, and no one is more aware of this than ministers and the officials involved in preparing forecasts. We now have many years of experience of the likely margins of error. These are well documented and substantial. Unfortunately, there is little sign of improvement over time despite significant technical and analytical developments. A similar pattern is evident in outside forecasts, which demonstrate similar, and often larger, errors. The Treasury took the lead in developing and publishing error margins derived from past experience.

Despite the remarkable growth in the number of independent forecasts, particular attention is given to the Treasury forecast. And because the results can be checked against what actually happens it is often viewed as the most important aspect of setting economic policy. But although the forecast is an important input, its role is usually overstated, not least because ministers are well aware of the frailty of the forecasts. Meanwhile, the other 1400 people in the central Treasury suffer the frustration of seeing their effort judged by the forecasts of 30 or so economists – and even for these economists the forecasts are only one aspect of their performance.

Much criticism is based on false expectations of what can be achieved by government. The Treasury is not, despite the old phrase, steering the economy. The weapons at its disposal are small in comparison to the natural momentum of the economy. When action is taken nothing happens for a long time. The lags are long. Little attention is given to similar problems in other countries. Much of the criticism is presented as if ours was the only country facing problems.

Supply side   Treasury officials are also very conscious that public comment usually accords far too much importance to the Treasury's role in macro- as opposed to microeconomic policy. Much of the Budget discussion is about the micro aspects of tax decisions; which taxes to reduce or abolish, or how to raise those taxes in a way that does least damage to the economy, pays due regard to distributional consequences and provides incentives to better economic performance.

Improving the growth performance of the economy – while it is helped by a stable macroeconomic environment – is above all a matter of improving the supply side. And improving the workings of markets and of supply performance is naturally seen as a key objective of the Treasury. For example, the Treasury has a close interest in labour market issues such as education and training. And the overall assessment of economic performance is affected by the rate of unemployment likely to result from policies designed to bear down on inflation.

In recent years most of the Treasury's contribution has come from pursuing with departments opportunities to increase competition; managing the Government's privatization policy; supporting departments responsible for trade policy and for reforming product, labour and capital markets; seeking to increase opportunities for private finance in public sector provision; and pursuing deregulation. It does this primarily by a distinctive supply-side advocacy within the Treasury in relation to the Treasury's own responsibilities.

In addition, from time to time the Treasury itself takes initiatives to promote supply performance if appropriate, even where other responsibilities provide no locus. Equally important, but more difficult, is to argue the case for supply-side interests where it might come into conflict with other public finance interests.

Public expenditure   Just as I spent the majority of my time as Chief Economic Adviser dealing with macroeconomic policy, I am now only too conscious of how much Treasury business lies outside this sphere. A large proportion of Treasury resources goes into the planning and control of public expenditure; and the Public Expenditure and Pay and Management groups are the largest two groups within the Treasury.

We try to do a number of things. We seek to assist ministers in determining their objectives for spending in total; in discussing priorities and settling plans for individual programmes within these totals; and in monitoring spending in the year to stay within agreed plans. The Treasury also briefs ministers on the policy proposals brought forward by other departments (for example, the Coal Review, NHS reforms and so on). The Treasury also helps departments in their pursuit of greater value for money and greater efficiency.

In the private sector, demand and supply are brought into balance by the price mechanism. For almost all public services this does not apply. It falls to the government to determine how much will be supplied, both in aggregate and of each individual service. This is rightly an intensely political process in all senses, and one in which ministers play a key role. Different governments will have different priorities. But all governments need objectives for total spending which are consistent with a coherent macroeconomic policy framework. The balance between a government's objectives for fiscal policy, the tax burden and public expenditure is a matter of economic as well as political significance.

The demand for public services may be a factor to be taken into account in deciding where to strike this balance. But decisions about the allocation of resources to programmes must, in principle, be subject to judgement about the appropriate overall level of spending. And while plans may change in successive

Surveys, the credibility of the planning process depends on effective control in delivering agreed totals. Upward pressures on both planning and control totals are always intense.

The Treasury's interests are wider than just the aggregate level of spending and having control mechanisms to ensure that agreed totals are not exceeded. Value for money, output and quality will always be important, as will suitable monitoring mechanisms to ensure that policies are fulfilled. It must also be concerned with the composition of spending as between current and capital, one sub-programme and another, and one form of income support or subsidy and another. Departments can take the initiative in improving the value for money and control of their programmes, but they cannot on their own settle their spending totals. In addition, much spending has significant implications for the functioning of the economy or interaction with the tax system.

As far as the Treasury is concerned, success depends on three crucial factors:

1. Having a sound principle of what ministers want to achieve. Complicated rules are possible but simplicity has its merits. (Elizabeth I's Treasurer had an effective policy: 'Beware thou spend not above three of four parts of thy revenue.'[1] It was successful enough to get him on to the 1992 Treasury Christmas card, the ultimate achievement for any financial statesman.)
2. The Treasury needs the opportunity to make its case whenever the Government wants to do anything costing money, and the clout and respect at the centre of Government to help it get a fair hearing. It is helped by the principle – first instituted as a Cabinet rule in 1924 – that 'no memorandum is to be circulated to the Cabinet or its Committees in which any financial issue is involved, until its contents have been discussed with Treasury'.[2]
3. The Treasury needs good relations with departments so that spending plans are discussed with them in the right way at the right time.

Pay and management of the civil service   Another of the Treasury's main responsibilities is for the pay and management of the civil service. This is an area that has been dealt with inside, outside and back inside the Treasury over the past 25 years. These responsibilities are currently shared with the Office of Public Service and Science (OPSS).

Unlike much Treasury work, pay and management involves substantial executive responsibilities; negotiating pay, setting allowances, awarding pensions and controlling the running costs of central government. It is an area where tasks, methods and the resources employed are changing rapidly.

The civil service used to be managed within a framework of top-down controls from the centre; now there is much greater decentralization and delegation. Decisions are more and more taken by those nearer to the coal face.

The Treasury is therefore currently delegating many of its responsibilities in this area, including pay, to departments and agencies. The aim is to achieve a significant shift towards strategic control – ultimately away from the pay and personnel controls of the past towards a budgetary control with decentralized decision-taking.

There will still be an important role for the Treasury here: almost £20 billion a year of expenditure on running central government must be controlled, and the structure and systems of the civil service must be efficient to serve the public, Parliament and ministers well. But the Treasury's role here is changing: it is at the same time contracting and growing more specialized and professional in carrying out its remaining very important tasks.

Financial supervision   The Treasury is also responsible for financial regulation, which is closely related to the Treasury's economic policy preoccupations, and reflects an underlying concern for the stability, integrity and efficiency of the financial system. This is an activity which has expanded enormously over the past decade, with the development and liberalization of financial markets and the implementation of major new legislation.

The Treasury has long had general responsibility for banking legislation. Since the 1992 election it has acquired responsibility for the regulatory structure under the Financial Services Act, giving it overall responsibility for financial services as is found in virtually every other Finance Ministry in Europe, North America and Japan. This has already eased the task of negotiating a number of key European directives, designed to facilitate the creation of a single market in financial services. It should in time be an advantage in other international and market access issues, as well as putting the Government in a better position to respond to developments in financial markets, where the boundaries between different products, activities and institutions are increasingly blurred.

The Treasury's role in this area is to develop an adequate and coherent framework for financial regulation. This is almost entirely a matter of policy and legislation and strategic oversight of the system. Operational responsibility for regulating individual institutions is for most practical purposes vested in, or delegated to, separate bodies, such as the Bank of England, the Securities and Investment Board (SIB) and the Building Societies Commission, the precise constitutional position of which varies, but which all operate, in this sphere at least, at arm's length from ministers.

International relations   Most of the Treasury's attention is directed towards home. But increasingly, as world and European economies become more integrated, the Treasury is closely engaged in a wide range of international matters.

The United Kingdom's membership of the European Community means that Treasury ministers have responsibility for the UK's role in negotiating the

Community Budget and the moves towards monetary union. The Treasury takes a full part in the process of discussing other countries' economic prospects and policies, in negotiation over financial supervision, and in all the many community policies with resource and trade implications.

This work requires frequent visits to Brussels, often for negotiations which result in legal texts; an extensive series of bilateral contacts, through visits and telephone calls, with the other member states (especially our opposite numbers in finance ministries); and close co-ordination with the Foreign Office. With so many issues having an important EC angle, increasing numbers of Treasury officials are getting heavily involved with the Commission and other member states.

The UK is also an active member of many other international bodies and organizations. This includes preparing for and attending meetings of the Group of Seven, at both ministerial and official level. The Treasury is closely involved in the determination of UK policy – how best to fulfil our objectives including limiting resource costs – in the IMF, EBRD and World Bank. Treasury officials appointed as directors of these institutions are in constant touch with the Treasury in London.

We also take an active role in issues of trade policy (such as non-tariff barriers and anti-dumping) because of our interest in competition and the supply side; legislation gives us a say in UK export credit policy to ensure that the taxpayers' interest is taken fully into account; and we take a close interest in the resource implications of UK policy in many parts of the world, ranging from dependent territories to the former Yugoslavia.

How the Treasury carries out its responsibilities: *central co-ordination*   Despite its range of responsibilities, the Treasury is not a large organization; comprising only five ministers with 1400 civil servants.

The Treasury's official role is as the main and continuing source of advice to the Chancellor of the Exchequer. Its job is partly procedural, partly substantive. It is mainly interested in the design of policy and in policy as a whole.

So it is the Treasury which pulls together all the strands of economic policy-making right across the Government's programme. The Treasury will almost always be present at the point at which ministers take explicit decisions. And it is very much in the business of trying to make sure that the different parts of policy fit together.

It has a key position at the centre of government. No department can spend money without the agreement of the Treasury, and it has a central role in advising ministers on any decisions about tax changes. This means it has a keen interest in much of the business of every department.

The general case for a central department like this, with a broad range of business is essentially as follows. It makes sense to relate the span of responsibility to the area over which co-ordination is required. In important respects the various functions and responsibilities of the Treasury all hang together. It is essential to understand all these areas if a good job is to be made of any one of them. Some organization needs to take an overview to ensure that the whole picture is being brought to bear on decisions about the parts. The Treasury is uniquely able to undertake these tasks. Detailed aspects of this case are discussed in the section below on proposals for change.

The skills of the people that work in the Treasury match this central co-ordinating position. They often have to work very quickly, they often find long hours unavoidable, and because each carries a wide range of responsibilities they are able to see the big picture and where everything fits in. In the battle for ideas this gives them a great advantage.

What the Treasury does not do   The Treasury simply cannot and does not try to do everything itself.

It spends very little money itself apart from the pay of its staff; the spending of money is done by other departments – notably the Department of Social Security (DSS), the Department of Health, the Ministry of Defence and the Department of Education – and by local authorities.

It collects no taxes; that is the job of the Inland Revenue and Customs and Excise, while DSS and local authorities between them collect significant revenues through NICs, business rates and the Council Tax. Of course, the Chancellor is the Minister responsible for the revenue departments, but it is their job, and not the job of the Treasury, to provide the detailed expertise on particular tax issues and to turn his decisions into practice.

Although the Treasury borrows money on behalf of the Government, it does not have the day to day operational responsibility for this. This lies with the Bank of England in the bond markets and the Department for National Savings in the personal savings sector.

Moreover, the Treasury has little direct contact with the financial markets; that is largely the responsibility of the Bank of England. Successive Chancellors have seen the Bank of England as a crucial source of monetary advice and rely upon it, rather than the Treasury, to turn decisions into practice.

Although it uses, interprets and forecasts some Government statistics, the Treasury does not, in most cases, produce them. That is primarily the job of the Central Statistical Office.

Relationships

The Treasury's relationships reflect its position at the centre of government but with few executive responsibilities. Since it does not have the power, it must rely on influence.

The relationship between No. 10 and the Treasury is key. Not surprisingly the Chancellor and Prime Minister see a great deal of each other; a weekly meeting between the two is the norm apart from the various Cabinet and Cabinet Committee meetings that take place all the time.

The relationship between the Treasury and the Bank of England is generally quite informal. Senior people meet their opposite numbers frequently. The Governor sees the Chancellor on a regular basis. The Bank and Treasury work very closely together at official level on monetary matters, even if, like all close relationships, occasionally there are tensions.

The relationship with the SIB is, of course, much newer to the Treasury, and differs in line with the statutory nature of the relevant responsibilities in this area. But, once again, the developing link is one of close, regular contact, a degree of informality and close co-operation.

Another critical relationship is with the Revenue Departments. These are two large professional bodies which provide detailed expertise on tax matters. They do not duplicate the Treasury; the vast majority of their staff are employed in the primary functions of assessment and collection, and they offer different skills (specialist tax knowledge as against packaging of combinations of tax proposals).

And finally, of course, there is a very close relationship between the Treasury and each of the government departments. Within the Treasury a group of officials is allocated to shadow each of the departments. They discuss with them any new policy proposals; they monitor their expenditure on agreed spending plans and are diligent in their search for economies. For departments the Treasury can occasionally be a convenient scapegoat, but the essence of the relationship is one of co-operation.

Changes in responsibilities and relationships
These arrangements have considerable strengths, as I have suggested. Not all our critics recognize this. This section discusses the main proposals critics have made, which usually involve reducing or dividing the role of the Treasury and handing some of its responsibilities to other organizations.

Earlier moves to achieve this include the establishment of a Civil Service Department with responsibilities for civil service pay and management, and a Department of Economic Affairs with responsibility for longer-term growth policy. More recently, suggestions have included the division of the Treasury between a Ministry of Finance and a Bureau of the Budget, and the establishment of an independent Bank of England responsible for the conduct of monetary policy.

Clearly, models other than the current one are possible. After all, they occur in some other countries. None of what follows is meant to suggest that change should be ruled out for all time. But at the same time it should be recognized that we are not dealing with a fixed and rigid system; changes have been taking place that have important implications for the way the Treasury does business.

Such changes include the new Unified Budget, changes in the handling of monetary policy (resulting in greater openness), and the development of more strategic approaches to public spending and civil service management.

There have also been transfers of functions between departments. It has been an important and continuing role of Treasury management to work continually to identify and focus on essential functions. Responsibility for regulation of financial services has been transferred *to* the Treasury. Responsibility for some functions not closely connected to our work has been moved *out*. This has now reduced the Treasury to what until now has been called 'central Treasury'; in terms of the simple headcount it has reduced the Treasury from over 3000 people in early 1982 to just over 1400.

The cumulative effect of these sorts of changes can be substantial. Some of them happen quickly; where they involve major or constitutional change, a gradual approach can have advantages.

The Treasury and monetary policy   Perhaps the most intense debate at the moment is on the Treasury's responsibility for monetary policy.

The conduct of monetary policy is inevitably a source of differences of opinion, especially in an open economy with a heavily traded currency, and particularly at a time of globalization of markets and financial deregulation. These differences have emerged during both periods of floating exchange rates and episodes of attempts at greater fixity. The appreciation of sterling in the early 1980s (coinciding with rapid growth of broad money) was seen by many as intensifying the recession. And yet the attempt to cap the sterling–DM rate at 3DM to the pound in the 12 months to March 1988 produced a massive inflow of reserves and was seen by others as a severe complication to the conduct of monetary policy. During most of the 1980s, and particularly from 1986 onwards, there was a strong body of business and political opinion that difficulties in the conduct of monetary policy could be overcome by membership of the ERM. But it proved to be unsustainable in Autumn 1992 when the floor set by German interest rates, at the level needed to handle the consequences of German unification, became increasingly inappropriate to the UK's cyclical position.

Apart from the acute differences of approach and judgement evident during the monetary debate, some question whether the present organization of the responsibilities for monetary policy makes it prone to certain kinds of policy errors.

By tradition, the conduct of UK monetary policy – and the responsibility for dealing with these conflicting pressures – is firmly in the hands of the Chancellor. He takes advice from the Bank of England and Treasury officials. Nigel Lawson notes in his book[3] that in the conduct of monetary policy he regarded both equally as advisers and sometimes took the side of the Bank of England in the event of disagreements. But as far as Parliament is concerned it is ministers who design and execute policy, and are accountable.

In a number of other countries there is a different tradition. In both the United States and Germany the central banks have explicit statutory responsibilities. Recently in New Zealand, the Government has handed over the day to day operation of monetary policy to the central bank within a carefully specified framework and set of objectives.

A number of reasons are advanced for taking the setting of interest rates out of the hands of ministers:

- there is some evidence that inflation performance is better in countries with greater central bank independence;
- in turn this is related to the ability of the central bank to concentrate on the objective of inflation, and to ignore political pressures that cause ministers to take other factors into account when making interest rate decisions;
- because of the increased credibility these arrangements bring it might be possible to keep inflation down with a smaller unemployment cost, and therefore further increase the credibility of policy;
- it is in line with policy in other areas to delegate responsibility to the appropriate agency within the framework of a well-defined set of objectives;
- this is the model that will form the basis of the European Central Bank; and if the UK is to move towards monetary union it will have to participate on this basis. This suggests making a move in this direction as soon as possible.

Although the demand for greater independence of the central bank has come to be the most popular single answer to the problem of inflation (once reserved for the ERM) there are complications:

- the evidence for improved inflation performance is weak;
- errors in the conduct of monetary policy have been related more to technical problems associated with innovations such as financial deregulation rather than political pressures; 'not the government' is not a guarantee of wisdom;
- in the short run there is a trade-off between the objectives of inflation and activity. Faced with uncertainty, choices have to be made. It is argued that these choices should be made by elected politicians;
- within the UK parliamentary system it is impossible to guarantee independence for all time, as no government can bind its successor. It is difficult to design a system of accountability to Parliament. If there is no accountability by those responsible for monetary policy to the government of the day, the political pressures could emerge in a different way;

- there are advantages in being able to design monetary policy alongside the setting of fiscal policy.

Nevertheless, there is a spectrum of options running from independence for the central bank to one where the decisions are taken exclusively by ministers with the function of the bank restricted to implementing decisions.

Treasury and supply performance   There is a suggestion that the Treasury should take on extra responsibilities for the supply side; and in particular that it should be more closely involved in the design of an industrial strategy. It is argued that the Treasury should use its position at the centre of economic policy to bring about faster change.

The first general point is that responsibilities for aspects of economic policy are spread among several departments: policy on human capital and labour market lies primarily with the Department for Education and the Department of Employment; policy on industrial strategy lies primarily with the Department of Trade and Industry. The Treasury can to some extent help to pull together interrelated policies which span several departments, without necessarily taking the lead in them.

The second point is that the Treasury does seek to have a positive bias towards policies that would improve the supply performance of the economy. Of course, there are times when that is in conflict with other objectives. For example, in a privatization, maximizing proceeds may conflict with bedding in a competitive structure for an industry; in public expenditure areas, the general need to constrain expenditure may conflict with the need to increase it in specific areas for supply-side reasons; in tax decisions, there may be conflict between revenue considerations and the supply side. In each case, the Treasury will seek objectively to analyse and weigh these conflicts, and to reach the optimum reconciliation rather than allowing its direct responsibilities to override, regardless, the broader and longer-term concerns.

The division between public expenditure and economic functions   A number of arguments are put forward for dividing the Treasury between the public expenditure and economic functions. Some say:

- that it would make a department with a more manageable range of duties and take some of the pressures away from the same group of ministers;
- that public expenditure control inevitably fosters a negative culture that is not at all suitable for the Treasury's other responsibilities;
- that it would enable the Economic Ministry to concentrate on policy proposals from the point of view of their impact on the performance of

the economy as a whole, rather than be dominated by the short-term public expenditure implications of proposals.

The main danger with the proposal is that it could well make overall public expenditure control less effective; it would make the total and content of public spending *less* subject to macroeconomic and supply-side influences and those responsible for it *more* susceptible to a negative culture. In addition there are important areas where the Treasury benefits from cross-fertilization of experience and knowledge. The Unified Budget, local government finance, social security finance and EC finance straddle these areas.

The present system, whereby the detailed public expenditure work is undertaken by the Chief Secretary under the overall authority of the Chancellor of the Exchequer, provides a strong support for public expenditure planning and control at the heart of government. This basic approach is followed in a number of European countries. It is the means by which the problem of pressures on ministers can be minimized.

A division of the public expenditure and economic responsibilities would require other means of giving support to the expenditure control system. For example, in the United States the Bureau of the Budget is bolstered by its status as part of the President's office; it is not just another department among many.

Alternatively, sometimes one comes across the suggestion that the 'finance' (in this context meaning tax and borrowing) and economic functions should be separated from the Bureau of the Budget (public expenditure) functions. In the UK, we are deliberately moving further in the opposite direction. The introduction of the new Unified Budget will help to increase the benefit we obtain from looking at spending and tax decisions together within a single department. This offers both a great challenge and a great opportunity for the Treasury.

The relationship between the Treasury and departments   A further suggestion is that the Treasury tries to be too closely involved in the management of individual departments; that it interferes too much. It is suggested that it should leave much more of the detailed financial management to departments, concentrating itself on the totals and the allocation between programmes. This is a fascinating dialogue that has gone on over many years.

The Treasury's role in relation to departments has changed over time and will continue to change. In the 1920s Warren Fisher, the then Permanent Secretary to the Treasury, promoted an active debate on whether the accounting officer in departments should be a Treasury man, a principal finance officer or a permanent head of department:

It is not only members of the public who have been misled by the phrase 'Treasury Control'; there have been times when even officials of the Treasury have, to its solemn refrain, conjured up a picture of themselves as the single-handed champions of solvency keeping ceaseless vigil on the buccaneering proclivities of Permanent Heads of Departments.[4]

Fisher believed that policy and expenditure were intertwined, and that the accounting officer should be the permanent head of department. At the same time he supported the view that department heads should also be seen as trustees of the taxpayer, and this should not be seen as the exclusive function of the Treasury.

Departments have a critical part to play in ensuring that taxpayers' money is well spent, in ways which accord with particular Government policies and also reflect the Government's general political stance. The Treasury should not seek to duplicate this role. But the image of the Treasury as the taxpayers' agent is a useful one.

Public services are often supplied by monopoly suppliers. In the absence of a market, it is particularly important to ensure that the taxpayer pays for well-managed products and services of the quality required. Rarely is the taxpayer in a position to achieve this directly. The Treasury can act for the taxpayer by providing guidance on best practice, and sometimes sharing in departments' work by direct support and assistance. It can also challenge where appropriate the value for money of the goods and services which departments provide.

In general there has been a move to a more strategic approach on public spending. The Treasury's role is increasingly that of exercising strategic-level supervision and control, helping ministers to determine priorities; helping to define strategic objectives and milestones; and monitoring progress and evaluating results. This all involves the Treasury much less in the details of programmes and rather more in the bigger question of priorities.

This has developed from the initiatives towards better financial management in government that have been underway for at least ten years. It has involved greater emphasis in defining the task to be done, coupled with delegation of responsibility to the lowest practicable level. It has also involved improved accountability and an agreement on key targets for financial performance, efficiency and quality of service.

At the same time new Survey arrangements have been introduced which reinforce these ideas. In the 1992 Survey a firm overall envelope for spending throughout the Survey period was set at the beginning, and a Cabinet remit was given to a group of ministers to propose allocations within it. There was then a need to squeeze some programmes to fit in the envelope, given other unavoidable demands. In other words, the whole process of allocation was, to a greater extent than before, one of strategic allocation.

As usual this involved some painful decisions along the way and some new procedures. Obviously key decisions still have to be informed by detail and must take account of the outputs and value for money of different activities and different levels of spending. But there was less comprehensive discussion of the detail of individual sub-programmes than there had been. From the Treasury's point of view it involved a significant development and clarification of roles, consistent with the strategic management approach. Moreover, by involving some other ministers more in fitting expenditure within the necessary envelope, there should be gains in terms of mutual scrutiny of each other's programmes and a wider recognition of the importance of public expenditure control.

Style

A second broad source of criticism has been in relation to the Treasury's style of doing business. It is suggested that the Treasury is secretive, unresponsive and unaccountable.

I do not accept these criticisms. Treasury officials have to be highly responsive to outside pressures in order to be at all effective in their work. In this sense, they have a much greater degree of accountability than their peers in the private sector. To be effective much of their work must, I believe, inevitably be carried out in conditions of confidentiality.

But we are nevertheless making changes in the way we work, as I explain below.

Ministers and officials

This issue reaches into the whole question of the relationship between ministers and officials.

Sir Humphrey   The dominant view held by commentators about the relationship between ministers and officials seems to be the one portrayed in 'Yes Minister'. In this:

- the scheming Sir Humphrey manipulates the innocent Jim Hacker;
- the department has strong views of its own which it insists on following, whoever may be the government. It forces its views on a naive minister either to protect the historical interests of the officials or to increase the power of the department and hence of the officials. Other views are stifled by secrecy, manipulation or misrepresentation;
- the Minister's prime purpose is to remain in power. Actions are judged in terms of whether they increase the reputation of the Minister. Ministers concentrate on presentation, taking initiatives and taking credit; they scheme against colleagues and are willing to pass the blame whenever they can;

- on important matters the officials are the puppeteers; and the Minister the puppet. Officials effectively take decisions in secret without being account-able; luckless Ministers have to carry the can.

Ministers are in charge   But this 'Yes Minister' version is nowhere near the truth. In the Treasury, ministers drive the main policy agenda. This is graphi-cally set out in Ministerial memoirs by Lords Lawson and Healey.[5] They were in charge; they commissioned work; they listened to others as well as Treasury officials; and they took decisions. This is my experience of other Chancellors too. There is a continuous stream of advice from outside, from universities, businesses, pressure groups, trades unions, political parties and journalists. Ministers devour it avidly.

The textbook version is more symmetrical. Basically:

- officials offer advice and ministers take decisions based on the advice of officials and the enormous range of comment and advice available from outside the civil service;
- the Minister is in charge and answerable to Parliament and the public. He holds his position as long as the Prime Minister wants him to and he and his party have enough votes in the Commons. His job is to examine the options, apply political judgement and take the decision;
- the job of officials is to offer confidential advice in private about a range of options about the stated government policy in a technical, non-political way, serving ministers of either party;
- the Minister takes responsibility for everything; the credit in good times; the blame in bad times; the official is loyal, invisible and voiceless.

The real officials   There is a lot of truth in this picture. In the end the Chancellor decides – just like it says in the textbooks. In practice much of the debate on policy is the battle for the Chancellor's mind. But the picture is under pressure in some ways. It is worth looking in more detail at the reality of the way in which policy advice is made and given.

We can distinguish two aspects of the role of officials, although in practice it is extremely difficult to separate the role of officials from that of ministers.

First, officials *contribute to the process of forming policy.* This means iden-tifying the issues in advance and making sure that the necessary work is done in good time for the point at which decisions have to be taken. It means co-ordinating the activities of many people who have an interest, and making sure that everyone who should know does know what is going on. It requires managing staff and having the right resources in the right place.

This not only involves much internal activity; it also means dealing with people outside the Treasury – including No. 10, the Cabinet Office, other government departments, overseas governments and institutions, the Bank of England, the Revenue Departments, industrialists, financiers, other managers throughout the public sector and academics and so on.

Officials' contributions to forming policy advice involve, as well as these management responsibilities, dealing directly with ministers as advisers. It is an enormous challenge to be part of the decision-making process for matters of such great importance.

When it comes to advice, senior officials can make their views known, and expect to be listened to. So, often, can more junior officials. Seniority provides no guarantee that the official's views will be accepted.

Of course, ministers do not take decisions without other sorts of constraints. There is a constant demand for ministers to take policy initiatives. But it only falls to government to change policy rarely. Governments fight elections; they have manifestos; policies have to be agreed by Cabinet. It is simply not possible to change policy on a whim – to duck and weave, forgetting about what you were trying to do yesterday.

Secondly, once the Minister decides a policy, the role of the official should normally switch to *implementation of that policy,* whatever view the official may have championed in the previous discussions. This means implementing policy decisions as effectively as possible; seeking to persuade other ministers and departments; and presenting the decisions to Parliamentary committees and generally to the outside world as the best available in the circumstances. It might also involve ministers delegating to officials the responsibility of taking further decisions, for which the officials are then accountable to the Minister.

Rather than seeking to frustrate decisions made by ministers, if anything the 'bias' among officials is to seek to sustain the policy framework once it has been established. It is far from unknown to see an official seeking to persuade a restless Minister to stick to an announced policy that the official had opposed in the first place.

Keeping the balance right between policy advice and implementation is crucial. One of the most important aspects of the job of senior Treasury officials, as in other departments, is being able to engage vigorously in debate about a policy proposal; but even when they find themselves on the losing side of the argument, to accept the conclusion and put all their energies into making the decision work.

In other words there is an implicit contract between ministers and officials when it comes to making decisions and implementing them.

Ministers set the policy agenda, often with help from officials, and make decisions within it. They seek, and officials offer, advice within the framework of this policy agenda. Officials are free to make observations about the likely results of policy proposals and to argue vigorously about the merits of various options until the point that the decision is made.

Once a decision is made, it is implemented and defended equally vigorously. In return for the privilege of being involved in the debate and having a chance to put their views, it is expected that officials subsequently keep their private views to themselves. And ministers take responsibility for the decisions they have taken.

Things work similarly in other organizations – and actually must do so. No organization can operate if the views of its members are made public in such a way that they can be used by outsiders to query or undermine the final decision.

Against this background, the reason why civil servants' policy advice to ministers should not be published emerges more clearly. To do so would undermine the effectiveness of the organization in defending and implementing decisions; and would damage civil servants' ability to serve ministers of a different party equally loyally. Confidentiality is essential for the political neutrality of the civil service; and it makes it easier for officials to provide and for ministers to accept 'fearless and frank' advice if both know that it will not be published.

Accountability and openness
In this context, how should we react to the criticisms and pressures?

Accountability   First, there is pressure for more accountability. There is growing pressure for more clarity about the responsibilities of organizations, particularly in the public service. 'Next Steps' has involved the creation of agencies with defined responsibilities. The question of whether departments are providing a professional and competent service is equally of natural public concern. The Citizens' Charter puts the spotlight on that.

Given the position of the Treasury at the heart of government, it is not surprising that these questions are also asked of it; there is a reasonable demand to know whether it is a professional and competent institution. But any change must address the central conundrum of how officials can be made more accountable for their advice when that very advice is confidential and it is ministers, not officials, that take decisions.

But there are ways of increasing accountability and openness within the present arrangements without doing too much damage to the principle of confidentiality of advice.

We have been putting effort into specifying objectives for the Treasury as a whole more clearly, and into describing how far the outcomes match the objectives. It is very difficult to get the balance right in setting objectives between what we have reasonable control over and what we are really aiming at. The former tends to be restricted to processes or intermediate aims; the latter to stray into economic developments subject to myriad factors outside our control.

The same basic impetus is reflected in the new arrangements for planning public expenditure. Setting a more definite remit for the Treasury at the start of the process allows clearer assessment as to how the Treasury performed. Similarly, we have set out our objectives for monetary policy, and are now committed to giving a clear account of the reasons for changes in, for instance, interest rates. This too will improve accountability.

Responsiveness and openness Secondly, there is pressure for more responsiveness and openness. This necessarily operates at the level of the individual official as well as of the organization as a whole. The image of the faceless official is changing. Officials are in practice no longer invisible or voiceless – they speak in front of Parliamentary Committees; they appear on TV and are profiled in the press; they negotiate here and abroad.

This is related to the increasing pressure to know how well civil servants have done their job of advising ministers and to want them to be answerable for the quality of their advice. There is particular concern about whether they offer disinterested advice; and whether they observe the correct constraints on advice by maintaining the traditional ethical and prudential standards which require officials at times to tell ministers what they may not want to hear. And people want to know the quality of the decisions taken by ministers faced with that advice.

There is also an increasing recognition that ministers cannot, in practice, be responsible for taking all decisions – for example, how a particular social security office might be run to best effect. For that reason the 'Next Steps' exercise has sought to establish across the civil service which matters are the responsibility of heads of agencies and other officials and has then made them accountable for those matters to ministers and, on behalf of ministers, to Select Committees.

We have taken steps to improve responsiveness – to listen to the views of others, engage in debate, and show whether and how far the views of others have influenced our thinking.

We have regular contacts at all levels with industrialists and economists, as well as with people in the financial sector, nationalized industries and local authorities at home, and officials, businessmen and commentators from other countries. The establishment of the Treasury forecasting panel is an important step towards ensuring that a range of views are presented to the Chancellor in a timely and manageable form. In practice, ministers have always devoured large amounts of material produced outside the Treasury; but greater formalization of consultation with outside organizations will help to ensure that their views are represented to ministers in a fair and open way.

The quarterly inflation report by the Bank of England, the move to publish the Treasury's monthly monetary report and the reasoning behind interest rate changes should also improve the quality of public debate.

There are many other channels of communication which can help. It is possible to envisage more participation by officials in conferences and seminars, and more background briefing on technical issues. The same trends will affect our relationships with other departments within government as well.

For reasons set out earlier, it is virtually impossible with a non-political senior civil service to disclose policy advice and debate on an ongoing basis. But without revealing confidential advice on policy given to ministers, we can do more to explain the background to decisions. Many of the changes described are relevant to that. In addition, one of the reasons for introducing the Treasury *Bulletin* was to offer a platform for background articles covering analysis of issues behind policy decisions.

Conclusion

Given the range and importance of its functions, it is not surprising that when things do go wrong it is the Treasury that receives the heaviest criticism. After all, who else is there to blame? Undoubtedly some of the criticism stems from a dislike of the Treasury's privileged position. At times, other criticism may focus on the Treasury when it is actually policy decisions taken by ministers with which the critics disagree. People dislike the secrecy; they dislike the extent to which the Treasury influences so much; and they dislike not knowing how decisions are taken.

To some extent this is the lot of the Treasurer. As King James said: 'All Treasurers, if they do good service to their masters, must be generally hated.'[6] Equally, the Treasury has to adapt to changing circumstances and the changing climate of opinion of what is expected from the civil service and its relationship with ministers.

It is the recognition of this that has caused us to look more clearly at the Treasury's role in the 1990s:

- to seek to identify the changing boundaries of the Treasury's core business;
- to seek to develop a clear focus on objectives;
- to question whether there is any bias within the Treasury towards the City and away from Industry;
- to see that staff are trained to take on the responsibilities and skills of the time;
- to have a communication system that enables these ideas to be known widely within the Treasury;
- to have an internal organization that reflects the balance of activities;
- to be more open about what we do generally, and have more contact with the outside world in particular.

Many challenges lie ahead for the Treasury, faced with demanding expectations for increased living standards, intensive scrutiny from those monitoring its activities and with an increasingly dynamic external environment. The Treasury must continue to change and adapt organically over time to meet these pressures, so that it can continue to provide its ministers with the high quality policy advice which they expect. My aim in this essay has been to demonstrate that the Treasury is aware of the criticisms and suggestions made about its role and style, which we consider carefully, albeit with a customary, critical eye; and that we are vigorously seeking to make what we see as useful changes where criticism has been well founded.

Notes

1. Lord Burghley, quoted in Henry Roseveare, *The Treasury: The Evolution of a British Institution*, Allen Lane, Penguin 1969, p. 29.
2. Cabinet 1924, quoted in Roseveare, p. 243.
3. Nigel Lawson, *The View from No. 11: Memoirs of a Tory Radical*, Bantam 1992, p. 464.
4. Sir Warren Fisher, in *Evidence to the Royal Commission on the Civil Service (1929–1930)*, 15 December 1930, p. 1270, para. 31.
5. Nigel Lawson, as above. Denis Healey, *The Time of my Life*, Michael Joseph 1989.
6. King James I, quoted in Roseveare, p.51.

4 UK unemployment revisited

*Robert M. Coen and Bert G. Hickman**

1. Introduction

The primary purpose of this paper is to investigate the relative importance of real wage rigidity and effective demand as determinants of excess unemployment in the United Kingdom during 1966–89. This is partly an update of our earlier work on the subject (Coen and Hickman, 1987, 1988), which only carried through to 1984. We have, however, introduced several changes in our methodology in the process of respecifying the medium-term econometric growth model on which the study is based. In a later publication we will present the results of complete-model simulations with endogenous wages, prices and activity variables, but this paper is limited to partial simulations of the model's labour-market blocs, so that it does not attempt directly to estimate the impact of changes in demand management or incomes policies on total unemployment or its classical and Keynesian components.

2. Alternate concepts of classical and Keynesian unemployment

In the standard fix-price model of price-taking competitive firms, Keynesian and classical unemployment are separate states according to whether notional product supply exceeds or falls short of market demand at the prevailing wage and price configuration, so that labour demand is either output-constrained and determined by the inverted production function (Keynesian unemployment), or firms are on their notional product supply and labour demand functions but the real wage exceeds the Walrasian full-employment (FE) level (classical unemployment). Thus labour demand is independent of the real wage in the Keynesian state and depends only on the real wage in the classical state (Patinkin (1956), Clower (1965), Barro and Grossman (1971), Malinvaud (1977) and Benassy (1975, 1982)).

Our conceptual framework assumes instead that imperfectly competitive firms price according to a mark-up rule and choose their inputs of labour and capital to minimize the cost of producing the output they expect to sell at the price they have set. The labour demand function is always conditional on both output and the real wage, and classical and Keynesian unemployment may therefore coexist. Keynesian unemployment exists when the economy is operating on an isoquant below that representing FE output, whereas classical

* The authors are, respectively, Professors of Economics at Northwestern and Stanford Universities.

unemployment occurs when the real wage exceeds its FE level either at or below FE output (Hickman (1987), Coen and Hickman (1987, 1988)).

Notice that these concepts refer to unemployment states rather than the shocks which induce them. A supply shock, for example, may lead to classical unemployment by raising the real wage above the FE level, but it may also depress aggregate demand and create Keynesian unemployment.

In order to quantify the impacts of high real wages and deficient effective demand on unemployment in our framework, it is necessary first to estimate the FE rates of unemployment, real wages, and output for comparison with the actual levels of these variables. We begin with the FE unemployment rate.

3. Specification and estimation of the natural rate of unemployment

Our specification of the natural rate of unemployment captures the influences of several factors. The natural rate is calculated as a weighted average of the natural rates for 16 age–sex groups, with weights proportional to the FE labour force in each group. Demographic changes can raise the natural rate insofar as they shift the composition of the FE labour force towards groups whose natural unemployment rates are normally relatively high. Demographic changes might also alter the natural unemployment rates of some groups; for example, disproportionate growth in the supply of younger workers might raise their unemployment rates insofar as it leads to a mismatch between the skills and work experience employers seek and those offered by younger job applicants. Another set of factors includes those altering the real product wage or creating a wedge between the real wage paid by employers and the real wage received by workers. These include indirect business taxes, employer contributions to social insurance, direct taxes on wage earnings, and changes in the relative price of consumption goods. The relative price of consumption goods in turn is affected by changes in indirect business taxes and import price shocks.

One age–sex group, a prime-age male group, is selected as the 'key labour force group', on the basis of its participation rate being relatively high and stable and its unemployment rate being relatively low and stable. Because of the key group's strong attachment to the labour force, its interests are likely to be very influential in wage negotiations. The natural unemployment rate of the key group is based in part on the notion that labour, as represented by the key group, and capital are engaged in a struggle over shares of aggregate income. Producers attempt to achieve a mark-up of price over unit labour costs to achieve their desired capital share, while workers seek a nominal wage that, in view of labour productivity and the price level, assures them of their desired income share. We assume that the bargaining strength of the key group is inversely related to its unemployment rate. Consistency of the desired income shares (they must sum to unity) is brought about by changes in the unemployment rate of the key group. Starting from a situation of equilibrium, a rise in taxes or import prices may create a distributional imbalance that would lead to spiralling inflation. The imbalance is removed by an increase in the natural rate of unemployment.

The natural rates of the other age–sex groups are related to the natural rate of the key group, according to elasticities estimated from data on actual rates. The underlying determinants of the key group's natural rate thereby also influence the natural rates of the other groups. These other rates are also dependent on demographic shifts, according to estimated elasticities of each group's observed unemployment rate to its share of the population. The overall natural rate is a weighted average of the age-specific natural rates.

The natural rate of the key labour force group

Our model of the natural rate is a variant of the 'Battle of the Mark-ups' approach epitomized by Layard *et al.* (1991). We assume that producers desire a capital share in income of γ and that the key labour force group (henceforth referred to simply as 'labour' or 'workers') desires a share of β. Suppose that the desired capital share is fixed, but that labour's desired share depends on the unemployment rate. A higher unemployment rate reduces workers' ability or willingness to bargain for higher wages, leading labour to settle for a smaller share.

If X is aggregate output, L labour input, W the nominal wage rate, and P the price level, then the desired capital and labour shares are, respectively:

$$\gamma = \frac{(PX - WL)}{PX} \tag{4.1}$$

$$\beta = \frac{WL}{PX}. \tag{4.2}$$

To obtain the desired capital share, producers wish to set the price level as a mark-up on unit labour costs, that is:

$$P = \frac{1}{1-\gamma} \frac{W^e L}{X}, \tag{4.3}$$

where the mark-up is on the expected wage and depends on the desired capital share.[1] The mark-up is assumed to be insensitive to changes in the level of activity, in view of the general finding in the literature that the elasticity of the mark-up with respect to changes in capacity utilization, orders and similar variables is small. To obtain the desired labour share, workers wish to receive a wage that is a mark-up on the expected price level, namely:

$$W = \beta \frac{X}{L} P^e. \tag{4.4}$$

The mark-up proportion here depends on the desired labour share and on the level of productivity. If, as we assume, the desired labour share itself is negatively related to the unemployment rate, U, then the mark-up proportion also depends on the unemployment rate For example, we might have:

$$\beta(U) = \beta_0 e^{-\beta_1 U} \tag{4.5}$$

in which case:

$$W = \beta_0 e^{-\beta_1 U} \frac{X}{L} P^e. \tag{4.6}$$

The desired factor shares will be consistent with one another only if they sum to unity. If capital and labour together desire shares that initially exceed unity, their interests are brought into balance by a rise in the unemployment rate, which reduces wage demands and makes labour content to settle for a smaller share. Given the specification of the desired labour share in (4.5), and imposing the condition that $\gamma + \beta = 1$, we can solve for the equilibrating, or natural, unemployment rate:

$$U^N = \frac{\ln \beta_0 - \ln(1 - \gamma)}{\beta_1}. \tag{4.7}$$

Equilibrium requires that actual unemployment is at the natural rate and that wage and price expectations are realized, so that the real wage desired by workers equals that set by employers in the pricing process. Dividing equation (4.3) by W and equation (4.6) by P and combining the equations yields:

$$U = \frac{\ln \beta_0 - \ln(1 - \gamma) - (\ln W - \ln W^e) - (\ln P - \ln P^e)}{\beta_1} \tag{4.8}$$

which may be rearranged as:

$$U = U^N - \frac{\left(\ln W - \ln W^e\right) + \left(\ln P - \ln P^e\right)}{\beta_1}. \tag{4.9}$$

Thus positive wage and price surprises drive U below the natural rate. On the assumption that the inflation rate follows a random walk, Layard *et al.* (1991, p. 15) show that the price and wage surprises are equivalent to changes in the rate of inflation, so that one can convert equation (4.9) to:

$$\Delta \ln P - \Delta \ln P_{-1} = -\frac{\beta_1}{2}\left(U - U^N\right) \tag{4.10}$$

if the wage and price surprises are of similar magnitude. Thus, given their assumption on the stochastic process generating inflation, U^N is a NAIRU.

While the natural rate in equation (4.7) is constant, variations in taxes or the relative price of consumption goods may affect the natural rate. Thus, suppose that the indirect tax rate is t_i, so that the price level, inclusive of indirect taxes, is $P = (1 + t_i)P_n$, where P_n is the price level net of indirect taxes. We might assume that the desired capital share pertains to income net of indirect taxes, that is:

$$\tilde{\gamma} = \frac{P_n X - WL}{P_n X}. \tag{4.11}$$

Substituting for P_n and rearranging, we have for capital's share in gross-of-tax income:

$$\gamma = \frac{PX - WL}{PX} = \tilde{\gamma} + t_i \frac{WL}{PX}. \tag{4.12}$$

Several factors account for the difference between the wage paid to a worker and his or her potential consumption. Employer contributions to social insurance create a wedge between the cost of labour to employers and the wage received by workers. Suppose that t_s is the social insurance tax rate paid by employers, so that the wage paid by employers is $W = (1 + t_s)W_n$, where W_n is the wage net of employer contributions. Similarly, the workers' disposable wage is $W_d = (1 - t_x)W_n$, where t_x is the combined employee social insurance and income tax rate on workers. Finally, there may be a wedge between the price of consumer goods, P_c (inclusive of indirect taxes) and the overall price level, P. Potential consumption is given by $W_d L/P_c$, where P_c is the price of consumption goods (inclusive of indirect taxes) and we have:

$$\tilde{\beta} = \frac{W_d L}{P_c X}. \tag{4.13}$$

Substituting for W_d and W_n and rearranging, we have:

$$\beta = \frac{WL}{PX} = \tilde{\beta} \frac{(1+t_s)P_c}{(1-t_x)P}. \tag{4.14}$$

For the desired shares to be consistent, we must have:

$$\gamma + \beta = \tilde{\gamma} + t_i \tilde{\beta} \frac{(1+t_s)}{(1-t_x)} \frac{P_c}{P} + \tilde{\beta} \frac{(1+t_s)}{(1-t_x)} \frac{P_c}{P} = 1 \tag{4.15}$$

or

$$\tilde{\beta} = \frac{(1-\tilde{\gamma})(1-t_x)}{(1+t_i)(1+t_s)\dfrac{P_c}{P}}. \tag{4.16}$$

Substituting from (4.5) and solving for U gives:

$$U^N = \frac{\ln \tilde{\beta}_0 - \ln(1-\tilde{\gamma}) + \ln(1+t_i) + \ln(1+t_s) - \ln(1-t_x) + \ln(P_c/P)}{\tilde{\beta}_1}. \tag{4.17}$$

Thus, the higher any of the tax rates, and the higher is the relative price of consumption goods, the higher is the natural unemployment rate.

A rise in the indirect tax rate leads producers to increase the price level in an effort to maintain capital's share, and the rise in the price level may cause workers to increase their wage demands. But for capital's share to be preserved, labour must be induced to accept a lower real wage and smaller share, which requires an increase in the unemployment rate. If the unemployment rate does not increase, the rise in the tax rate sets off an inflationary spiral as each group attempts to maintain its share by successive price and wage increases. Thus, our natural rate of unemployment may be viewed as one that is consistent with a stable price level or inflation rate in the face of fluctuations in indirect taxes.

The immediate impact of a rise in the employers' social insurance tax rate is to raise labour costs and reduce capital's share. To restore capital's share, producers will want to reduce the wage, but labour will accept a lower wage (and share) only at a higher unemployment rate. Should labour resist a lower wage, producers will seek to recoup the added tax and reduce the real wage by raising prices. Again, without a rise in the unemployment rate, an inflationary spiral will result.

An increase in workers' personal income or social insurance tax rates will reduce their disposable incomes and potential consumption and create upward pressure on wages, prices and unemployment.

A rise in the relative price of consumption goods causes labour to demand higher wages in order to maintain potential consumption. If they are successful, capital's share declines, leading producers to raise prices, and so on. Once again a rise in the unemployment rate is required to coax labour into accepting a smaller share. There are two major factors affecting P_c/P. Differentially higher indirect taxes will tend to raise the relative price of consumer goods, since capital goods are not much affected by such taxes. Import price shocks may also drive up the real price of consumption goods.

The above analysis assumes that capital's share is invariant to changes in tax rates and relative prices, but this need not be so. To the extent that capital bears portions of these taxes and accepts a smaller share, the changes in the unemployment rate will be smaller. For example, in the extreme case where capital's share is reduced by the full amount of the taxes, the unemployment rate would be independent of the tax rates. An additional consideration arises in the case of social insurance taxes. To the extent that workers view these taxes, including the employer portions, as purchases of fairly priced annuities which they would desire to purchase privately if they were not publicly provided, then tax increases should not lead to higher wage demands. Thus, the sensitivity of the natural unemployment rate to changes in taxes and relative prices is not clear *a priori* and needs to be studied empirically.

Empirical implementation
In our empirical implementation, we assume a log-linear relationship between the observed unemployment rate of the key group, which is 35–44 year old males, and its determinants.

$$\ln(U_{k,t}) = c_0 + c_1 \ln(t_{i,t}) + c_2 \ln(t_{s,t}) + c_3 \ln(t_{x,t}) +$$
$$c_4 \ln s_m(P_{m,t}/P_t) + c_5 \ln(z_t) = v_t, \qquad (4.18)$$

where z_t is a capacity utilization variable (described in Appendix A) and v_t is a stochastic disturbance. We have substituted the real import price (weighted by the share of imports in GDP) for the real consumption price in order better to identify external supply shocks to the natural rate. As noted above, P_c/P responds primarily to changes in t_i and P_m/P. The final choice of the estimated equation uses a log-linear combination of the tax variables as a regressor and omits the import price variable, which was insignificant (see Appendix B).[2]

Finally, to estimate the natural rate, we purge the observed rate of its cyclical and stochastic components by setting z_t to unity and v_t to zero in (4.18).

Natural rates of unemployment for other groups
Natural rates for other population groups are computed from regressions of their unemployment rates on the key unemployment rate and the population ratio of the group. The equations are in log form. For age–sex group i, the regression equation is:

$$\ln(U_{i,t}) = c_0 + c_1\ln(U_{k,t}) + c_2\ln(N_{i,t} / N_t) + w_t, \qquad (4.19)$$

where N is population and w_t is a stochastic disturbance. Thus, cyclical variations and tax or price-induced variations in the age–sex-specific rates are related to variations in the key group's rate. The population ratios are included to allow for influences of labour market mismatches on the age–sex specific rates (Wachter, 1976). A rise in the proportion of young workers might, other things equal, increase their unemployment rates, insofar as employers do not regard them as good substitutes for older, experienced workers. Also, minimum wage legislation or other factors may prevent adjustments in demand favouring untrained and lower-skilled young workers.

To compute the natural rates from these regressions, we purge the observed rates of their cyclical and stochastic components by setting the unemployment rate of the key group on the right-hand side to its natural level and setting the disturbance to zero.

The aggregate natural rate
The aggregate natural rate, U^N, combines the age–sex-specific rates with weights equal to each group's share of the natural labour force:

$$U_t^N = \sum_{j=1}^{16} U_{j,t}^N \frac{L_{j,t}^N}{L_t^N}, \qquad (4.20)$$

where L^N refers to the natural labour force.

4.   Prices and wages
In this section we amplify on the theoretical specification of the price mark-up equation, discuss the empirical estimation of the equilibrium FE mark-up and relate it to the real wage gap, and refer briefly to the Phillips curve for nominal wage determination.

Theoretical specification of the mark-up equation

In order to highlight the distributional issues in wage and price determination, in section 3 we defined the mark-ups in terms of the income shares of capital (γ) and labour (β), with the price mark-up equal to $1/(1 - \gamma)$. What factors may determine γ and how does $1/(1 - \gamma)$ relate to other mark-up specifications? These issues will be discussed in the context of our empirical model, which features a Cobb–Douglas technology with constant returns to scale and imperfect competition.

We assume a representative firm with value-added C–D function and neutral technical progress at rate ρ:

$$X = A\ e^{\rho t} K^{\alpha} L^{1-\alpha}. \tag{4.21}$$

The market demand function is:

$$X = BP^{-\phi_1} Y^{\phi_2} \tag{4.22}$$

where Y is aggregate income and $\phi_1 > 1$. Profit maximization yields the expression for optimal long-term price:

$$P = [1 - (1/\phi_1)]^{-1} AC \tag{4.23}$$

where

$$AC = A^{-1}\ \alpha^{-\alpha} (1 - \alpha)^{-(1-\alpha)}\ e^{-\rho t}\ Q^{\alpha}\ W^{1-\alpha}. \tag{4.24}$$

Equation (4.24) (the cost dual to equation (4.21)) is the expression for the minimum long-run average cost, AC, as a function of the production parameters, the wage rate, W, and the rental price of capital, Q. It is also the long-run marginal cost (MC) function under constant returns to scale. Thus the profit-maximizing condition ($MR = MC$) is represented in equation (4.23) as a mark-up on average cost, including the cost of capital as well as labour (Nordhaus, 1972). The mark-up is a function of ϕ_1, the elasticity of demand for the product, and its magnitude is determined by $[1-(1/\phi_1)]^{-1}$, or the 'degree of monopoly'.[3]

Average cost may also be expressed, however, as $AC = [1/(1 - \alpha)]\ ULC$,[4] so that equation (4.23) may be transformed to:

$$P = \left[1 - \left(1/\phi_1\right)\right]^{-1} \left[1/(1 - \alpha)\right] ULC = \left(\frac{\theta}{1 - \alpha}\right) ULC \tag{4.25}$$

where $ULC = WL/X$ and θ symbolizes the degree of monopoly. Equation (4.25) shows that the mark-up over ULC basically depends on α, the relative contribution of capital to production, and the elasticity of product demand ϕ_1. Comparing the mark-up coefficients in equations (4.3) and (4.25), and assuming the producers' wage expectations are satisfied shows that:

$$\gamma = 1 - \left[\left(1 - \frac{1}{\phi_1}\right)(1 - \alpha)\right] = \alpha + \frac{(1 - \alpha)}{\phi_1}. \tag{4.26}$$

Suppose that demand were perfectly elastic, with $\phi_1 = \infty$. In that case labour and capital would be paid their marginal products, so that $\gamma = \alpha$. If $\infty > \phi_1 > 1$, however, labour and capital are paid their marginal revenue products and $\gamma > \alpha$, as labour's share is reduced and 'capital' receives a monopoly profit to augment its total interest return. In this model, then, there is stability over the long run in the income shares if the degree of monopoly and the marginal productivities are constant.[5]

The 'capital' share γ in equations (4.l) and (4.3) includes a (monopoly) profit component as well as interest and depreciation. In a two-factor model, the profit has to be imputed to 'capital'. but there is still a sharp distinction between the interest component as a cost of capital services and the profit component.

To see this, note that the value of total output under imperfect competition is:

$$PX = \theta[WL + P(r + \delta)K] \tag{4.27}$$

where $P(r + \delta) = Q$ is the rental price of capital services (under the simplifying assumption that the price of capital goods is the same as the price of output) and θ is again the degree of monopoly. Thus the value of output exceeds total factor cost in the ratio θ, and both the wage and interest shares are reduced by the extraction of monopoly profits. If the monopoly rent π is imputed to K, we have:

$$\pi PK = PX - \left[WL + P(r + \delta)K\right] = PX - \frac{PX}{\theta} = \left(\frac{\theta - 1}{\theta}\right)PX \tag{4.28}$$

so that:

$$\pi = \left(\frac{\theta - 1}{\theta}\right)\frac{X}{K}. \tag{4.29}$$

The optimal input of capital services is determined by the *MRP* condition that the rental price of capital equals the marginal revenue product of capital:

$$P(r + \delta) = P\left(1 - \frac{1}{\phi_1}\right)\alpha \frac{X}{K}. \tag{4.30}$$

Rewriting equation (4.27) as:

$$PX = P(\pi + r + \delta)K + WL \tag{4.31}$$

and making use of (4.29) and (4.30) to solve for the labour share yields:

$$\frac{WL}{PX} = \left(1 - \frac{1}{\phi_1}\right)(1 - \alpha). \tag{4.32}$$

The expression on the right-hand side of equation (4.32) is the wage share when labour is paid its marginal revenue product. We have now shown that the wage share is the complement to the non-wage share $\gamma = [P(\pi + r + \delta)K]/PX$ defined to include profit as well as interest and depreciation, verifying equation (4.26).

Empirical implementation of the price equation
Equations (4.23)–(4.25) refer to long-run equilibrium with firms on their production functions (no adjustment lags) and long-run cost curves. The actual mark-up may deviate from equilibrium because capital and labour inputs are not fully adjusted to the equilibrium levels and firms are not operating on their long-run cost curves, or because of changes in the degree of monopoly associated with changes in demand pressure or capacity utilization.

For the master price equation we assume the existence of a constant, long-term equilibrium mark-up of price over unit labour cost and model the variations around the equilibrium mark-up by an error-adjustment mechanism. The adjustment variables include changes in the rate of capacity utilization, intended to capture the relatively small cyclical fluctuations in the mark-up, and changes in unit labour cost, the indirect tax rate, and lagged prices (see Appendix B).

The equilibrium mark-up is estimated by the mean of the actual mark-up (*P/ULC*) during 1960–72 and is plotted against the actual mark-up in Figure 4.1. This period was chosen because it preceded the powerful supply shocks of the 1970s and 1980s, which may have distorted the 1960–89 average as an estimator of the long-term equilibrium. The actual mark-up fluctuated moderately about the equilibrium during the 1960s, but the deviations were much larger during the turbulent 1970s and 1980s.[6]

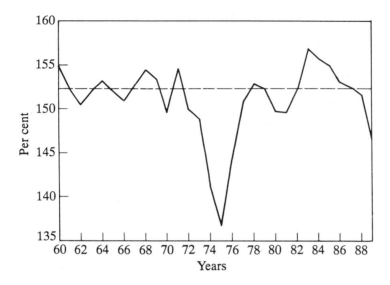

Figure 4.1   Actual and equilibrium mark-ups

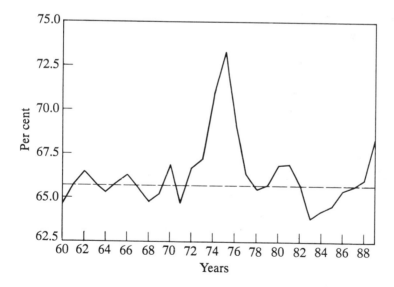

Figure 4.2   Actual and equilibrium wage shares

The reciprocal of the actual mark-up is, of course, the labour share (Figure 4.2). Evidently there are powerful forces tending to reverse deviations of the income distribution from its long-term equilibrium, but the departures may persist for many years and attain large amplitudes. The equilibrating forces include demand management and incomes policies, as discussed in section 7.

In addition to the master price equation for the aggregate price level, the model incorporates a set of auxiliary equations to explain the sector deflators as functions of the aggregate price index and other determinants.

The real wage gap

We measure the real wage gap in relative terms as WR/WRF, where $WR = W/P$ and WRF is the real wage that would prevail under FE conditions. In our model, the FE path implies an equilibrium income distribution, since otherwise the resulting wage/price pressures would be incompatible with maintaining a steady state growth path. The value of the long-run equilibrium mark-up over ULC compatible with optimal employment of labour and capital was defined as $\theta/(1 - \alpha)$ in equation (4.25), and the equation can be rearranged to give $WRF = [(1 - \alpha)/\theta] \, PRODF$, where $PRODF$ is the level of labour productivity at full employment. Given a constant value for the equilibrium price mark-up, the real wage would grow at the same rate as productivity along the FE equilibrium path, and the equilibrium labour share would be constant at $WRF/PRODF = [(1 - \alpha)/\theta]$, shown by the dashed line in Figure 4.2.

As we have already seen, the actual mark-up fluctuates widely around the FE mark-up, implying correspondingly wide inverse fluctuations in the labour share. The actual labour share equals $WR/PROD$, where $PROD$ is realized labour productivity. Thus the ratio of the actual and equilibrium labour shares is $(WR/PROD)/(WRF/PRODF) = (WR/WRF)/(PRODF/PROD)$, and the real wage gap (WR/WRF) will approximately equal the ratio of actual and equilibrium labour shares if $PRODF \approx PROD$. It appears from Figure 4.2, then, that the wage gap was positive during the mid-1970s and negative in the mid-1980s.

Phillips curve

The wage equation in the complete macromodel is a standard Phillips curve:

$$W = a - b(U_t - U_t^N) - c(U_t - U_{t-1}) + d(p^e) + e(p_{mw}) \qquad (4.33)$$

where W is the rate of wage inflation, p^e is expected inflation, p_{mw} is the weighted rate of change of the real import price, and U and U^N are the actual and natural unemployment rates. (This equation is not used in the partial simulations reported in this paper.) An import price shock may affect wage inflation directly through the p_{mw} term as well as indirectly by affecting U^N. The change in actual unemployment is included to test for persistence or hysteresis. Full hysteresis requires $b = 0$ and $c > 0$, so that wage inflation depends only on the change in U, and there is no equilibrium NAIRU. If $b > 0$ and $c > 0$, there is persistence, implying loops around the Phillips curve of the Lipsey (1960) type, but not full hysteresis.

In the estimated equation p_{mw} is lagged one year and p^e is an average of current and lagged inflation. The unconstrained coefficient on p^e is not significantly different from unity. Three alternative specifications are tested for the unemployment gap $(U - U^N)$, namely the current gap, the lagged gap, and an average of the current and lagged gaps. The current gap is only weakly significant, but the weighted and lagged gaps are significant at the 5 per cent level. In all three cases the corresponding terms for the change of unemployment are statistically insignificant, implying at most a weak tendency towards persistence or hysteresis.

5. Determination of FE output

We define FE output as the output that would be required to achieve full employment of labour at the natural rate of unemployment, if the real wage were at its FE level. Estimates of FE output, the FE real wage and the natural rate of unemployment[7] are obtained by solving a simultaneous system of labour demand and supply equations that also determines the FE levels of the labour force and labour-hours. We first describe the specification of the equations on each side of the labour market and then indicate how the system is closed. Parameter estimates and regression statistics for the principal equations are shown in Appendix B.

Labour supply

Labour supply, measured in labour-hours, is the product of annual hours per worker and the number of employed persons, the latter depending on the unemployment rate and the size of the labour force. Labour force participation equations are estimated by sex for eight age groups. A logistic form is used in which the dependent variable is the logarithm of the participation rate (LP) divided by one minus the participation rate. The principal determinants are the employment–population ratio (E/N), the real after-tax consumption wage (WRC), and average hours (H). The employment–population ratio, an indicator of the probability of finding work, captures what are commonly referred to as discouraged-worker effects, while the after-tax real consumption wage measures the opportunity cost of leisure.

Denoting FE levels of variables by the suffix 'F', the FE participation rate for the ith group in year t is given implicitly by:

$$\ln\left(\frac{LPF_{i,t}}{1 - LPF_{i,t}}\right) = c_{1,i} + c_{2,i}\frac{EF_t}{N_t} + c_{3,i}WRCF_t + c_{4,i}HF_t + c_{5,i}T66 + c_{6,i}\frac{N_{i,t}}{N_t}. \quad (4.34)$$

T66 is a time trend beginning in 1966, and N_i is the population in group i. Additional trends and dummies are included for some groups. The aggregate labour force, aggregate employment and private employment at full employment are given by the following identities:

$$LAF_t = \sum_{i=1}^{16} N_{i,t} LPF_{i,t} \tag{4.35}$$

$$EF_t = \left(1 - \frac{U_t^N}{100}\right) LAF_t \tag{4.36}$$

$$EPF_t = EF_t - EG_t \tag{4.37}$$

where *EG* is the exogenous level of government employment.

Our average hours equation is a hybrid relation combining both supply and demand factors. Hours per worker depend on the real after-tax consumption wage, which is presumed to affect workers' labour supply decisions, and on cyclical variations in labour demand as measured by the unemployment rate, *U*. FE hours are given by:

$$HF_t = c_1 + c_2 \, WRCF_t + c_3 \, U_t^N + c_4 \, T82 + c_5 \, D73ON_t + c_6 D65_t \tag{4.38}$$

where *D65* is a dummy variable for 1965, *D73ON* is a dummy variable for years after 1972, and T82 is a time trend beginning in 1982. FE private labour-hours are then computed as:

$$LF_t = (HF_t)(EPF_t). \tag{4.39}$$

The system of equations (4.34)–(4.39) can be solved for *LAF*, *EF*, U^N, and *LF*, conditional on the real wage and exogenous variables.

Labour demand

The demand for labour-hours is derived on the assumption that firms choose labour and capital inputs to minimize the expected costs of producing expected output, subject to a Cobb–Douglas production function with constant returns to scale, as in equation (4.21). Thus, desired labour-hour input depends on expected output, expected relative factor prices, and the level of total factor productivity. Because of adjustment costs, firms are assumed to close only a fraction of the gap between desired and actual labour-hours each period. Denoting expected values by the superscript '*e*', the disequilibrium demand function is:[8]

$$L_t = \left[\left(\frac{\alpha}{1-\alpha} \right)^{-\alpha} A^{-1} \left(\frac{W_t^e}{Q_t^e} \right)^{-\alpha} X_t^e e^{-\rho t} \right]^{\lambda} L_{t-1}^{1-\lambda} \qquad (4.40)$$

where W is the private wage, Q is the implicit rental price of capital, X is private non-residential output, and λ is the speed of adjustment of labour-hours. The expected rental price is:

$$Q_t^e = P_{I,t}^e (r + \delta_t) TX_t \qquad (4.41)$$

where P_I is the investment price deflator, r is the discount rate, δ is the depreciation rate and TX captures the influence of business income taxation and investment subsidies.[9] The discount rate is a constant equal to 4 per cent per annum, which is a rough estimate of the average ex-post real after-tax return on capital and can be thought of as the target return firms seek on new investment. We find that this specification gives superior fits for the labour input and investment functions to formulations using nominal or real long-term market interest rates before or after taxes. Expected values of wages, prices and output are generally determined by predictions from autoregressions.

Full-employment output
Let *XF* be the FE level of *X* and *WRIF* be the FE real investment wage. Substituting *LF* for *L* on the left-hand side of (4.40), and *XF* for X^e and *WRIF* for W^e/P_I^e on the right, we can invert the labour demand equation to obtain the following expression for FE output:

$$XF_t = A \left(\frac{\alpha}{1-\alpha} \right)^{\alpha} \left(\frac{WRIF_t}{(r+\delta_t)TX_t} \right)^{\alpha} e^{\rho t} LF_t^{1/\lambda} L_{t-1}^{-(1-\lambda)/\lambda}. \qquad (4.42)$$

FE GDP is obtained by adding income originating in housing, *YH*, and government *YG*:

$$XGDPF_t = XF_t + YH_t + YG_t. \qquad (4.43)$$

Note that *XF* is a function of both the real investment wage and the real consumption wage, the latter being a determinant of *LF*. To close the system (4.34)–(4.39) and (4.42)–(4.43), additional equations are needed to determine these FE real wages. We determine the FE real *product* wage, *WRXF*, as the reciprocal of the equilibrium FE mark-up times FE labour productivity:

$$WRXF_t = \left(\frac{1}{\text{MARKUPF}_t}\right)PRODF_t = \left(\frac{1}{\text{MARKUPF}_t}\right)\frac{XF_t}{LF_t}. \quad (4.44)$$

Since we assume that the FE mark-up is constant, equation (4.44) implies that WRXF grows at the same rate as FE productivity and that the FE labour share is constant and equal to the reciprocal of the FE mark-up. Thus for reasons discussed in section 4, our concept of the FE path imposes an equilibrium income distribution as well as a cleared labour market at the FE real wage.

Changes in real consumption and investment wages may differ from those in the real product wage for several reasons. First, there may be differential rates of technical progress in the two sectors. Secondly, consumption and investment goods prices may respond differently to external shocks, such as changes in energy prices. Finally, consumption and investment prices may display different patterns of cyclical behaviour.

Changes in actual relative prices will, of course, be reflected in observed factor demands and supplies. To allow for their influence on the FE path, we express the FE real consumption wage as the FE real product wage multiplied by the actual ratio of the output deflator to the consumption deflator, and similarly for the FE real investment wage:

$$WRCF_t = WRXF_t\left(\frac{P_{X,t}}{P_{C,t}}\right) \quad (4.45)$$

$$WRIF_t = WRXF_t\left(\frac{P_{X,t}}{P_{I,t}}\right). \quad (4.46)$$

Thus, we build into the FE path all observed changes in the relative prices of consumption and investment goods, although it would be preferable to abstract from purely cyclical changes. One result of this specification is that our empirical measures of real wage gaps are identical, whether they are expressed in terms of the output deflator, the consumption deflator or the investment deflator.

6.   Theoretical unemployment decomposition

Our theoretical decomposition of unemployment is illustrated in Figure 4.3, where we abstract from variations in average hours, which are taken into account in the empirical estimates, and measure labour demand and supply in numbers of workers. Figure 4.3 depicts a state of excess unemployment. *LDF* is the (log linear) labour demand schedule at FE output. The FE labour force is *LF* (drawn as wage-inelastic for simplicity), and the FE wage *WRF,* would clear the labour market at the natural rate of unemployment *(LF – EF)/LF.*

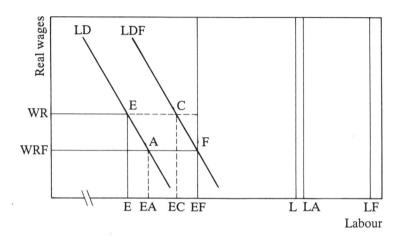

Figure 4.3

LD is the actual labour demand function whose position depends on current output and lagged employment. *E* persons are employed at the current real wage, *WR.* There is a shortfall of *(EF – E)* between actual and FE employment. The actual or measured labour force, *L,* depends on the level of *E,* owing to the dis-couraged-worker effect, which generates hidden unemployment of *(LF – L).* Actual or measured unemployment is *(L – E),* and the measured unemployment rate is *(L – E)/L.* The larger is the elasticity of labour force with respect to employment, the larger will be the increase in hidden unemployment and the smaller will be the increase in measured unemployment for a given decline in labour demand.

We adopt for our analysis the 'adjusted unemployment rate', *(LF – E)/LF,* obtained by adding hidden unemployment to the numerator and denominator of the measured rate. The magnitude of discouraged-worker effects varies over time and among countries, and the adjusted unemployment rate facilitates intertemporal and international comparisons. The gap between the measured and natural unemployment rates shows the magnitude of excess unemployment, whereas the gap between the adjusted and measured rates shows the importance of hidden unemployment.

Given that $WR > WRF$, unemployment of $(EF - EC)$ would exist even if actual and FE output, and hence LD and LDF, were equal. This is classical unemployment due to real wage rigidity and the failure of the labour market to clear. It may occur because of labour market bargaining on behalf of union members ('insiders') or because price-setters are also efficiency-wage-setters. This can be estimated empirically by substituting WR for WRF in the LDF function .

In past work we estimated the classical component by a counter-factual experiment in which WR was reduced to WRF with aggregate demand and output unchanged.[10] This increased employment to EA, so that of the original employment shortfall of $(EF - E)$, $(EA - E)$ was the classical component, attributable to the wage gap $(WR - WRF)$, and $(EF - EA)$ was the Keynesian element, assignable to deficient product demand. Given our constant-elasticity log-linear labour demand function, it appears from Figure 4.3 that $(EF - EC) = (EA - E)$. This is misleading, however, because the labour demand function is actually specified for labour-hours rather than employees, and average hours are themselves an endogenous variable in the model. The partial wage elasticity of average hours is negative (the income effect dominates the substitution effect) so that the direct result of the hypothetical wage reduction is to increase average hours along with total labour-hours, thereby nullifying some of the stimulus to employment. Moreover, since the induced rise in employment from E to EA would encourage some workers to re-enter the labour force, the latter would increase from L to LA, damping the fall in unemployment from the hypothetical wage reduction. We now prefer to estimate the classical component directly at the disequilibrium wage – that is, by $(EF - EC)$ – so that the difference in labour-hour input due to real wage rigidity and the failure of the labour market to clear is attributed exclusively to a difference in employment at the existing levels of average hours and hidden unemployment.

In the situation depicted in Figure 4.3, the adjusted unemployment rate is decomposed into its natural, classical and Keynesian components as follows:

$$(LF - E)/LF = (LF - EF)/LF + (EF - EC)/LF + (EC - E)/LF. \quad (4.47)$$

Figure 4.4 illustrates the five possible states of the decomposition. Point F shows the FE equilibrium, where there is neither Keynesian nor classical unemployment and measured unemployment is at the natural rate. Points E, B, H and J refer to the four disequilibrium employment states, and L, LB, LH and LJ are the corresponding labour supply functions reflecting the various degrees of employment-induced labour force change affecting hidden unemployment.

Two states are possible when the wage gap is positive, according to whether aggregate demand (AD) and hence LD fall short of (point E) or exceed (point

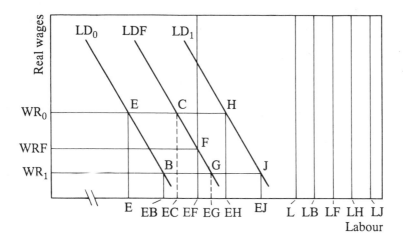

Figure 4.4

H) their FE levels. Classical unemployment (*EF − EC*) is the same in both cases, but excess Keynesian unemployment adds to total unemployment at point *E*, whereas at point *H* the classical unemployment arising from the wage gap is more than offset by the excess labour demand stemming from high aggregate demand. At point *H* the unemployment decomposition becomes:

$$(LF - EH)/LF = (LF - EF)/LF + (EF - EC)/LF + (EC - EH)/LF. \quad (4.48)$$

The two remaining states involve a negative wage gap and either a negative (point *B*) or a positive (point *J*) *AD* and *LD* gap. In both cases excess demand for labour would exist at point *G* on *LDF* even if the *AD* and *LD* gaps were zero, and hence classical unemployment (*EF − EG*) is negative. The corresponding decompositions are:

$$(LF - EB)/LF = (LF - EF)/LF + (EF - EG)/LF + (EG - EB)/LF \quad (4.49)$$

where (*EG − EB*) is the employment shortfall from deficient aggregate demand, and:

$$(LF - EJ)/LF = (LF - EF)/LF + (EF - EG)/LF + (EG - EJ)/LF \quad (4.50)$$

where $(EG - EJ)$ is the employment surplus or negative shortfall from excess aggregate demand.

7.   Empirical findings

Natural rate of unemployment
Figure 4.5 depicts our estimates of the natural rate of unemployment and the unemployment gap $(U - U^N)$ during 1966–1989. The paths of the actual and natural rates were basically flat during the 1960s and early 1970s, increased two-fold during the first oil shock and its aftermath in the mid and late 1970s, and spurted markedly higher in the 1980s. The estimated gap fluctuated narrowly about zero until the 1980s, averaging 0.33 per cent between 1966 and 1980, spurted sharply to a higher plateau during 1981–86, when it averaged 2.67 per cent, and then declined considerably to an average level of –1.37 per cent in 1987–89.

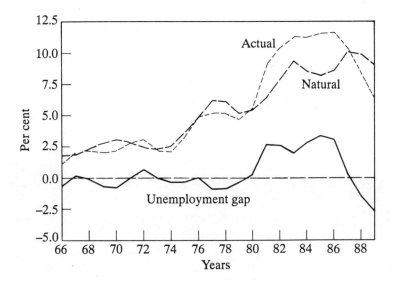

Figure 4.5   Actual and natural unemployment rates

These estimates may be compared to those of Layard *et al.* (1991, p. 436) (see Table 4.1).

Table 4.1. Estimates of unemployment by different authors

	Coen and Hickman		Layard *et al.*	
	1969–79	1980–88	1969–79	1980–88
Actual	3.39	9.87	4.30	10.32
Natural	3.80	8.21	5.15	7.92
Gap	–0.41	1.66	–0.85	2.40

Our data on actual unemployment differs conceptually from Layard *et al.* (see Appendix A) and our gap estimates are somewhat lower, but both studies conclude that the natural rate rose substantially in the 1980s.

Output and wage gaps
Actual and FE output and the utilization ratio or output gap are shown in Figure 4.6. The FE path is not as smooth as most published measures of potential output, because our concept is disturbed by shocks to the real investment wage and by changes in taxation, both of which affect the rental–wage ratio in equation (4.42), by shocks to the real consumption wage, which affects *LF*, and by trend breaks

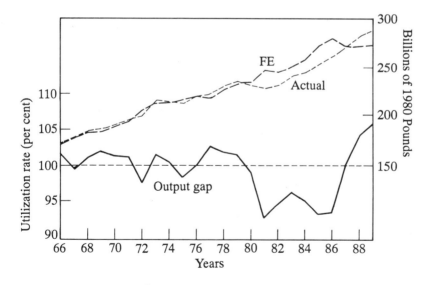

Figure 4.6   Actual and FE output

in technical progress. The path is also quite sensitive to previous departures from full employment, which affect FE output in proportion to the gap between current FE labour input and lagged actual input. Finally, we specify a stochastic concept of FE output, in which we add to the FE expressions for labour demand (as inverted in equation (4.42)) and supply the current disturbances from the corresponding equations for actual demand and supply for labour.[11]

The utilization ratio fluctuated within a range of about 2 per cent above and below its baseline of 100 per cent during 1966–1980. It became severely depressed in 1981–86, when it averaged only 94 per cent, but recovered strongly to average 103 per cent in 1987–89. As is apparent from Figures 4.5 and 4.6, these amplified fluctuations in the unemployment and output gaps occurred in a period of continuously rising output during 1981–1989.

The output and unemployment gaps in Figures 4.5 and 4.6 are negatively related, as predicted by Okun's Law (Figure 4.7). The absolute slope coefficient in the depicted regression line is 2.2, indicating that on average a decline of 2.2 per cent in aggregate output will be accompanied by an increase of one percentage point in the unemployment rate. Interestingly enough, at 2.2 the estimated Okun coefficient is virtually the same as in our US model.

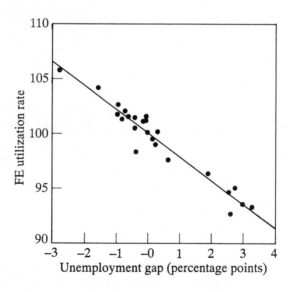

Figure 4.7   Output versus unemployment gap

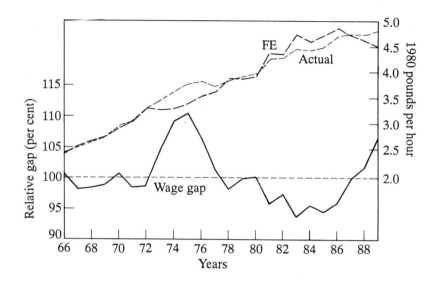

Figure 4.8   Actual and FE real product wages

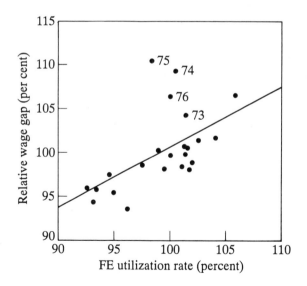

Figure 4.9   Wage versus output gap

The actual and FE real wage rates diverged substantially during much of the period covered by our study (Figure 4.8). The relative wage gap was small in 1966–72, but a positive gap opened during 1973–80 and was especially large in 1973–76. In contrast, the wage gap turned substantially negative during 1981–86, before recovering strongly to positive territory in 1987–89.

The scatter diagram and regression line in Figure 4.9 show a positive relationship between the wage and output gaps. This positive correlation indicates that the real wage is procyclical, in the sense that fluctuations of actual output about *FE* output induce corresponding fluctuations of the real wage relative to the *FE* real wage. Thus the fluctuations in the wage gap are normally associated with corresponding fluctuations in aggregate demand.

This was clearly not the case in the mid 1970s, however.[12] In 1973–75 the wage gap was driven sharply upwards in the face of relatively stable output and unemployment rates by depreciation of the pound, labour militancy over incomes policies and the first oil shock. The subsequent acceptance of voluntary pay restraints by the trades unions facilitated the reduction of the wage gap during 1976–78 without the introduction of severe deflationary demand policies. The traces of these wide swings in cost-push factors are clearly evident in the comparison of Figures 4.6 and 4.8 and in the high wage-gap outliers in the central portion of Figure 4.9.

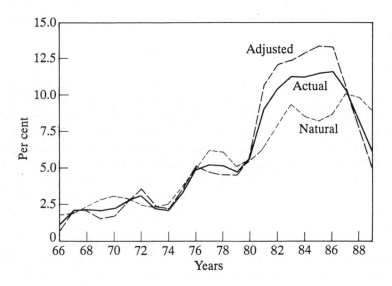

Figure 4.10   Adjusted, actual and natural unemployment rates

The 1980s are another story, because the movements in FE utilization and the wage gap were primarily induced by fiscal and monetary policies. The Thatcher Government came into power in May 1979 and quickly instituted the Medium-Term Financial Strategy of steady disinflation through monetary and fiscal restraints, and the policy remained in place through the rest of the decade. Demand restraint was combined with microeconomic supply-side policies to reduce wage pressure and improve productivity and competitiveness. On the whole these policies accomplished their objectives. The inflation rate dropped from 18 per cent in 1980 to 7 per cent in 1982 and averaged 4.5 per cent in 1983–87 and 6.5 per cent in 1988–89. After declining initially during the 1980–81 recession, production increased through the rest of the decade, and was accompanied by rising employment after 1983 and an overheating economy in 1988–89. The tight demand-constraints of the early 1980s did lead, however, to the large unemployment, output and wage gaps observed in Figures 4.5, 4.6 and 4.8, and the subsequent overshooting in 1988–89 was partly induced by a relaxation of monetary policy in 1987–88 in the aftermath of the stock market crash.

Decomposing unemployment

Figure 4.10 shows the relationship between the adjusted, actual and natural unemployment rates over our sample period. The gap between the adjusted and actual rates is comprised of hidden unemployment due to the discouraged-worker effect, whereas that between the actual and natural rates is excess unemployment.

Hidden unemployment may be either negative or positive. As shown in Figure 4.4, it will be negative when the actual labour force at *LH* or *LJ* exceeds the FE labour force at *LF* owing to an excess of actual employment *EH* or *EJ* over the full-employment level, *EF*. Negative hidden unemployment usually occurs in periods when aggregate demand exceeds its *FE* level (the utilization rate exceeds 100 per cent), as in 1968–71, 1977–79, and 1988–89. The average rates of hidden unemployment in those periods were –0.4, –0.5 and –0.9 per cent. Substantial positive hidden unemployment occurred in 1972–76 and 1980–87, averaging respectively 0.2 and 1.1 per cent in the two periods.

Excess unemployment may also be positive or negative. According to our estimates, it was negative during most of 1966–79, positive in 1980–87, and again negative in 1988–89. The corresponding average rates of excess unemployment were respectively –0.3, 2.1 and –2.0 per cent.

The adjusted unemployment rate and its natural, demand and wage components is shown in Figure 4.11. It is apparent that fluctuations in the demand component dominated the variations in excess unemployment during 1966–89. The largest fluctuation in classical unemployment occurred during 1973–76, but its effects on adjusted unemployment were largely nullified by a counterbalancing fluctuation in Keynesian unemployment, so that most of the rise in the adjusted rate was due to a rise in the natural rate. Increases in both the natural rate and Keynesian unemployment raised the adjusted rate during 1981–86, whereas most of the subsequent reduction in the adjusted rate is attributable to increasing demand stimulus.

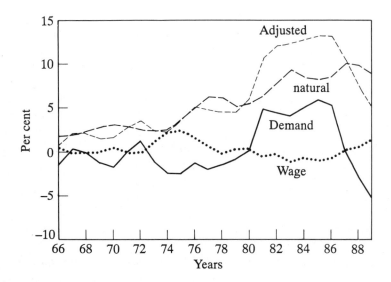

Figure 4.11   Adjusted unemployment and components

Table 4.2.   Adjusted unemployment and its natural, Keynesian and classical components (%)

	1966–72	1973–76	1977–80	1981–86	1987–89
Level					
Adjusted	2.0	3.3	4.9	12.3	7.7
Natural	2.5	3.4	5.8	8.2	9.5
Keynesian	−0.5	−1.9	−1.1	4.9	−2.5
Classical	0.0	1.8	0.2	−0.8	0.7
Change					
Adjusted	n.a.	1.3	1.6	7.4	−4.6
Natural	n.a.	0.9	2.4	2.4	1.3
Keynesian	n.a.	−1.4	0.8	6.0	−7.4
Classical	n.a.	1.8	−1.6	−1.0	1.5

Table 4.2 summarizes our findings on the contributions of the natural, classical and Keynesian components of adjusted unemployment. The sub-period averages in the upper panel indicate the dominance of the natural rate in total unemployment. The period to period changes in the lower panel tell a different story, however. The principal factor in the rise of unemployment during 1973–76 was a large increase in classical unemployment, and the subsequent decline in the classical component offset much of the increase in the other components during 1977–80. Perhaps of greater interest is the observation that a rise in the Keynesian component accounts for most of the increase in the adjusted unemployment rate between 1977–80 and 1981–86, and its subsequent fall similarly dominates the decrease in the adjusted rate from 1981–86 to 1987–89.

These findings differ in two major respects from our earlier studies covering the period through 1984 (Coen and Hickman, 1987, 1988). First, the natural rate explains a much larger portion of total unemployment in the 1970s and 1980s, since our earlier estimate of natural unemployment was not a NAIRU and did not allow for an increase in the natural rate of the key labour force group after the 1960s. Secondly, the classical component was positive, though small, in our original estimates for the early 1980s, owing to an estimated positive wage gap under our earlier methodology.

8. Conclusions

Our revised concept of the FE growth path reflects a heightened concern for price stability as well as efficient production, and therefore incorporates the requirement of an equilibrium income distribution in addition to cleared markets for labour and capital. The path is also sensitive to previous departures from full employment, to stochastic disturbances in the labour market, and to supply shocks which alter the natural rate of unemployment and FE labour supply and may also affect FE productivity by changing relative factor prices and the capital–labour ratio. One consequence of these characteristics is considerable year to year variability in the FE output path, including negative growth at times. In these respects our FE path specification resembles real business cycle theory, with the crucial difference that we do not assume continuous market clearing and hence do allow for departures of actual inputs and output from their FE levels.

Our estimates of the natural rate of unemployment do not attempt to take account directly of such factors as changing mismatch in the structure of unemployment (except to the extent that it is captured by demographic shifts) or changes in unemployment benefits or union power.[13] They are not, however, far out of line with similar estimates in the literature, and the substitution of these estimates (or of an atheoretical definition of the natural rate as a moving average or fitted trend of the actual rates) would not substantially alter our empirical findings about the output and wage gaps and the associated measures of Keynesian and classical unemployment.

The estimates indicate that substantial excess capacity existed in product as well as labour markets during 1982–86, and it may be tempting to conclude that a smaller degree of demand restraint would have reduced employment losses without much inflationary cost. It is true that the positive association between the output and wage gaps implies some offset from the classical component, and average working hours would also have been higher; but those effects would have been of second order, and unemployment would have been smaller were aggregate demand higher. According to our price equation, it is also the case that higher capacity utilization has only a marginal effect on the price mark-up. Wage inflation would have been higher at the lower level of unemployment, however, and in the absence of complete model simulations we cannot estimate the trade-off between inflation and unemployment. That will be an important component of the next stage of our research.

Notes

The generous financial support of the Jubiläumsfonds of the Austrian National Bank is gratefully acknowledged.
1. For simplicity, we specify the mark-up as determined by actual rather than smoothed productivity despite the fact that most econometric models assume normal cost pricing on the basis of trend productivity. Similarly, in equation (4.4) the desired wage depends on actual productivity.
2. The high correlation between the import and tax variables (0.75) probably masks the separate role of import price shocks.
3. The usual expression for the degree of monopoly is $(P - MC)/P$, so that the measure is zero under perfect competition and ranges to unity under monopoly, whereas our form is P/MC, and the measure is unity under perfect competition and ranges upward without bound. In either metric, monopoly power is greater and the mark-up larger, the less elastic is demand (as long as it exceeds unitary elasticity).
4. See Hymans (1972). The transformation involves multiplying the right-hand side of equation (4.24) by $(Ae^{\rho t}K^\alpha L^{1-\alpha})/(X^\alpha X^{1-\alpha})$, collecting terms to yield $AC = \alpha^{-\alpha}(1 - \alpha)^{-(1-\alpha)}(QK/X)^\alpha(WL/X)^{1-\alpha}$, making use of the marginal revenue productivity conditions $Q/P = [1-(1/\phi_1)]\,\alpha(X/K)$ to eliminate (QK/X) and $W/P = [1-(1/\phi_1)]\,(1 - \alpha)(X/L)$ to eliminate $(WL/X)^{-\alpha}$, and collecting terms. Note that this derivation shows that in the long-term equilibrium of our system, the configuration of inputs, output and prices will maximize profits as well as minimize costs, even though our factor demand specification is based solely on cost minimization.
5. The foregoing development is closely related to target-return pricing formulas, which assume that price is set to cover unit labour cost and a target rate of return on unit capital cost, both at a standard rate of output, and where the target rate includes profit as well as interest. See Eckstein (1964), Eckstein and Fromm (1968) and Ball and Duffy (1972).
6. The hypothesis of a unit root in the mark-up is rejected at the 10 per cent level in an Augmented Dickey–Fuller test. A unit root cannot be rejected in the corresponding co-integrating regression for P and ULC, however.
7. The disaggregated natural rates of unemployment by age and sex do not depend on variables endogenous to the labour demand and supply equations, but the aggregate natural rate depends on the natural level of the labour force and its composition (see equation (4.20)).
8. There is a similar disequilibrium demand function for capital input, which shares common parameters from the underlying production function. To honour restrictions arising from the

production function, we estimate the labour demand function first and then impose the implied production parameters in estimating the investment equation.

9. See Appendix A for details on the measurement of these and other variables.

10. This procedure was followed because *LD* would not necessarily coincide with *LDF* under the potential output concept which we employed in the earlier studies. In those studies potential output was defined along a natural growth path of continuous equilibrium, so that the labour demand function at potential output depended on $EF(-1)$, whereas the actual labour demand function depended on $E(-1)$, and *LD* would not coincide with *LDF* unless the lagged unemployment terms were equal. See Hickman (1987) and Coen and Hickman (1987) for this distinction and the related concept of carry-over unemployment.

11. The reason for adopting the stochastic specification of FE is as follows. Suppose that the actual value *Y* (for example, of labour input) depends on *X* and the residual *e*, so that $Y = a + bX + e$. If the corresponding FE value *YF* were computed as $YF = a + bXF$, and if $XF = X$, *YF* would equal *Y* only if *e* were zero. To ensure that $YF = Y$ whenever $XF = X$, the disturbance *e* must be added to the right-hand side of the *YF* equation.

12. Our interpretation of economic events and policies in the remaining portion of this section has been checked against the contemporary analyses contained in the annual issues of the OECD Economic Surveys of the United Kingdom.

13. See Layard and Nickell (1986) for a more exhaustive study of the determinants of the natural rate.

References

Ball, R.J. and Duffy, M. (1972), 'Price formation in European countries', *The Econometrics of Price Determination.* Board of Governors of Federal Reserve System and Social Science Research Council, 347–68.

Barro, R.J. and Grossman, H.I. (1971), 'A general disequilibrium model of income and employment', *American Economic Review,* March, 82–93.

Benassy, J.P. (1975), 'Neo-Keynesian disequilibrium theory in a monetary economy', *Review of Economic Studies,* **42**, 503–23.

Benassy, J.P. (1982), *The Economics of Disequilibrium,* New York: Academic Press.

Clower, R.W. (1965), 'The Keynesian counterrevolution: a theoretical appraisal' in Hahn, F.H. and Brechling, F.P.R. (eds), *The Theory of Interest Rates,* London: Macmillan.

Coen, R.M. and Hickman, B.G. (1987), 'Keynesian and classical unemployment in four countries', *Brookings Papers on Economic Activity,* **1**, 123–93.

Coen, R.M. and Hickman, B.G. (1988), 'Is European unemployment classical or Keynesian?', *American Economic Review,* **78** (2), 188–93.

Eckstein, O. (1964), 'A theory of the wage–price process in modern industry', *Review of Economics and Statistics,* October, 267–86.

Eckstein, O. and Fromm, G. (1968), 'The price equation', *American Economic Review,* **58** (5), Part 1, 1159–83.

Hickman, B.G. (1987), 'Real wages, aggregate demand, and unemployment,' *European Economic Review,* **31**, 1531–60.

Hickman, B.G. and Coen, R.M. (1976), *An Annual Growth Model of the US Economy,* Amsterdam: North-Holland.

Hymans, S.H. (1972), 'Prices and price behavior in three US econometric models', *The Econometrics of Price Determination,* Board of Governors of Federal Reserve System and Social Science Research Council, 309–24.

Layard, R. and Nickell, S. (1986), 'Unemployment in Britain', *Economica,* **53**, S121–S169.

Layard, R. Nickell, S. and Jackman, R. (1991), *Unemployment,* Oxford: Oxford University Press.

Lipsey, R.G. (1960), 'The relation between unemployment and the rate of change of money wage rates in the United Kingdom, 1862–1957: A further analysis', *Economica,* February, 1–31.

Malinvaud, E. (1977), *The Theory of Unemployment Reconsidered,* Oxford: Blackwell.

Nordhaus, W.D. (1972), 'Recent developments in price dynamics', *The Econometrics of Price Determination,* Board of Governors of Federal Reserve System and Social Science Research Council, 16–49.

Patinkin, D. (1956), *Money, Interest and Prices,* 2nd edn, New York: Harper and Row.

Poterba, J. M., and Summers, L.H. (1983), 'Dividend taxes, corporate investment and "Q"', *Journal of Public Economics,* **22**, 135–67.

Wachter, M.L. (1976), 'The changing cyclical responsiveness of wage inflation', *Brookings Papers on Economic Activity,* **1**, 115–59.

Appendix A: data sources and methods
The principal sources of data are the OECD's *Flows and Stocks of Fixed Capital* (*FC*), *Labour Force Statistics* (*LFS*), and *National Accounts* (*NA*). All real variables are in billions of 1980 pounds. Population, labour force and so on, are in thousands of persons.

Population, labour force and unemployment
Population by age and sex were supplied in special tabulations by the OECD. Aggregate civilian labour force and unemployment and their male and female components are from *LFS*. The male and female totals were distributed by age in accordance with participation and unemployment rates by age and sex published in *LFS*. The aggregate unemployment rate and age–sex-specific unemployment rates are measured as ratios (in per cent) of unemployment to total labour force, including armed forces (also from *LFS)*. The OECD also publishes a standardized aggregate unemployment rate, which is intended to be better suited for international comparisons. We use the non-standardized rate, however, to be consistent with the labour force and unemployment levels in the OECD reports.

Output
The measure of output in our aggregate production function is private non-residential product, which is real GDP less GDP originating in government and housing, all from *NA*.

Capital stock, price of capital goods, and implicit rental price
The real net stock of business fixed capital (*K* in our aggregate production function) is the aggregate net capital stock minus the net stocks of dwellings and government capital, all from *FC*. The depreciation rate is computed as the rate implicit in the capital stock identity, $K_t = I_t + (1 - \delta_t)K_{t-1}$. *I* is real gross private non-residential fixed investment, calculated as aggregate fixed investment from *NA* minus fixed investment in housing and government, given in *FC*. The price of capital goods is the implicit deflator for *I*.

The tax component of the rental price of capital is $(1 - DEPSAV)/(1 - TXBR)$, where *DEPSAV* is the present value of tax savings resulting from one pound of current investment and *TXBR* is the statutory corporate income tax rate. For 1960–82, *DEPSAV* is from Poterba and Summers (1983), smoothed to eliminate influences of temporary tax changes, which we find improves the fit of the factor demand system. Thereafter, we compute *DEPSAV* from information on tax reform legislation of 1984 reported in *The Economist,* March 17, 1984. For most years prior to 1984. tax allowances were so generous that *DEPSAV* is very nearly equal to *TXBR* and the tax component is very close to one.

The discount rate in the rental price was determined by examining the ex-post real return on fixed capital, calculated from the identity expressing nominal private non-residential product as the sum of labour compensation, the total return to capital, and indirect taxes. The total return to capital is the rental price times the quantity of capital. All components of the identity are observable, except for r, which can therefore be inferred. We find that a rate of return of 4 per cent per annum fits this identity well. The calculation is admittedly crude, because our estimate of capital stock does not include land or inventories.

Capacity utilization

We assume that if firms are increasing their net capital stock, this is an indication that they are using their existing stock more intensively than is optimal. Given our adjustment hypothesis for capital, capacity utilization can thus be measured as the ratio of the current to the lagged stock of capital, raised to the reciprocal of the speed of adjustment of capital, which is estimated to be 0.080. (See Hickman and Coen, 1976, pp. 12–17, for the theoretical specification of the short-run production function and the rate of capacity utilization.) In order to isolate the cyclical component from the secular trend of capacity utilization, the original series is detrended non-linearly to provide the normalized capacity utilization index used in the study.

Aggregate labour-hours, average hours and the wage rate

Annual hours per worker are special estimates prepared by the OECD covering the entire economy. We assume that average hours are the same for private and public workers.

The hourly wage measures private employee compensation per hour (including social insurance taxes). The numerator is aggregate employee compensation minus government employment compensation, both from *NA*; the denominator is average hours times the number of private employees, which is total employment minus (1) the number of self-employed (from the UK Central Statistical Office's *Annual Abstract,* and (2) the number of government employees (from *NA*). The after-tax hourly wage takes into account social insurance taxes paid by employers and employees and personal income taxes. Effective tax rates are computed using data on tax revenues from the OECD's *Revenue Statistics.*

Appendix B: equation estimates

In the following listings, numbers in parentheses under regression coefficients are absolute values of t-statistics. 'RSQ' is the R^2 adjusted for degrees of freedom, 'SEE' is the standard error of estimate, and 'D–W' is the Durbin–Watson statistic. Ti is a time trend beginning in year i. Dij is a dummy variable with a value of 1 in years i through j, zero otherwise. Other variables are as defined in the main text. The information in parentheses following the title of each equation refers to the number of its theoretical counterpart or the section in which it is discussed in the main text.

1. Unemployment rate of males 35–44 (equation 18)

$$\ln(UM3544_t) = 13.289542 - 1.7492120*\ln(z_t)$$
$$ (9.312) \qquad (1.916)$$
$$+ \; 0.6273413^*(\ln(T_{s,t}) + \ln(T_{i,t}) + \ln(T_{x,t}))$$
$$(1.297)$$
$$+ \; 1.2210129^*(\ln(T_{s,t-1}) + \ln(T_{i,t-1}) + \ln(T_{x,t-1}))$$
$$(2.835)$$

Sample: 1966–87
RSQ: 0.912381
SEE: 0.192481
D–W: 1.163562

2. Master price equation (section 4)

$$\ln(P_t/P_{t-1}) = 0.0025366 - 0.3324943^*(\ln(MARKUP(-1))-0.4203478)$$
$$\phantom{\ln(P_t/P_{t-1}) =} (0.418) \qquad (2.777)$$
$$+ \; 0.6872339^*\ln(ULC_t/ULC_{t-1}) + 0.0867471^*\ln(T_{i,t-2}X/T_{i,t-3})$$
$$(12.60) \qquad\qquad\qquad\qquad (1.306)$$
$$+ \; 0.0811469*\ln(z_t/z_{t-1}) + 0.2316804^*\ln(P_{t-1}/P_{t-2})$$
$$(1.345) \qquad\qquad\qquad (3.145)$$

Sample: 1963–87
RSQ: 0.950628
SEE: 0.012044
D–W: 2.412297

Notes: $0.4203478 = \ln(MARKUPL)$, where $MARKUPL = 1.522491$, the 1960–72 average of MARKUP.

3.   Average hours (section 5)

$$H = 2081.3899 - 162.71016*(W^d/P_c) - 9.5232885*U$$
    (59.57)   (9.313)   (5.417)
$$+ \ 11.433495*T82 + 27.036815*D73ON + 28.992842*D65$$
    (5.512)   (2.675)   (2.369)

Sample: 1965–87
RSQ: 0.986922
SEE: 10.65088
D–W: 2.452321

4.   Labour demand function (equation 40)

$$\ln(L_t/L_{t-1}) = 0.0848326 + 0.2227564*\ln(Q^e/W^e) + 0.7397890*\ln(X_t/L_{t-1})$$
        (0.582)   (4.624)   (8.551)
$$- \ 0.0245320*T55 + 0.0049178*T74 + 0.0076413*T81 - 0.4668520*v_{t-1}$$
        (6.112)   (1.916)   (3.202)   (2.016)

Sample: 1963–87
RSQ: 0.787920
SEE: 0.013305
D–W: 2.130225

Notes: v_{t-1} is the lagged residual.
Implied structural parameters are:
    λ = .739789
    α = .301108
    ρ= .033161 for 1963–73
    ρ= .033161 –.006648 = .026513 for 1974–80
    ρ= .033161 –.006648 – .010329 =.016184 for 1981 on

5.   Expected wage equation (section 5)

$$\ln(W_{n,t}) = 0.0390873 + 1.6407661*\ln(W_{n,t-1}) - 0.6449072*\ln(W_{n,t-2})$$
        (1.935)   (9.716)   (3.778)

Sample: 1962–87
RSQ: 0.997896
SEE: 0.044409
D–W: 1.979880

Notes: The expected wage, net of employer contributions to social insurance, W_{ne}, is the predicted value from this autoregression. The expected wage in the labour demand function is $W^e = (1 + t_s)W_{ne}$.

6. Expected price of capital goods (section 5)

$$\ln(P_{I,t}) = \ \underset{(0.253)}{0.0034713} + \underset{(17.05)}{1.8619653^*\ln(P_{I,t-1})} - \underset{(7.817)}{0.8710436^*\ln(P_{I,t-2})}$$

Sample: 1962–87
RSQ: 0.998369
SEE: 0.029839
D–W: 1.565380

Notes: The expected price of capital goods is the predicted value from this auto-regression.

5 Structural adjustment in the UK Economy: the effect of North Sea oil
Bill Robinson

1. Introduction

Jim Ball has made many distinguished contributions in the field of applied economics, but his best work has been in the area of inflation and the balance of payments. Many of us who grew up in the world of fixed exchange rates had grown used to thinking of the exchange rate as a policy instrument which should be used to ensure that the balance of payments would balance. When the world moved over to floating exchange rates in the 1970s, it became apparent that changes in the exchange rate did not necessarily have much effect on the current account, but they usually had a dramatic effect on the rate of inflation.

The Keynesian economic models of the day, constructed in the era of fixed exchange rates, were rather slow to adjust to the new reality. The London Business School (LBS) model, originally Jim Ball's creation, became an honourable exception. In his theoretical work (Ball and Burns, 1976; Ball *et al.*, 1977), Jim was able to show the important role played by exchange rate changes in the transmission of inflation in small and medium sized economies, and to translate theory into serviceable equations which could be used in a forecasting model (Ball *et al.*, 1980).

The LBS model came to play a prominent role in the economic policy debate from the second half of the 1970s onwards. The key issue at the time was the need to defeat inflation. Monetary targets were in place. But the idea that the exchange rate might have an important role to play in the process of getting inflation down was not generally accepted. The Treasury view at that time held that while monetary policy should be used to get inflation down, the need for a competitive exchange rate remained paramount.

Budd and Burns (1977), in an influential paper, argued that the reduction in inflation would be frustrated if the exchange rate was not allowed to appreciate. Thereafter, the LBS became identified with a 'strong exchange rate' view of the world. Econometrically estimated price elasticities for exports and imports suggested that trade volumes were less responsive to exchange rate movements in a floating rate world than they had been under fixed rates. By contrast trade prices were more responsive.

The conclusion, reluctantly accepted then but now at the heart of Treasury thinking, is that a policy of exchange rate depreciation does not deliver competitive advantage. It merely delivers higher inflation. Conversely, a firm exchange rate helps to achieve lower inflation, while having much less impact on the current account than previously supposed.

In the early 1980s the new policy framework was put to the test. The results broadly supported the above conclusions. A strong exchange rate helped to secure a remarkable deceleration of inflation against a background of current account surplus. That surplus did however owe a great deal to the North Sea oil revenues, and to the fall in imports in the 1980–81 recession. So the strong exchange rate policy, which made life extremely difficult for many of Britain's traditional manufacturing exporters, was highly controversial.

The events of the early 1980s launched a debate which continues to this day about the role of manufacturing industry in the UK economy. A constant refrain in that debate has been the idea that manufacturing is uniquely important. Another is that it was allowed to shrink too far in the early 1980s and needs rebuilding against the day when North Sea oil runs out. Both ideas were expressed vigorously in the report of the Aldington Committee (House of Lords, 1985).

The ink was scarcely dry on the Aldington Report when the oil price fell sharply and the value of Britain's oil revenues halved. That, together with the sharp rise in imports in the boom of the late 1980s, pushed the current account from surplus to large deficit. Moreover, the deficit has persisted into the early 1990s, despite another long recession, prompting new fears of a balance-of-payments 'constraint' on the recovery.

In his earlier work, Jim Ball was one of the first to point out that there is no such thing as a balance-of-payments constraint, and that a current account deficit is only a symptom of an underlying supply constraint. In his more recent writings (Ball, 1992; Ball and Robertson, 1993), Jim Ball has returned to balance-of-payments issues and the role of the manufacturing sector. He remains sceptical of the claim that 'an industrial economy as mature as the United Kingdom could be "balance of payments-constrained". He also notes that manufacturing competitiveness, whether measured by productivity gains or by the share of UK exports in world trade, improved in the 1980s.

This paper offers an interpretation of the events of the 1980s and early 1990s which is very much in line with this thinking. It shares Jim Ball's view that an economy cannot be balance of payments-constrained, only supply-constrained. It shares his scepticism about the special importance of manufacturing, and his belief that the real exchange rate will always adjust to eliminate large deficits or surpluses in the balance of payments.

It differs from Jim Ball's analysis in assigning much more importance to the role of oil as an agent of structural change in the economy. The basic fact about UK manufacturing industry is that it shrank dramatically in the early 1980s, but has grown healthily since then. The fall and rise of manufacturing was to some extent the mirror image of the rise and fall of UK oil revenues.

The purpose of this paper is to show how the arrival of North Sea oil changed the structure of UK output, and to explore the (delayed) effect of the fall in oil revenues since 1985. The theme of the paper is that these structural changes were the result of large economic forces and not, as many have claimed, of Government policies. These forces led to a relative decline in manufacturing output in the 1980s. The logic of the argument points to a relative expansion of the manufacturing sector in the 1990s.

2.   The thesis

The thesis can be briefly stated. North Sea oil provided the UK with an endowment income. Like any income it could be spent (on better living standards) or saved. At the macroeconomic level there were two key mechanisms whereby the living standards of the British consumer could be raised: by an appreciation of the real exchange rate or by a reduction in the tax burden. So the extent to which the North Sea endowment was spent rather than saved depended on the behaviour of the exchange rate (and relative inflation rates) and on fiscal policy.

In the early 1980s fiscal policy was tight, which meant that some of the oil wealth was saved and invested overseas. But in this period the real exchange rate also rose. The UK's terms of trade, the real income of consumers, and living standards all benefited. The improvement in living standards involved a shift of resources from manufacturing to services.

In the second half of the 1980s oil income was dramatically reduced. According to theory, that shock should ultimately have produced a fall in the real exchange rate, a reduction in public expenditure or an increase in the tax burden, and a shift of resources back into manufacturing.

As so often in economics, however, the reality was more complicated than the theory. The predicted adjustment did not happen immediately, and was complicated by another shock: the 'Big Bang' of financial deregulation which led to rapid growth, especially in the service sector of the economy.

The period of rapid domestic demand growth in the late 1980s was associated with a large inflow of capital from abroad, much of which served to finance a sharp increase in business investment. This inflow of capital made it possible to delay the adjustment of living standards (and the associated structure of production) to the lower oil price. The other side of the capital account surplus was a current account deficit which reflected the fact that the output of other tradeable goods had not yet expanded to replace the lost oil revenues.

However, the process of adjustment, which will involve even stricter control of public expenditure, an increase in the underlying level of public sector saving, a lower real exchange rate and a consequent increase in the share of manufacturing in the economy (all compared with the levels of the late 1980s), will not be delayed indefinitely. It is likely that the 1990s will see an unwinding of many of the structural shifts of the early 1980s.

3. The theory: resource shocks and temporary shocks

There are two theoretical tools which we can use to analyse what has occurred. The first is the theory of a resource shock, which analyses what happens to an economy on the discovery of a natural resource, such as gold or oil or other minerals. The effect of the discovery can be analysed in a simple model of the economy in which output is allocated between three kinds of good: the resource (which is typically a tradeable primary product), secondary goods (typically manufactures, also tradeable), and non-tradeable services. The discovery of the resource causes a structural shift in the pattern of output. A greater proportion of output, by value, is accounted for by the primary sector. A greater proportion is also accounted for by the tertiary sector. It follows that a smaller proportion must be devoted to the production of tradeable manufactures.

The second relevant piece of theory concerns the rational response to a windfall. How will the consumer respond to a temporary increase in his income? The answer is that consumption depends not on actual but on permanent income. If income increases by £1000 for a period of five years, and if the total (anticipated) windfall of £5000 can be invested at 5 per cent to produce £250 per annum, it is by that amount that consumption should increase. It follows that when the first £1000 of extra income arrives, a high proportion of it will be saved. It also follows that when the last £1000 of extra income has gone, consumption will still be higher than it was before the windfall arrived.

The relevance of these two theories to the UK economy is obvious. The arrival of North Sea oil was a resource shock. It was also a temporary shock. It was always known that the flow of oil would fall off after a few years. That is why the adjustment of living standards to the arrival of North Sea oil was fairly gradual.

4. Adjusting to the arrival of North Sea oil

The process of adjustment to the resource shock emanating from the North Sea was complicated by sharp changes in the price of oil. The period of maximum oil production occurred in Mrs Thatcher's first term of office, which was also a period of high oil prices, as shown in Table 1.5

Table 5.1   Output and price of North Sea oil

	Output (m. tonne)	Price (£/tonne)	Value (£bn)	% GDP
1976	12	14	0.5	0.4
1981–85	112	37	15.5	5.0
1986	128	18	8.6	2.2
1987–91	102	22	7.9	1.6
1992	91	20	9.9	1.7

During that period, in which the sterling exchange rate was strong, manufacturing industry experienced a sharp decline in output, and it became fashionable to talk of deindustrialization. But though British manufacturers may have found North Sea oil more of a curse than a blessing, it made a major contribution to the welfare of the British people. At their peak, oil revenues amounted to some 6 per cent of GDP. Although there were some costs of extraction, the bulk of this revenue amounted to an unearned endowment income for the average citizen. It was as though the family on an income of £20 000 p.a. suddenly found itself with £21 000. That extra income was spent, among other things, on extra services. So the British economy had to be geared up to produce more restaurant meals, retail and hotel services, transport and so on.

If we look at the structure of UK production in 1976, and ask what would be the effect of the arrival of oil, we can make the simple calculations shown in Table 5.2. This shows primary production increasing its share of UK output by four percentage points, which is what actually happened when oil production came on-stream between 1976 and 1985. The third and fourth rows show the effect on the construction and service sectors of this increase, assuming people to be 4 per cent better off with a 4 per cent higher demand for construction and services. The manufacturing sector is then calculated as a residual. The inevitable counterpart of a larger oil sector and a larger services sector is a (relatively) smaller manufacturing sector.

Table 5.2   The effect of oil on the structure of UK production (shares of total output, per cent)

	Before North Sea oil (1976 actual)	After North Sea oil Predicted	1985 actual
Primary production	8.6	12.6	12.6
Manufacturing output	28.6	22.1	23.5
Construction	6.6	6.9	6.0
Services	56.0	58.2	57.8

Source: Blue Book, Table 2.1.

The reason why it is the manufacturing sector that has to adjust in this way is that its output is tradeable and can be replaced from abroad. This simple but powerful explanation, based on the 'resource shock' theory outlined above, was put forward in an influential article by Forsyth and Kay (1980). Table 5.2 illustrates the essence of their argument. The figures in the first two columns are calculated as described above and show the *predicted* shift of resources out of the manufacturing sector. The third column shows the shift that actually occurred. The shrinkage of the manufacturing sector was actually rather less than might have been expected. The share of manufacturing output in GDP actually stopped falling in 1981, and in absolute terms manufacturing industry expanded steadily for the rest of the decade.

There were two key insights in the Kay/Forsyth analysis. The first was that in order to consume the fruits of the oil endowment, the economy had to undergo a structural change. More resources would be required in the service sector because richer people would demand more services. But where were these resources to come from? Would not a richer people demand more of everything, including more manufactured goods? They would but, as noted above, these could be supplied from abroad.

Kay and Forsyth's second key insight was that resources could only be released for the supply of extra services to the British consumer if manufacturing exports fell and/or manufacturing imports rose. And that could only be achieved by an appreciation of the real exchange rate.

The role of the exchange rate in the process had already been noted by Budd and Burns (1977). The key point was that the arrival of North Sea oil turned the *terms of trade* sharply in Britain's favour. This meant that the UK could pay for increased imports with a smaller volume of exports. The terms of trade gain thus satisfied the desire of the newly enriched consumer for more (imported) goods and services at a reduced real cost in terms of UK exports. The resources freed from the export sector were able to move into the UK service sector, to satisfy the increased demand for services.

Table 5.3   Exports and imports of manufactures (% of GDP)

	1975	1985	1991
Exports			
Semi-manufactures	6.4	5.6	5.0
Finished goods	10.1	9.1	9.6
Total	16.5	14.7	14.6
Imports			
Semi-manufactures	5.6	5.7	5.2
Finished goods	7.0	10.0	10.0
Total	12.6	15.7	15.2
Balance	3.9	−1.0	−0.6

Source: Pink Book, Table 3.1.

Table 5.3 shows the startling extent of these shifts. Between 1975, when there was no oil production, and 1985, the year of peak production, the share of GDP devoted to exports of manufactures shrank by nearly 2 per cent, while the share of manufacturing imports rose by over 3 per cent. The terms of trade shift increased the quantity of manufactures available for domestic consumption by nearly 5 per cent of GDP. That is how the increased *demand* for manufactures was met, despite the fall in share of manufacturing in total output as resources shifted into the service sector.

5.   The loss of oil revenue

A salient feature of Table 5.3 above is that the deterioration in Britain's manufacturing trade balance which took place during the oil bonanza has not been reversed since. The same is true of the associated growth in the service sector, as Table 5.4 shows.

Table 5.4   Shares of national output for different sectors

	1976 (pre-oil)	1985 (peak oil)	1991 (lower oil production and price)
Primary production	8.6	12.6	7.5
Manufacturing	28.6	23.5	20.9
Construction	6.6	6.0	6.8
Government services	16.9	15.6	17.0
Private services	39.1	42.2	47.7

Source: Blue Book.

This may seem surprising at first sight, because the value of Britain's oil revenues fell sharply in 1986 when the oil price halved. Oil output also peaked that year, and it has declined by nearly 30 per cent since. Together these changes meant that the value of oil output, which had averaged 5 per cent of GDP in the period 1981–85, fell to only 2.2 per cent.

As a consequence of this reduction in oil income we might have expected to see, in the late 1980s, a reversal of the trends observed in the first half of the decade – an expansion of manufacturing at the expense of services, a reduction in the deficit in manufacturing trade (as predicted, for example, in Robinson and McCullough, 1986). There was indeed some reduction in the share of GDP accounted for by imports of manufactures, but this was insufficient to offset the loss of oil revenues. Meanwhile the appetite of British consumers for services continued to grow (see Table 5.5).

Table 5.5   Consumer spending on services (at constant 1985 prices)

	1976	1985	1991
Share (per cent)	23.8	28.1	33.2

So despite a much improved export performance, the UK current account moved into deficit in the second half of the 1980s, as Table 5.6 shows.

Table 5.6   Oil and the balance of payments

	North Sea oil		current balance	
	value (£bn)	% GDP	£bn	% of GDP
1976	0.5	0.4	−0.8	−0.6
1981–85	15.5	5.0	4.0	1.3
1986	8.6	2.2	0.1	0.0
1987–91	7.9	1.6	−13.1	−2.6
1992	9.9	1.7	−13.2	−2.5

The deterioration in the current account in the second half of the decade compared with the first half (which amounts to nearly 4 per cent of GDP) is of the same order of magnitude as the decline in the value of UK oil revenues (nearly 3.5 per cent of GDP). These comparisons cover periods of five years and reflect an *underlying*, rather than a cyclical, deterioration.

What happened, in essence, was that the underlying deterioration in the oil trade balance was not offset by any improvement *in net non-oil trade volumes* (even though exports rose strongly in the late 1980s). And that had a great deal to do with the movements in relative prices shown in Table 5.7. The arrival of oil resulted, as we have seen, in a sharp improvement in the UK's terms of trade in the early 1980s. When the oil price fell in 1986, the nominal exchange rate also, at first, fell. For a brief while it looked as though this might be part of the mechanism required to reverse some of the oil-induced changes. But, in the event, the fall in the exchange rate proved only temporary. The gains in competitiveness were eliminated by a rising exchange rate and rising inflation.

The story revealed by Tables 5.6 and 5.7 (which are designed to smooth the huge cyclical swings in the current account reflecting the boom of the late 1980s and the subsequent recession) is clear. The price signals which had encouraged a pattern of consumption and production appropriate to an oil-rich economy were not reversed after the oil had shrunk in value. So imports remained buoyant. The share of GDP devoted to the production of services continued to grow. In short, there was no real adjustment to the changed circumstances. The lost oil revenues were simply replaced by an inflow of capital from abroad.

Table 5.7   Terms of trade and competitiveness (1985 = 100)

| | Terms of Trade (1985 = 100) | Competitiveness | |
		Relative costs	Relative prices
1976	88	88	84
1981–85	100	106	101
1986	96	95	97
1987–91	100	100	104
1992	106	107	107

6.   The effects of the boom

What happened in the late 1980s was that the surge in economic demand delayed the adjustment to the lower oil price that seemed to have begun in 1986. Ironically this period of rapid growth itself – which was a world-wide phenomenon – had its origins in the fall in the oil price. That lessened the inflation constraint and encouraged policy-makers around the world to adopt easier monetary policies. (The stock market crash in the autumn of 1987 gave further urgency to this monetary easing.) The fall in the oil price also reduced the costs of manufacturing, and industry embarked on a period of rapid expansion.

The boom came relatively early to Britain (which had tended to lead the world economic cycle all through the 1980s and early 1990s). It was brought forward and strengthened by the fall in the nominal exchange rate and by the second major exogenous shock to hit the economy in this period: *financial deregulation* which had both a macro- and a microeconomic impact. The macroeconomic impact came from the one-off portfolio adjustments which followed deregulation. It became easier to borrow and to spend, and the resulting boost to demand helped to sustain the economy on a rapid growth path. Since fast-growing economies attract capital inflows, it was no coincidence that the nominal exchange rate reversed its earlier decline as the recovery gathered pace.

Financial deregulation also had a microeconomic impact. It directly encouraged the growth of the financial services industry. It also diverted resources into the property market, and encouraged the growth of the associated service industries (mortgage lenders, estate agents, interior decorators, carpenters and plumbers). It thus provided a countervailing force, at the microeconomic level, to the decline in the value of oil production, which required the *contraction* of the service sector.

The boom in demand for services led to a boom in investment in the service industries. Total business investment in the late 1980s increased its share of GDP by an astonishing four percentage points. Some of the new investment – for example the arrival of Japanese firms making colour televisions and cars for export – clearly benefited the manufacturing sector. But casual observation suggests that a great deal of the investment in this period went into the service sector in the form of new shopping centres and new office blocks.

The statistics set out in Table 5.8 confirm the anecdotal impressions. Between 1985 and 1991 total investment increased by 20 per cent, or £12 billion at 1985 prices. The overwhelming bulk of that increase took place in the service sector. This is entirely consistent with the picture shown in Table 5.4, which shows the production of services increasing sharply as a share of GDP over the same period. For the reasons given above, Britain was clearly becoming a more service-oriented economy in this period, and the investment flows reflected this trend.

Table 5.8   Investment by industry (£bn at 1985 prices)

	1985	1991	Change 1985–91
Primary	8.0	10.2	2.2
Manufacturing and			
construction	10.7	10.8	0.1
Services	26.8	38.3	11.5
'City'	7.1	12.2	5.1
Dwellings and land	14.8	13.3	–1.5
Total	60.3	72.5	12.2

Source: Blue Book.

7.   North Sea oil and the invisible balance

It is often asserted that the structural changes brought about by the arrival of North Sea oil damaged the UK's ability to earn its way in the world. The issue is whether a country can replace manufacturing export earnings with exports of services and with other invisible earnings.

In theory it obviously can. Many services – insurance, shipping, air travel – are internationally traded. So a structural shift from manufacturing to services does not necessarily reduce the UK's export capacity. In theory, too, it is possible to balance the external account with fewer exports of goods *and* services if there is more property income from abroad.

In practice it looks as though the increase in the productive capacity of the services sector had very little impact on the services balance of trade. On the other hand, the external surpluses earned in the early years of North Sea oil *did* have a significant effect in generating extra property income from abroad.

Table 5.9 shows what has happened to the balance of trade in services. Since 1985 exports of services have fallen as a share of GDP – continuing a trend established in the late 1970s – while imports have remained broadly constant. The balance of services has accordingly deteriorated. The large investment in services in the late 1980s was mainly in non-tradeables.

Table 5.9   Exports and imports of services (% of GDP)

	1975	1985	1991
Exports			
Sea transport	2.6	0.9	0.6
Civil aviation	0.8	0.9	0.7
Travel	1.4	1.5	1.2
Financial and so on	3.0	3.3	2.8
Total	7.8	6.6	5.3
Imports			
Sea transport	2.5	1.0	0.7
Civil aviation	0.7	0.8	0.8
Travel	0.8	1.4	1.7
Financial and so on	1.5	1.3	1.0
Total	5.5	4.5	4.2
Balance	2.2	2.1	1.1

Source: Pink Book 1992.

But the story is different for the other key component of the invisible balance: interest profits and dividends (IPD) from abroad, which reflect past capital outflows and inflows. Outflows invested abroad produce a stream of remitted profits, dividends and interest payments which benefit the current account. Inflows invested in the UK produce a corresponding outflow of IPD payments.

An important part of the North Sea oil story is the effect of the revenues in boosting capital outflows. As noted above, the oil revenues caused a sharp reduction in public borrowing. Other things being equal, a reduction in borrowing by government will lead to a reduction in borrowing (or an increase in lending) by the nation as a whole.

The use of oil revenues to reduce the PSBR thus contributed to the emergence of a current account surplus as oil production built up. The abolition of exchange controls in 1979 removed a major obstacle to a market-led investment of these surpluses overseas. The additional UK investment abroad produced a long-term balance-of-payments benefit in the form of an enhanced flow of net interest, profits and dividends.

During the years of maximum oil revenues current account surpluses totalling over £20 billion were recorded. These surpluses were invested abroad by private investors seeking to maximize the returns on their capital, with the result that net IPD income rose from £1 billion in 1976 to £5 billion in 1986. After the oil price collapsed the current account moved into deficit. More capital flowed into the UK than flowed abroad, IPD outflows rose sharply and the net surplus disappeared.

These movements in the external accounts conform exactly to the theory of the adjustment of consumers to a windfall described in section 3. When the UK's windfall arrived, some of it was saved but consumption did adjust upwards. When a large part of the windfall disappeared, consumption was not immediately cut. Instead, the UK drew on the savings it had accumulated in the good years, which afforded it the luxury of a relatively gradual adjustment to the fall in oil revenues.

8 Adjusting to lower oil revenues

That adjustment meant reversing some of the changes in the structure of production and trade that occurred in the early 1980s. Figures 5.1–5.3 provide some evidence that the adjustment, though delayed, has begun. Figures 5.4 and 5.5 provide further evidence that it may continue.

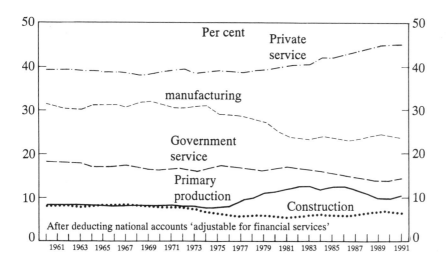

Figure 5.1   Shares of gross domestic product at constant factor cost

Figure 5.1 shows the structure of UK production. The salient features are the decline of the share of manufacturing between 1970 and 1981, the rise in the share of services in the 1980s, and the sharp oil-induced rise and fall in the share of primary production between 1976 and 1986. The interpretation of these changes put forward in this paper is that the rise in oil output accelerated the trend decline in the share of manufacturing, and initiated the rise in the share of private services. The fall in the share of oil output will in due course reverse both these changes, but the effect has been delayed by the effect of the boom on the demand for housing and financial services.

Figure 5.1 shows that as soon as oil production reached its peak, the share of manufacturing stabilized (and in absolute terms therefore grew strongly in the 1980s). It also shows that the share of services in GDP, which rose steadily for ten years or more, first because of the North Sea oil effect and subsequently because of the boom, has started to level off.

Figure 5.2 also bears out the thesis that the period of most rapid decline in manufacturing coincided with the build-up of North Sea output. The share of GDP devoted to manufacturing exports fell sharply as oil output came on-stream, but reached a floor in 1983 and has since trended upwards.

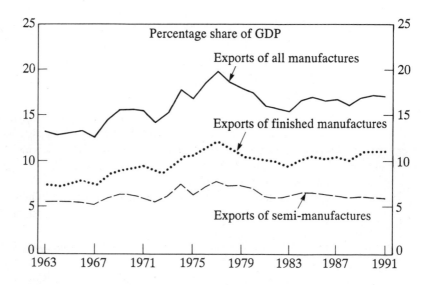

Figure 5.2   UK exports of manufactures

On the import side, the upward trend in manufacturing import penetration continued after oil output had started to decline in value, but this was the continuation of a long-established trend that was intensified by the boom of the late 1980s. Figure 5.3 shows that the steady rise in the proportion of imported manufactures peaked in 1989 and has since gone into reverse.

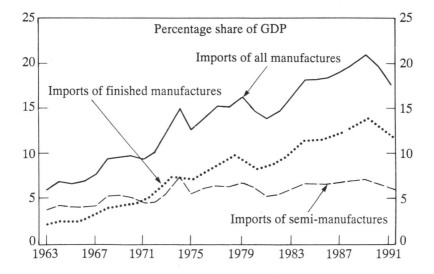

Figure 5.3   UK imports of manufactures

Figures 5.2 and 5.3 both suggest the beginning of a process of replacing foreign tradeable goods with British ones. That process will continue as long as UK firms are competitive. In this regard it is constructive to look at Figure 5.4, which shows the behaviour of the share of world markets taken by UK exporters. After a long period of decline, that share stabilized in the 1980s.

That was a remarkable performance under the circumstances, because, as Figure 5.5 shows, British firms were suffering a price handicap compared to their position in the 1970s.

One way of interpreting these events is that in the 1980s, *non-price competitiveness* improved in all sorts of ways. Industrial relations improved, fewer days were lost in strikes, working practices improved and products were better designed and delivered on time. These improvements in non-price competitiveness were sufficient to outweigh the loss of price competitiveness revealed in Figure 5.5.

The improvements in non-price competitiveness are still in place. The recession may have reduced output and investment, but there is no evidence

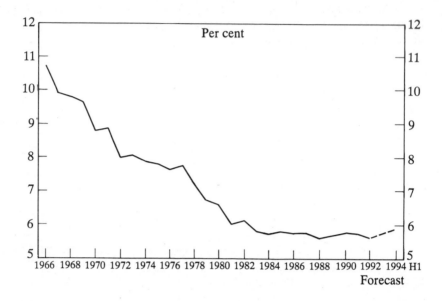

Figure 5.4   UK volume share of world trade in manufactures

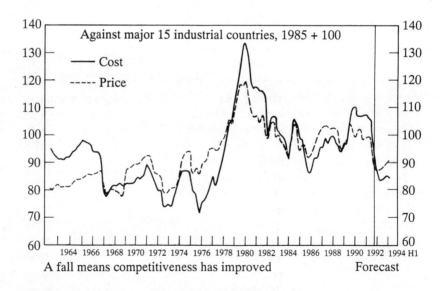

Figure 5.5   Export price and cost competitiveness

that the improvements in working practices, the advances in technology and so on of the 1980s have been reversed. So Britain in the mid-1990s will enjoy the levels of non-price competitiveness that enabled her to hold on to market shares in the 1980s despite a relative price handicap, while also benefiting from a level of price competitiveness close to the average of the 1970s. It would be surprising if this conjunction of price and non-price competitiveness did not lead to an increase in market share.

9.   North Sea oil and the public finances

Changes in the terms of trade were an essential part of the process whereby the income generated by North Sea oil was converted into real increases in living standards, but they were not the only mechanism in play. The oil boom also had an important influence on public finances. The revenue from the North Sea was subject to a special tax regime. The combined effect of corporation tax, petroleum revenue duty and oil royalties meant that roughly half of total North Sea profits were creamed off for the benefit of the British taxpayer.

It was always known that the oil revenues would not remain for long at the peak levels of the early 1980s. On the permanent income theory, therefore, it might have been expected that much of the early flow of revenue would have been saved and reinvested. The income from this investment, together with a proportion of the continuing income from the North Sea, would then have permitted a permanent modest increase in consumption (rather than the alternative of spending the North Sea revenues up to the hilt for a few years and then cutting back on consumption as the oil ran out).

It was this sort of thinking which lay behind the repeated calls that the Government should spend the North Sea revenues on domestic investment, for example, on improving the infrastructure. That idea was based on the false assumption that the government knows better than the private sector how much investment is needed. It also reflected a confusion between saving and investment. The amount of investment that can usefully be undertaken in the economy does not depend on the amount of money available to finance it. It depends on the rate of return – that is, on the number of profitable investment opportunities. The number of such opportunities (outside the oil sector) did not magically increase when the oil revenues came on-stream – though it did, in a sense, when exchange controls were lifted.

But what the Government could do was to influence the amount of North Sea revenue that was saved. In theory it could have stood back from that decision as well, allowing all the revenues to pass into private hands, and leaving it to the private sector to decide how much of the windfall should be saved rather than spent. In practice a large amount of North Sea oil revenue passed through Government hands, and so it became an issue in public finance whether the revenue was passed straight back to the private sector by reducing other taxes and/ or increasing public spending, or whether, by leaving other taxes and spending unchanged, the North Sea revenues were effectively used to reduce the national debt and thereby saved.

Table 5.10 shows what actually happened. Up to 1985, when oil revenues were at their maximum, other taxes were increased and the overall tax burden rose. The public sector financial deficit was cut. National savings increased and, as recounted in section 6, were invested overseas.

Table 5.10   The public finances and the balance of payments (% of GDP)

	Expenditure	Revenue		PSFD	Current
		North Sea	Total		account[1]
1976/7	45.2	0.1	40.8	5.8	–0.6
1981/2 – 1985/6	46.0	3.0	43.0	3.1	1.3
1986/7	43.7	1.2	41.3	2.1	0.0
1987/8 – 1991/2	40.6	0.6	39.9	0.4	–2.6
1992/3	44.5	0.2	36.9	7.6	–1.5

1. Calendar years.

In the second half of the decade a rather different picture emerged. Public spending had until then continued to increase as a share of GDP. But the rapid growth of the late 1980s steadily reduced spending as a share of GDP. So notwithstanding the fact that oil revenues had fallen sharply, it was possible to cut taxes and still balance the public finances. However, the loss of oil revenues *was* reflected in the balance of payments, which was in surplus in the first half of the decade, and moved into substantial deficit in the second half, as Table 5.10 shows.

Of course, changes in tax receipts from the North Sea are just one influence among many on the Government's finances, and such changes do not feed automatically into the balance of payments. But the data in Table 5.10 are consistent with assertions frequently made in the mid-1980s that the Government had used the North Sea revenues to get the PSBR down, and that its actions, in not cutting taxes on the back of its new oil revenues, led directly to a current account surplus – which was invested overseas.

In the second half of the 1980s, with the public finances in balance (indeed increasingly in surplus) and public spending falling as a share of GDP, an overall fall in the tax burden became possible. So even though North Sea revenues had fallen, there were a series of reductions in income tax rates. The basic rate came down from 30 to 25 per cent. The higher rates were consolidated in a single rate of 40 per cent. The move to independent taxation reduced the tax on investment income of women. And the introduction and extension of various tax breaks for savings (PEPs, TESSAs, personal pensions) further reduced the average rate of tax on income.

But despite these tax cuts the public sector deficit did not increase. The most important reason was that public spending was absorbing a far smaller share of the national income in the second half of the 1980s than in the first half of the decade. But there was also an upswing in non-North Sea taxes. Corporation tax in particular, following the 1984 reforms, proved a buoyant source of revenue, increasing by nearly 2 per cent of GDP.

One way of interpreting these events might run as follows. Oil revenues in the 1990s are expected to be lower than they were at their peak in 1985/86, to the tune of around 3 per cent of GDP. Other things being equal, that requires either a permanent cut in public spending or a permanent increase in non-oil tax revenues (as a share of GDP). That does not necessarily imply an increase in tax *rates*, since the non-oil tax *base* should expand as the oil sector shrinks (just as it shrank as the oil sector expanded). However, the boom of the late 1980s deferred the need for this adjustment, just as it deferred the adjustment of the real exchange rate, by producing a strong *cyclical* improvement in Government finances.

The estimates for 1992/93 suggest that the recession of the early 1990s has caused some deterioration in the public finances. Public spending has risen sharply as a share of GDP, helped, among other things, by a rising debt interest burden, and Corporation Tax revenue, which is extremely sensitive to the economic cycle, has fallen back sharply. The public sector deficit, at 75 per cent of GDP, is more than double the average level of the early 1980s.

However, the underlying deterioration is nowhere near as great as this. Just as the boom flattered the public sector finances, so the recession makes them look a great deal worse than they really are. When the economy is back on trend, public spending (which still absorbs a lower share of GDP than in the early 1980s) will absorb a lower share than at present, and tax revenue, notably from corporation tax, will be higher. There has clearly been some *underlying* reduction of public spending as a share of GDP compared with the early 1980s, and hence a sustainable reduction in the tax burden.

But that still leaves the problem of the disappearing North Sea oil revenues. Table 5.11 shows the main sources of tax revenue. If we compare the current year with the early 1980s, income tax revenue is down by nearly 1.4 per cent of GDP, oil revenues are down by 2.8 per cent, and local taxes are down by 0.4 per cent. General Government revenue has fallen by over 6 per cent of GDP since the early 1980s. It is doubtful whether the underlying fall in public spending is as large. Unless this problem is addressed by tax increases or spending cuts, public and private consumption will continue to absorb a greater share of GDP than in the early 1980s – without the oil revenue to pay for it. The result will be a continuing current account deficit.

Table 5.11   Taxes as percentage of money GDP

	Income tax and NIC	VAT and specific duties	Corporation tax, capital tax and stamp duties	Local taxes	North Sea
1978/9	17.2	10.5	2.9	3.4	0.3
1981/2 – 1985/6	17.4	12.3	2.9	4.1	3.0
1986/7	16.8	12.2	4.2	4.1	1.2
1987/8 – 1991/2	16.3	11.6	4.7	4.0	0.6
1992–3	16.0	12.0	3.0	3.7	0.2

Table 5.12   Public and private consumption as share of GDP

Year	Share of GDP (%)
1976	79.6
1981–85	82.7
1986	82.8
1987–91	84.2
1992	86.7

The solution to the problem is to reduce the share of consumption in GDP by restraining the growth of public and private spending to below the rate of growth of GDP. The increase in the share of consumption has built up slowly over a number of years (Table 5.12). The reduction in share can take place equally slowly. Living standards can continue to rise, but they will rise more slowly than national output.

10.   Summary and conclusions

It is time to pull the threads together and draw some conclusions. When oil came on-stream in the late 1970s it caused a rise in the real exchange rate, an expansion of the service sector, and a relative decline in manufacturing. The expansion of services was necessary in order that a richer population could consume more out of its oil wealth. The relative decline in manufacturing was an inevitable counterpart to the growth of the service sector – the resources *had* to come from somewhere, and they *could* come from manufacturing because the oil surplus reduced the need for manufactured exports.

In theory the run-down in oil production in the late 1980s, and the sharp fall in its price in 1986, should have reversed this switch and led to a contraction of the service sector and an expansion of manufacturing. That in turn might have involved a fall in the real exchange rate (to stimulate both foreign and domestic demand for UK manufactures), and a reduction in domestic demand (to reduce home demand for services and free resources to move into manufacturing).

However, such adjustments take time – and may be delayed by other shocks. In the event both the fall in the real exchange rate and the reduction in domestic demand were effectively frustrated by the financial deregulation of the late 1980s and the boom which followed it. The exchange rate fell in 1986, when the oil price collapsed, but it subsequently recovered when the boom attracted inflows of foreign capital.

The boom also postponed the need for any fiscal adjustment to the loss of oil revenues. When output was growing rapidly in the late 1980s there was a surge in tax revenue, particularly from corporation tax, which replaced much of the lost oil revenues. Moreover, during this period public spending fell steadily as a share of GDP, making it possible to cut tax rates and still show a fiscal surplus.

At the same time, deregulation directly stimulated the growth of financial services and led indirectly to the property boom. So demand for services remained high and investment flowed into the service sector. The share of services in both output and consumption continued to grow.

The consequence was that much of the demand for manufactures continued to be met from abroad. The capital inflows associated with the boom made it easy to finance the resulting current account deficit, so consumers did not have to adjust immediately to the loss of oil revenues that occurred in 1986. The required expansion of the UK manufacturing sector, and the associated reduction of the service sector, was postponed.

However, there are signs that the long-delayed adjustment to the lower oil revenues is now taking place. The fall in inflation and improved price and cost competitiveness should mean a sustainable improvement in the output of tradeable goods. The correction of the public finances was begun by adopting a new system of public spending control in the 1992 Autumn Statement and continued with the pre-announced tax increases in the 1993 Budgets.

The recession itself, widely acknowledged to be concentrated in the south and in the service sector, has been one part of the adjustment process. Many of those who became unemployed during the recession came out of service industries. Unemployment is always a regrettable waste of resources, but a period of *transitional* unemployment is almost inevitable when resources are being shifted on a major scale between one sector of the economy and another.

As the upturn gathers pace and prospects improve for employment in the manufacturing sector, the economy will embark on the second leg of the process of adjustment to the fall in North Sea revenues. It will take the form of renewed growth led by the manufacturing sector.

References

Ball, R.J. and Burns, T. (1976), 'The inflationary mechanism in the UK Economy', *American Economic Review*, **66**, September.

Ball, R.J., Burns, T. and Laury, J.S.E. (1977), 'The role of exchange rate changes in balance of payments adjustment: the United Kingdom Case', *Economic Journal*, **87**, March.

Ball, R.J., Burns, T. and Warburton, P.J. (1980), 'The London Business School Model of the UK Economy: an exercise in international monetarism', in Ormerod, P. (ed.), *Economic Modelling*, London: Heinemann.

Ball, R.J. (1992), 'Manufacturing industry, economic growth and the balance of payments', in Ball, C.J. (ed.), *The Economics of Wealth Creation*, Aldershot: Edward Elgar.

Ball, R.J. and Robertson, D. (1993), 'Manufacturing industry and balance of payments adjustments: the UK Case', *CEF Discussion Paper DP2-93*.

Budd, A.P. and Burns, T. (1977), 'Why the exchange rate must be set free', *Economic Outlook*, London Business School, April.

Forsyth, P.J. and Kay, J.A. (1980), 'The economic implication of North Sea oil revenues', *Fiscal Studies*, **1**, (3), 1–28.

House of Lords (1985), *Report From the Select Committee on Overseas Trade*, Volume 1.

Robinson, P.W. and McCullough, A. (1986), 'Manufacturing Prospects after OPEC III', *Economic Outlook*, October.

6 Bank risk and the level playing field
Harold Rose*

Introduction

At the heart of bank regulation today is the principle of a required minimum ratio of book capital to total 'risk-adjusted' assets, the latter being the sum of a bank's assets (in book value terms) weighted by risk coefficients for different classes of asset as prescribed by the supervisors. The system, which was first developed by the Federal Reserve Board and the Bank of England, became enshrined in the December 1987 agreement of the Group of Ten countries meeting as the Basle Committee on Banking Regulation and Supervisory Practice.

This approach to the question of capital adequacy has been criticized by academics for appearing to assume either that banks are optimally diversified – in which case the system would not be needed, for regulators could simply prescribe the required minimum overall ratio – or that asset risks are linear and additive,[1] which is true only if the correlation between different asset class returns is unity. The system is also open to criticism for giving all loans to the private non-bank sector, other than residential mortgages, the same risk weighting, irrespective, for example, of their industrial composition.[2] But the main objective of the Basle Committee was to obtain international agreement as to minimum capital ratios in order to ensure that competition in international markets between the banks of different countries was not distorted by differences in regulatory requirements – the aim of a so-called 'level playing field' – and it is this which is the main focus of this paper. Its place in this Festschrift reflects the role of James Ball as Director of an international bank as well as economist, business school Principal and insurance company Chairman.

The main questions discussed in this paper are whether the level of banking risk is substantially the same in different countries and, in particular, the possible implications for risk of cross-border banking. Particularly because of the lack of reliable data, only a crude first approximation of answers to these questions is possible here, and the statistical findings should be regarded as illustrating the issues rather than resolving them.

Is banking risk the same in all countries?

The function of bank capital is to reduce the probability of insolvency to some acceptable level; and bank risk arises primarily from the uncertainty of returns

* I am grateful to Professor R.A. Brealey for comments on this paper, to Maria Vassalou for statistical assistance and to Andrew Ball, of Barclays Bank Economics Department, for providing data.

from bank assets, including, of course, the uncertainty of future loan losses. *Expected* losses due to default on new loans will be reflected in provisions for bad debts on the loan portfolio and, therefore, in the gross loan margin. The classic case for mandatory capital ratios is that bank failure, or the threat of it, has external costs in the shape of a run on other banks, including solvent banks, and of the interruption of the supply of loans to solvent borrowers, who, because of asymmetry of information, may find it difficult to obtain an immediate replacement for their unused loan facilities provided by a bank which has failed. Asymmetry of information is also held to justify the prescription of minimum capital ratios for the protection of depositors. If the latter are instead protected by deposit insurance, the main function of minimum capital ratios becomes that of restricting the losses of the insurer.

Whatever the force of these arguments, if the risk weightings prescribed by regulators do not accurately reflect the pattern of risk, the imposition of the same risk weighting for banks in different countries will not achieve the desired result of 'fair' competition. The Basle system, by using the same risk weight for a given class of asset across countries, especially bank loans, implicitly assumes that the riskiness – that is, degree of uncertainty – of returns on bank loan portfolios is substantially the same in all countries, or at least is not so different as to outweigh the convenience of having a simple uniform minimum ratio. The Basle Committee might well argue that it was a substantial practical achievement to obtain international agreement at all and that a more complicated approach would only have caused time-consuming or fruitless dissent. Academics, however, are not bound by such constraints.

The measurement of banking risk is no simple matter, even if the question is confined to bank assets with no regard to their relationship to the character of bank liabilities, for example, with respect to possible interest rate, currency and other risks. If the probability distribution of rates of return on bank assets, as reflected in historical volatility, were a normal – or log-normal – one, some inference could be drawn from the standard deviation of returns earned by banks as to the probability that the value of bank assets and, therefore, bank capital would drop below some critical level. In addition, however, banks need to form an estimate of the possible magnitude of extreme adverse experience and, because the cumulative effect of relatively moderately poor experience can ultimately prove fatal, the effect of a run of even moderately unfavourable years on the capital ratio. Apart from all this, the underlying process generating returns on bank assets may not be stable, and returns estimated from published accounts are subject to various forms of profit-smoothing and other accounting devices that vary from country to country. Hidden reserves have been maintained especially in Germany, the Netherlands and Switzerland, and until recently in Japan; and in all countries loan provisions may be subject to delay[3] or an element of smoothing. Valuation rules relating to bad debts, securities and physical assets also vary between countries; and in no country do banks' published accounts value all assets fully on the estimated market value basis needed for a true assessment of profitability and solvency.[4]

The statistics shown in the various Tables in this paper, therefore, are only a first approximation to the data needed for a comparison of banking risk in different countries, even in the narrow sense of the relative variability of rates of return, the measure of which on which this paper concentrates.

National differences in the variability of bank rates of return

The data in Table 6.1 are subject to the usual reservations due to the relatively small number of annual observations and to differences in accounting treatment. But there appear to be material differences between the lowest annual values of profitability and between the standard deviations of rates of return.

Table 6.1   Bank profits (before tax) as a percentage of total assets in different countries 1975–90

	Lowest value %	Mean %	Standard deviation %	Coefficient of variation	First order serial correlation
Canada	0.48	0.82	0.37	0.45	0.01
France	0.19	0.30	0.12	0.40	0.51
Germany	0.61	0.74	0.25	0.34	0.51
Italy	0.39	0.70	0.32	0.46	0.81
Japan[1]	0.26	0.42	0.16	0.38	0.58
Netherlands	0.22	0.60	0.25	0.42	0.62
Spain	0.84	1.17	0.45	0.38	0.77
UK[2]	0.67	1.10	0.51	0.47	0.03
USA	0.59	0.67	0.29	0.43	–0.55

[1] 1979–90.
[2] 1980–90.

Sources: J.S. Revell, 'Costs and Margins in Banking – An International Survey', OECD 1980. 'Bank Profitability 1981–1990', OECD 1992.

Although portfolio risk can generally be represented by standard deviation of return, the mean expected rate of return is also relevant to the assessment of solvency. If two countries have the same standard deviation of return but different means, the probability that the capital ratio will fall below a given critical level is higher in the country with the lower rate of return. Because of this, the coefficient of variation gives a better immediate indication of the ranking of risk than does the standard deviation alone. On this basis Table 6.1 suggests that, of the countries listed, British and Italian banks have had the highest level of 'normalized' variability of return and German banks the lowest.

The implication of Table 6.1 is that crude capital ratios should vary between countries. However, the published information concerning asset composition does not enable a test to be made as to whether this difference in apparent riskiness corresponds to the pattern of risk-adjusted weightings prescribed under the Basle agreement. Bank risk is probably dominated by the proportion of assets taking the form of loans, but there is little correlation between published loan proportions and either the standard deviation or the coefficients of variation of the countries listed in Table 6.1.

For some countries, as Table 6.1 shows, rates of return are subject to serial correlation, probably due to book profit smoothing and/or the serial correlation in asset levels, the main exceptions being the low serial correlation for Canada and the UK (with significance levels of 0.97 and 0.92 respectively). The negative serial correlation for banks in the USA mainly reflects the impact of large but irregular provisions for LDC debts in the 1980s. Because of serial correlation and because the variability of *changes* in rates of return is a better measure of uncertainty, Table 6.2 gives results for first differences of book rates of return, the aspect on which most of this paper concentrates.

Table 6.2   Bank profits before tax as a percentage of book assets in different countries 1975–89 – first differences

	Mean %	Standard deviation %	Coefficient of variation	First order serial correlation
Canada	–0.08	0.372	4.65	–0.39
France	–0.02	0.150	7.50	–0.06
Germany	–0.05	0.252	5.04	–0.13
Italy	–0.08	0.183	2.29	–0.18
Japan	–0.02	0.105	5.25	0.33
Netherlands	–0.03	0.281	9.37	0.01
Spain	–0.11	0.462	4.20	–0.22
UK	–0.04	0.679	16.98	–0.54
USA	–0.03	0.459	15.30	–0.52

The period, 1975–89, was one of falling bank profitability in most countries, but there was a wide degree of dispersion in first differences. Using these rather than levels results as usual in higher standard deviations and in an altered ranking order of apparent risk, with banking in the UK and the USA heading the list in this period by a wider margin than in levels if the coefficient of variation is taken as the most relevant measure. Further investigation would be needed to establish the extent to which this was the result of differing degrees of accounting profit-smoothing, which are probably much greater in continental countries and in Japan than in the UK and the USA.

The extent to which bank risk varies between countries would not matter to the aim of securing a 'level playing field' if international competition between banks were an insignificant proportion of banking business; although it might affect the share of banks in financial transactions within different countries. But, as Table 6.3 shows, bank cross-border lending is a significant activity for some countries. As bank risk varies between countries, equality of international treatment should require capital ratios specifically to take into account the risks of international lending, which can differ from those of domestic lending; and the importance of cross-border lending to a country's banks differs from country to country.

Table 6.3   Foreign assets of banks in different countries end-1991 ($bn)

Country of residence	Total	Cross-border claims on		Domestic claims on private sector
		banks	non-banks	
Canada	46	34	12	339
France	460	309	151	1271
Germany	403	278	125	1687
Italy	106	95	11	527
Japan	943	751	192	4416
Netherlands	189	140	49	271
Spain	82	65	17	371
UK	983	714	269	1238
USA	656	577	79	2549

Source: 'International Financial Statistics', IMF. 1993 Yearbook.

Cross-border lending to non-banks is small compared with domestic lending in most countries, the main exception being the UK, where, because of its entrepôt role, the figure is as high as 22 per cent. Of greater potential significance to banking risk in most countries is the volume of cross-border inter-bank lending. At the end of 1991 this was equivalent to 52 per cent of bank domestic private sector claims in the case of the Netherlands, and 58 per cent in the case of the UK.

The risks of cross-border inter-bank lending depend on a variety of factors, such as the term of lending; and most inter-bank loans are of a short term with relatively low default risk. But the relative profitability of banks in different countries must have *some* influence on the default risk of international banking activities, to an extent which will depend partly on the correlation between changes in bank profitability in different countries, which will determine the effects of diversification across countries. Table 6.4 therefore shows, for first differences in national book rates of return, the correlation between the returns on banks in individual countries and those in the rest as a group (the Appendix records the full correlation matrix between individual countries).

Table 6.4   First differences of profits as a percentage of total assets 1975–90 – correlation and sensitivity coefficients between the rest of the group and individual countries

	Correlation coefficient	Sensitivity coefficient[1]	t-value	Durbin–Watson statistic
Canada	0.72	0.45	3.70	2.26
France	0.61	1.06	2.80	2.93
Germany	0.79	0.77	4.60	2.34
Italy	0.41	0.59	1.63	2.15
Japan	0.09	0.14	0.29	3.37
Netherlands	0.49	0.45	2.04	2.81
Spain	0.70	0.35	3.53	2.89
UK	0.73	0.21	3.65	1.73
USA	0.71	0.36	3.65	1.73

[1] The b-coefficient in the regression equation, in first differences: (Rate of return overseas)$_t$ = a + b(national rate of return)$_r$ + u.

Table 6.4 also shows the 'sensitivity' of changes in return in the rest of the group to changes in the rate of return on individual countries, the b-coefficient in a simple linear regression, in first differences, of the rate of return of banks overseas as a group (unweighted) on that of banks in each country. (That is to say, returns of banks overseas are being used as a proxy for returns on the overseas assets of banks resident in a particular country.) When weighted by the proportion of assets overseas, the b-coefficient would represent an estimate of the proportionate contribution of foreign assets to the variance of changes in return on bank portfolios.[5]

It should be noted that it has not been possible to correct bs due to the fact that, for banks in some countries, profit on overseas assets may represent a significant proportion of the reported profits on which the 'national' rate of return is based. This factor, which causes spurious correlation, probably helps to account for the relatively high correlation coefficients for the UK and USA.

The implication of these coefficients is that international banking for the group of countries concerned reduces risk, but to varying degrees. The low 'sensitivities' for the UK and the USA on the face of it, imply that the proportionate contribution of overseas activities, as mirrored by the return on banks overseas, to total portfolio risk is relatively small for these countries. The sensitivity coefficient for Japan is the lowest, but is not statistically significant.

Cross-border lending risk

If, instead of taking the variability of book rates of return on assets as a whole, we were to investigate the risks specifically of cross-border lending, statistics of returns on loans would be needed. These are not available in the form required, but we can derive some information from the narrower measure of provisions as a proportion of outstanding loans, again using first differences. Here, the effect of international diversification appears to be even stronger than that for overall bank profitability (Table 6.5). For some countries, the correlation coefficient between the change in the provision ratios of its banks and that of the rest of the group is actually negative (implying that the correlation coefficients for the remaining elements of profitability are strongly positive). The main exceptions are the UK and the USA, where the correlation coefficients are relatively high and are of the same order of magnitude as for overall rates of return.

Table 6.5 First differences of provisions as a percentage of loans 1975–90 – correlation between individual countries and the remainder

	Correlation coefficient
Canada	0.40
France	−0.24
Germany	0.12
Italy	−0.55
Japan	−0.69
Netherlands	−0.56
Spain	−0.14
UK	0.86
USA	0.84

The use of book value ratios

Finally, there remains the fact that capital ratios are prescribed on a book value basis, the minimum required equity capital ratio being 4 per cent of so-called *risk-adjusted* book assets. There was some relationship between mean *unadjusted* book capital ratios and volatility of return over the period 1975–90 (see Appendix 3). However, the relationship between book value and the market value of bank equity varies between countries and is not stable over time, as Table 6.6, which has had to be based on a more limited period, shows.

Table 6.6   Percentage ratios of market to book values of equity of banks in different countries 1986–91

	1986	1987	1988	1989	1990	1991
Australia (3)	96	82	106	111	77	114
Canada (6)	104	87	118	128	100	121
France (5)	88	112	99	128	81	68
Germany (3)	164	109	138	186	262	134
Japan (7)	886	890	1080	750	370	411
Spain (4)	217	237	239	212	158	140
Switzerland (3)	248	147	134	152	88	95
UK (4)	93	81	80	117	92	121
USA (35)	113	99	112	123	77	112

Note: Number of banks in brackets. The ratios represent medians except for Australia and Switzerland, for which unweighted means are shown.

Source: Salomon Brothers Publications.

A belief that securities markets are generally 'efficient' would be accompanied by the view that it is the capital ratio on a market value basis which is generally the more significant, reflecting the market's view of a bank's future profitability and future risk as well as its current performance (and accounting practices). A listed bank should be able to reinforce its capital by making a new issue at close to the current market price; and required capital ratios could easily be defined in market value terms for listed banks.

Bank supervisors can reply by saying that they can take market values into account, prescribing different capital ratios for different banks, and that they have more information about bank solvency than do outsiders (a claim which, however, can be disputed in the light of BCCI and cases where bank share prices have fallen in advance of regulatory action). But if asymmetry of information *is* the problem, banks could be obliged to give more information to the public concerning, for example, the industrial composition of loan portfolios and the weight of relatively large loans to single borrowers. Rules on published provisions could also be tightened up.

Regulators can argue that the volatility of Japanese bank share prices in particular demonstrates the possible danger of relying on market values. The rise in Japanese share prices in the 1980s now looks like a long 'bubble', and it is possible to combine a belief that markets ensure an 'efficient' pattern of *relative* price valuation, as between securities, with periodic bubble-like behaviour by the level of prices as a whole. However, even after their sharp fall in 1992, Japanese share prices remain above book values, whereas on a book value basis several Japanese banks are close to or below their minimum required ratios.

The interesting question is whether it is possible for a bank to be relatively close to insolvency on a 'today' basis, because the realizable value of its *present* assets is not much above the value of its *present* liabilities, and yet be valued in the equity market on a higher basis relative to today's assets because the market expects the bank to be able to acquire *new* assets in the future (perhaps with characteristics different from those of its existing assets), with an expected market value well in excess of its expected new liabilities.

Such a situation is theoretically possible and may justify a cautious attitude in some circumstances on the part of supervisors towards some banks with an apparently adequate capital ratio on a market value basis. Whereas the regulators' obligation is to protect the claims of depositors, bank shareholders, like those in any geared firm, are in the position of having a call option on a bank's assets; and the value of that option depends on the variance of the value of those assets and not on some lower bound to their value, which is what is relevant to a bank's solvency. But whether this justifies the use of *book* values is a separate matter. It is hard to believe that wide international differences in the ratio of market to book value do not, at least to some degree, reflect actual differences in the margin of present as well as expected future solvency. Only if the bank's envisaged 'future' operations are expected to earn more than the bank's cost of capital would a bank's growth prospects add to the market value of the bank's equity today (and profitable growth prospects should make it easier to raise additional equity today if necessary).

Conclusions

The published data on bank profitability and loan provisions are subject to important reservations concerning accounting practice and statistical significance. But the varied picture of risk they present, in the admittedly narrow sense of historical variability, argues against the case for a uniform minimum capital ratio for banks in different countries; and it is doubtful whether the Basle system of risk-adjusted capital fully allows for this. That banking risk can be shown to vary from country to country would not matter much if international banking played a uniform part in banking risk. But the effect of cross-border transactions on banking risk varies from country to country, not only because of differences in scale, but more interestingly because the correlation between banking experience at home and that abroad, even in the same overseas country, is not uniform for banks in different home countries.

The prescription of a common book capital ratio, even on a so-called risk-adjusted basis, is hard to reconcile with the wide differences that have existed between the ratio of equity market values to book values. Objections can be made to relying on market values, but even so it does not follow automatically that the prescription of common minimum book ratios is any more appropriate.

Notes

1. See, for example, Schaefer, S., 'Financial regulation: the contribution of the theory of finance', in *Lectures on Regulation*, Centre for Business Strategy, London Business School, 1992.
2. See, for example, Rose, H., 'Bank regulation and industry risk', ibid.
3. For example, major provisions for LDC bad debts were not made until 1987 in the USA and UK, despite the Mexican debt moratorium of 1982 and the clear evidence of the severe deterioration in the quality of most LDC debts well before 1987.
4. The closest approach to market value accounting has been followed by banks in Denmark. See Bernard, V.L., Merton, R.C., and Palepu, K.G., *Mark-to-Market Accounting for US Banks and Thrifts: Lessons from the Danish Experience.* Working Paper 93-04, Harvard Business School November 1992.
5. The *absolute* contribution of an asset to the risk (variance of return) of a portfolio is given by the covariance between returns on the asset and those on the portfolio, multiplied by the weight of the asset. The *proportionate* contribution to portfolio risk is this divided by the variance of the portfolio return. This is the same as the asset's weight multiplied by its 'sensitivity' coefficient.

Appendix 1: Correlation matrix – rates of return on total assets 1975–90

Canada	1.00	0.45	0.26	0.36	0.43	0.21	0.64	–0.14	0.68
France	0.45	1.00	–0.40	–0.19	0.37	–0.19	0.70	–0.43	0.44
Germany	0.26	–0.40	1.00	0.61	0.26	0.52	0.16	–0.12	0.27
Italy	0.36	–0.19	0.61	1.00	0.32	0.03	0.58	–0.53	0.86
Japan	0.43	0.37	0.26	0.32	1.00	0.11	0.27	–0.24	0.89
Netherlands	0.21	–0.19	0.52	0.03	0.11	1.00	–0.03	–0.18	–0.22
Spain	0.64	0.70	0.16	0.58	0.27	–0.03	1.00	–0.55	0.02
UK	–0.14	–0.43	–0.12	–0.53	–0.24	–0.18	–0.55	1.00	0.70
USA	0.68	0.44	0.27	0.86	0.89	–0.22	0.02	0.70	1.00

Appendix 2: Correlation matrix – rates of return on total assets – first differences 1975–90

Canada	1.00	0.60	0.52	0.07	0.12	0.51	0.62	0.68	0.47
France	0.60	1.00	0.46	0.35	0.29	0.61	0.81	0.24	0.21
Germany	0.52	0.46	1.00	0.55	–0.33	0.74	0.60	0.62	0.64
Italy	0.07	0.35	0.55	1.00	–0.39	0.21	0.41	0.34	0.43
Japan	0.12	0.29	–0.33	–0.39	1.00	–0.11	0.09	0.21	0.15
Netherlands	0.51	0.61	0.74	0.21	–0.11	1.00	0.64	0.23	0.12
Spain	0.62	0.81	0.60	0.41	0.09	0.64	1.00	0.33	0.25
UK	0.68	0.24	0.62	0.34	0.21	0.23	0.33	1.00	0.91
USA	0.47	0.21	0.64	0.43	0.15	0.12	0.25	0.91	1.00

Appendix 3: Mean capital ratios and standard deviations of profits/assets 1975–90

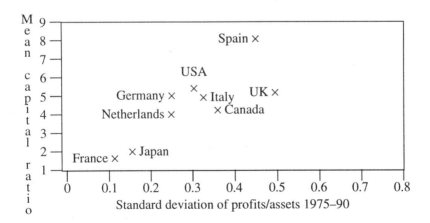

PART II

ISSUES IN ECONOMIC MODELLING

7 The UK macroeconometric modelling tradition: expectations and learning

*David Currie and Stephen Hall**

1. Introduction

It is a great pleasure for us to contribute to this volume of essays in honour of our colleague, Sir James Ball. His career is remarkable in spanning three distinct areas of professional life: first, the academic, being the leading British pioneer in applied macroeconometrics and macromodel-building; second, academic administration in his role as Principal of the London Business School; and, third, business, notably as Chairman of Legal and General. In the first of these roles, he established the Centre for Economic Forecasting at the London Business School, funded from both public and private sources, and produced the first UK forecasts based on a fully estimated and computerized macroeconometric model. These forecasts have now been produced for more than a quarter of a century. As the current Director and Research Director of the Centre, we have benefited enormously from his legacy in this area. In his role as Principal of the London Business School, he ensured the growth of the School in its first decade or so, and established the strong academic and market reputation which continues to grow. In the third phase of his career, we continue to benefit from his valuable contribution and incisive comments as a colleague.

Our topic in this paper is the role of expectations in empirical macroeconometric models. This is appropriate for this volume for two reasons: First, the analysis and modelling of expectations have come to play a major part in the tradition of macroeconometric modelling which Sir James Ball did so much to establish. Secondly, his own early writings showed an acute awareness, unusual for that time, of the key role of expectation in macroeconomics: his book on *Inflation and the Theory of Money* (1964), for example, refers to the role of expectations with regard to prices, wages, demand, permanent income, investment and profits. In this, he followed the lead of the great economists, such as Marshall, Walras and Keynes, who were always aware of the crucial role of expectations.

An important advance in the two decades since the publication of *Inflation and the Theory of Money* has been the development of techniques for giving a formal analytical treatment of expectations in both theoretical and empirical models. This paper has a very specific aim: to survey the development of the

---

* Centre for Economic Forecasting, London Business School

treatment of expectations in empirical models over this period. We will not attempt to survey the developments at a theoretical level: many such surveys already exist, for example, Shiller (1978), Begg (1982), Attfield *et al.* (1985) or Holden *et al.* (1985). Nor will we discuss the econometric issues of estimation or identification when expectations are treated explicitly (see Pesaran, 1987, or Cuthbertson *et al.*, 1992 for such discussions). We will rather focus instead on the impact which the changing treatment of expectations has had on macro-economic models, on policy analysis and on forecasting.

Much early empirical work on expectations centred around attempts to provide direct measures of agents' expectations, for example, Katona (1951, 1958), Tobin (1959), Eisner (1965), and Ball and Drake (1964), and the thrust of much of this research was towards a psychological understanding of individual expectations formation. Direct measures of expectations were undoubtedly useful in forming economic forecasts. However, this approach was limited by two inherent problems. First, gathering direct measures of expectations was very expensive and the data became rapidly outdated. Secondly, and perhaps even more important, direct measures of expectations gave little insight into how expectations would change as policy changed. Thus, although the importance of expectations to economic policy was stressed by the economic theorists, direct measures of expectations helped little in determining what the correct economic policy should be. The breakthrough which allowed a much more general approach to expectations modelling came with the realization that expectations could be treated as an unobservable component. This implied that expectations could be substituted by their determinants once an explicit rule for expectations formation was assumed. One of the earliest examples of this treatment was the specification of the adaptive expectations hypothesis by Cagan (1956) and Nerlove (1958): this was an important departure because it allowed the treatment of expectations to be made explicit for the first time in an empirical setting. The major disadvantage of this approach quickly emerged, however, when it was realized that an agent who used this method to determine expectations would, in many circumstances, make entirely predictable errors even in the very long run. It is hard to believe that such a feature could be true of an intelligent economic agent, and hence these developments led quite quickly and naturally to the suggestion of rational expectations (RE). While there had been some early precursors to the proposal of RE (for example, Grunberg and Modigliani, 1954), Muth (1961) is widely regarded as the founder of this approach. RE was not, however, to be widely adopted for more than a decade after Muth's work was published. Indeed, far from being viewed as a criticism of the adaptive expectations approach, the main perception throughout the 1960s of Muth's work was primarily that it justified adaptive expectations as being rational under certain conditions. It was only some 10–15 years later that it began to be appreciated how restrictive these special conditions were and that an alternative empirical approach was needed.

Empirical work incorporating expectations was given an important boost by the work on the expectations augmented Phillips curve (Friedman, 1968) and the empirical models which implemented such ideas (Lucas and Rapping, 1969). The adaptive expectations approach both illustrated that expectations could be treated in an explicit way in an empirical model and opened up the way for alternative approaches. A rapid explosion occurred in theoretical work incorporating RE, and RE became linked very closely with the new-classical approach to macroeconomics. Some of the main contributions in this area were Walters (1971), Lucas (1972a, 1972b, 1973, 1975), Sargent (1973, 1976), Sargent and Wallace (1973, 1975, 1976), Barro (1976, 1977) and Kydland and Prescott (1977). The perceived connection between classical economics and RE became very strong at this time, to the extent that many saw the two approaches as largely synonymous.

The late 1970s saw the development of the first macroeconomic models with RE. The initial models (for example, Sargent, 1976 and Taylor, 1979) were essentially more elaborate versions of the simple theoretical models and not true empirical ones. The first estimated macroeconomic models incorporating RE were Anderson (1979) which included only current dated expectations of current dated variables, and Fair (1979) which was a fairly large model (84 equations) including expectations of future prices in the bond and stock markets. The introduction of RE terms into the Fair model, in particular, required the development of new model solution procedures, which had been discussed, but not implemented, in Anderson (1979).

A clear distinction then developed within the literature between the treatment of linear and non-linear models. Blanchard and Kahn (1980) developed a closed form solution for linear models with RE which allowed detailed theoretical analysis of the properties of linear RE models, and this spawned a large literature investigating the consequences of RE within a linear framework. The development of non-linear models and RE, on the other hand, required a range of new numerical techniques to be developed to allow their solution and analysis.

It is perhaps worth stressing that, while the formal treatment of expectations has changed enormously and has often been controversial, the importance of expectations in forecasting and policy analysis has never been seriously questioned. This is illustrated by the stress which has often been put on obtaining direct measures of expectations; for example, Klein (1987) or Pesaran (1985).

We will begin in section 2 of this paper by discussing some basic concepts in the treatment of expectations (for example, adaptive expectations, the Lucas critique, RE and so on). Section 3 will then examine the developments which have been made within a linear framework, while section 4 will consider the development of expectations effects in non-linear models. Section 5 will draw some conclusions and outline likely directions for future research.

2.   Background to expectations mechanisms

In this section we will discuss the developments of some of the background concepts which underlie the treatment of expectations in both linear and non-linear models.

The hypothesis of adaptive expectations, first proposed by Cagan (1956), is mainly important for the simple fact that it allowed the first explicit introduction of expectations terms into formal empirical models. If we define $(_{t-1}x_t^e)$ as the expectation of the value of x in period t formed in period $t-1$ then the adaptive expectations hypothesis states that:

$$(_{t-1}x_t^e - _{t-2}x_{t-1}^e) = \Phi(x_{t-1} - _{t-2}x_{t-1}^e) \qquad 0 < \Phi < 1. \qquad (7.1)$$

That is, an individual holds a series of expectations for the variable x and at each point in time the expectation for the future is revised in a proportional way with the most recently observed error. By simply rearranging (7.1) we can get:

$$(_{t-1}x_t^e) = \Phi x_{t-1} + (1 - \Phi)_{t-2}x_{t-1}^e, \qquad (7.2)$$

and of course by successively substituting out for the lagged expectation we can get:

$$(_{t-1}x_t^e) = \Phi x_{t-1} + \Phi(1 - \Phi)x_{t-2} + \Phi(1 - \Phi)^2 x_{t-3}... \qquad (7.3)$$

and so we may model the unobservable expectation purely in terms of past observations of x. At first sight this seems intuitively appealing, as it says that our expectations of the future are a simple extrapolation of the past. It is, however, easy to construct examples where this rule makes consistent and growing mistakes. Consider the case when x grows at a constant 10 per cent rate – in this case the adaptive expectations model would always underestimate the level of x and what is more it would do so by an increasing absolute amount over time. It is, of course, possible to generalize the adaptive expectations model to overcome this specific problem and to produce an extrapolative rule which would cope with growing variables, or indeed any other specific form of time-series behaviour. Many suggestions have been put forward for such schemes; for example, Flemming (1976) and Pesaran (1985) define a broad class of expectations mechanisms which make use of past information as extrapolative expectations. But as a general statement, all fixed parameter extrapolative rules are liable to perform poorly in one circumstance or another. For example, if a rule is chosen which copes well with stationary behaviour in x, that rule will generally not cope if the behaviour in x changes to become non-stationary. Any fixed parameter rule will therefore be likely to perform badly in the face of a change in the regime generating x. This is the heart of the Lucas critique.

The Lucas critique (Lucas, 1976) essentially emphasized the idea that policy regimes and particular policy rules will affect the reduced form solution for all the endogenous variables in a model. If agents are rational, even if only in the weak sense that they will not make systematic errors, then agents' expectations rules will change as the policy rule changes. Hence any model which either uses fixed parameter extrapolative rules or, even worse, does not explicitly model expectations at all, will not be structurally stable across regime changes and will not be a suitable vehicle for policy analysis. This point can be easily illustrated in a very simple example. Suppose a government controls an instrument G and that agents want to form expectations about a variable X which is simply the sum of G and Z:

$$X_t = G_t + Z_t, \tag{7.4}$$

where we might think of X as total demand and Z as non-government demand. Assume that Z is determined as follows:

$$Z_t = \alpha X_t + \varepsilon_t. \tag{7.5}$$

Now under one regime where G is simply held fixed, a reasonable expectations rule to form expectations about the future value of X would simply be:

$$\left(_t X^e_{t+1}\right) = \frac{G_{t+1}}{1 - \alpha} \tag{7.6}$$

if the next period value for G was part of the information set, or if this was not the case then simply:

$$(_t X^e_{t+1}) = X_t. \tag{7.7}$$

In this case a simple form of adaptive expectations rule would work well. But to see the force of the Lucas critique, suppose the government changed its policy rule and decided that from now on G would grow at 10 per cent per period. Although equation (6) would still be valid, equation (7) is no longer appropriate as the growth in G would now imply that:

$$(_t X^e_{t+1}) = 1.1 X_t. \tag{7.8}$$

The regime change has, then, left the structural equations unchanged but has changed the reduced form equations of the system and has rendered the appropriate extrapolative rule of expectations formation invalid. The general point is that if agents are intelligent and avoid making consistent mistakes in their expectations, then any fixed parameter extrapolative expectations model will be unable to cope adequately in the face of policy or other regime changes. One answer to the Lucas critique (although, as we will argue below, not the only answer) is to make use of the RE assumption.

Muth (1961) introduced the notion of a rational expectation to be 'essentially the same as the prediction of the relevant economic theory'. In many formal contexts this is taken to mean the conditional expectation of the relevant stochastic system of equations, although Hall (1988) argues that in the case of non-linear systems the mathematical expectation may not always be a good measure of an agent's expectation. In the full, or strong, form of the RE hypothesis, it is assumed that the economic agent has a complete knowledge of the economic system about which he needs to form expectations. This knowledge includes both the functional form, the parameters of the system and any exogenous process which is entering the system. Under this extreme assumption about the degree of information available to an agent, the optimal expectations formation mechanism becomes the model's own prediction of what will take place. In terms of the simple example above, the rational expectation of X would be given by either the structural form (7.6) or by the correct reduced form, that is (7.7) for the first regime or (7.8) for the second regime. By construction there is always an extrapolative rule which is equivalent to the RE, but the advantage of the RE approach is that it can cope with regime changes and other structural shifts automatically while the extrapolative model would have to be continually respecified. The main disadvantage of the RE approach is the extreme assumption which is required about the information available to the economic agent.

An alternative approach to making this extreme assumption would be to assume that agents' expectations are on average correct, but not to make any specific assumption about how agents arrive at these expectations: we define this as weak rationality. This represents a small generalization of the usual notion of weak rationality, for example, Feige and Pearce (1976) in which agents are assumed to use only a univariate model to form their expectations. The notion that agents do not make consistent predictable mistakes is an appealing one but, as noted above, it is not a property which any fixed parameter expectations rule will generally have. We must therefore move to a class of models which, while not containing full information, is able to adapt to regime changes and in effect to 'learn' about the economic environment.

The question of learning is also important in the context of the RE assumption where, in particular, the question of how agents come to know the true model is simply not addressed. As a consequence, learning has received increasing attention in the theoretical literature over the last decade. Learning can be modelled on the basis of a number of assumptions about the underlying knowledge which agents possess. The most extreme assumption, underlying much of the earlier theoretical literature, gives rise to the rational learning models: Friedman (1975), Townsend (1978, 1983), Bray (1983), Frydman (1982) or Bray and Kreps (1984). The assumption made here is that agents know the true structure of the model but that some of the parameters of the system are unknown. As the true structural equations are known, the agents' learning problem is essentially one of estimating the parameters of the system. As long as a consistent estimation procedure is used we would expect the system to converge on a full rational expectation equilibrium (REE), and indeed most of the theoretical investigation of small analytical models has shown this to be the case. Rational learning models, however, still make very stringent assumptions about the degree of knowledge which agents have of the structure of the system.

A slightly weaker assumption gives rise to the boundedly rational learning models. Here the general assumption is that agents use some 'reasonable' rule of learning to form expectations and that the form of the rule remains constant over time. In fact choosing a rule which all agents regard as reasonable is rather difficult, and almost always the choice has been the reduced form of the whole system: for example, DeCanio (1979), Radner (1982), Bray and Savin (1986). Thus it is assumed that agents know the reduced form of the whole system as it would exist under RE but, again, do not know some or all of the parameters. The move to bounded rationality in this form may seem to be a rather small one, and yet it has important consequences for the behaviour of the system. The reason for this is that even in the absence of regime changes the reduced form of the model is a combination of the stable structural equations and the changing parameters of the expectations rule, so that it is time varying. The boundedly rational agent is usually assumed to be attempting to parameterize a stable reduced form system and so is actually trying to estimate a misspecified model. Under this assumption Bray and Savin (1986) are able to show that, for a simple cobweb model, the model sometimes converges to the RE equilibrium and sometimes cycles or diverges from the RE equilibrium.

When we consider more realistic models (and in particular when we allow for the Lucas critique), a further important complication is that the behavioural equations may themselves be undergoing structural changes. So even if the learning process is able to converge on the true model, it may, in effect, be chasing a moving target and so it may not converge to a stable set of parameters.

More recently, however, we have come to appreciate that the behaviour of the parameters in the learning rule gives an important insight into the form of equilibria which may emerge from the system. Marcet and Sargent (1988) summarize the main results. The concept of learning is characterized as a mapping of the parameters of the agents' expectations rule. A fixed point of that mapping is then a situation where the parameters of the expectations rule cease changing. So suppose an agent has a rule which is a linear function of a set of parameters, D, and the learning process (assumed to be some form of least squares learning) is represented by a mapping, S, such that $D_{t+1} = S(D_t)$, so that the learning process produces a sequence of parameters of the expectations rule. A fixed point of the mapping is represented by convergence of this sequence to some fixed value, this point is sometimes referred to as an expectations equilibrium, or an E-equilibrium. Then Marcet and Sargent (1989a) demonstrate that this fixed point is also a full rational expectations equilibrium. Furthermore, Evans (1983, 1985, 1986a, 1986b), Woodford (1990) and Marcet and Sargent (1989a, 1989b) demonstrate that the least squares learning procedure actually rules out many of the undesirable rational equilibria which can arise in conventional rational expectations equilibria. When a fixed point of the mapping is found, then we not only have an RE solution but we also have one which is not dependent on an arbitrary terminal condition.

This section has considered the conceptual developments in the treatment of expectations which underlies the empirical implementations which will be discussed in the next two sections.

3.   Expectations and linear models

One important strand of the literature has worked with linear models. The strength of this approach is that in many applications it admits an explicit analytical solution (following Blanchard and Kahn, 1980), permitting a greater extension of analytical ideas to model questions of credibility in policy. The disadvantage is the assumption of linearity, which excludes the additional phenomena arising in non-linear dynamics, including chaotic motion. Since non-linearities in economics are usually poorly founded, and since convincing empirical examples of chaotic behaviour are not easy to find (particularly at the quarterly frequency that is the usual concern of macroeconomists) this may not be too great a price to pay in return for the analytical advantages. To take advantage of the benefits of linearity, one approach to large-scale non-linear models is to linearize these models, and then apply linear control methods to the linearized model. This approach is developed and applied in Barrell *et al.* (1992), in the context of an application to the Global Econometric Model (GEM).

Following Blanchard and Kahn (1980), consider the general linear model given by:

$$\begin{bmatrix} Z_{t+1} \\ x^e_{t+1,t} \end{bmatrix} = A \begin{bmatrix} Z_t \\ x_t \end{bmatrix} \tag{7.9}$$

where **Z** is a vector of predetermined variables (defined as variables that change only slowly, for example, the capital stock) and **x** is a vector of non-predetermined variables (such as the exchange rate or asset prices, which can change instantaneously: most (but not quite all) linear RE systems can be put in the form of (7.9)). Excluding unstable bubble processes, it is straightforward to show (as Blanchard and Kahn do) that the rational solution to (7.9) is given by:

$$x_t = BZ_t .$$ (7.10)

For an appropriate choice of B, (7.10) determines non-predetermined variables (for example, asset prices) in terms of predetermined variables, and implies a rule for private sector expectations. Then the solution to (7.9) is given by

$$Z_{t+1} = (A_{11} + A_{12} B) Z_t,$$ (7.11)

which describes the dynamics of the system. These dynamics are determined by the number of predetermined (slow-moving) variables in the system.

Part of the dynamics of the system in (7.9) may arise from the policy rules of the authorities (for monetary and fiscal policy, for example). Hence the rules in (7.10), which specify how expectations are formed, will depend on the form of policy rule adopted by the authorities. This represents the Lucas (1972a) critique of non-expectational macromodels: that the expectational rules implicit in such models will shift in the face of policy shifts, giving rise to instability in model structure.

The endogenicity of B also greatly complicates the problem of formulating optimal policy. Since B depends on the type of policy adopted, it is necessary to take account of this in determining optimal policy: the authorities in the control problem act as a Stackelberg leader, taking account of the reactions of private sector expectations.

It also gives rise to a rather deeper problem, namely that of time inconsistency (Kydland and Prescott, 1977). An optimal policy formulated at time, *t*, in full knowledge of future events may become sub-optimal at a later date, *T*, simply with the passage of time and no new information. The authorities therefore have an incentive to renege on the previous policy. But an intelligent private sector can anticipate this, so that original policy lacks credibility.

This insight has generated a rich literature on policy credibility and the scope for precommitting policy to avoid the problems of time inconsistency. Since the gains from precommitted policies can often be quite large (see, for example, Currie *et al.* 1987), there are considerable benefits from effective forms of precommitment that enhance credibility. One means is to enhance the costs of reneging, whether by political announcements that raise the political costs or by external commitments (for example, the ERM or G7 policy co-ordination) that may incur costs in relations with trading partners. The presence of stochastic noise also enhances credibility (Currie and Levine, 1987), as may the formulation of simple rules for the conduct of policy (Levine and Currie, 1987).

Four additional developments from this policy literature have also been relevant. First, there has been the attempt to relax the stringency of the RE assumption by weakening the informational requirements to only partial or diverse (across individuals) information. It turns out that the implementation of this whilst retaining the rationality assumption is highly complex, even in linear models (see Pearlman *et al.*, 1986). The implied level of calculation by agents is therefore much higher, making its plausibility as a description of behaviour somewhat doubtful, this branch of the literature may push the rationality assumption too far.

A second strand concerns the design of robust policy rules (see Vines *et al.*, 1983; for a discussion in a non-RE context, see also Currie, 1985). Policy rules should if possible, perform well in a wide range of circumstances, so that uncertainty about future shocks, economic structure and agents' expectations do not seriously impair policy. Substantial work is in progress in this area (see, for example, Kemball-Cook, 1992), but the benefits of this research have yet to be realized.

A third area concerns the application of dynamic game theory to empirical macromodels (see, for example, Currie *et al.* 1987). Multi-player games are much easier to analyse in a linear context than a non-linear one, and this represents an exciting area of research (see Currie *et al.* 1992). However, the benefits are more in terms of insight than precise empirical estimates: it may be that this literature pushes the empirical models rather further than their empirical basis warrants.

Finally, an important area of research concerns the incorporation of learning into empirical models (see Driffill and Miller, 1992, and for a recent contribution see Kemball-Cook, 1992). This is also an active area of research in a non-linear context, as we discuss later. But an advantage of the linear framework, as Kemball-Cook demonstrates, is that it allows issues of learning to be combined with other important issues such as credibility and uncertainty. In principle, these issues could be addressed in a non-linear context, but the computational problems are considerable. The simplifying assumption of linearity allows greater richness in policy analysis along other dimensions. For this reason, we expect research on linear models to flourish alongside that on non-linear models.

4.   Expectations and non-linear models

This section will deal with the development of expectations effects in large non-linear models. It will begin by considering some general issues of specification and assessing the importance of expectations effects. It will then consider the problem of solving models with consistent expectations, and will move on to policy formation and the time inconsistency problem. The conceptual problems of information sets, historical tracking and uncertainty will then be considered. Finally, we will examine the development of learning models of expectations formation in large models.

Fair (1979) is in many ways the natural departure point for our account. This model was the first sizeable model to be solved under model consistent expectations and so it was the first time a modeller had been faced with the new technical problems which this assumption posed. The Fair model has, however, been isolated amongst US domestic models as the only one to adopt RE as a regular tool of solution. The main focus of development switched from the US to the UK with the publication in 1980 of the first results from the Liverpool model (see Minford *et al.*, 1984). From this point on, developments in solution techniques and the analysis of non-linear models with rational expectations occurred mainly in the UK. Holly and Corker (1984) reported on the introduction of model consistent expectations into the exchange rate and financial sector of the London Business School model. Hall and Henry (1985,1986) reported on the introduction of RE into both the exchange rate sector and the real side of the National Institute model. Westaway and Whittaker (1986) discussed the introduction of RE into HM Treasury's model. The late 1980s saw the spread of RE: Murphy (1989) introduced expectations effects into an Australian model and Lahti and Viren (1989) reported on the introduction of RE into a model of the Finnish economy. Masson *et al.* (1988) discussed the first introduction of RE into an international model, the IMF Multimod, and Gurney (1990) introduced RE into the GEM. A large amount of work then began in order to understand fully the implications of these changes for the models, surveys of some of this work may be found in Fair (1984), Hall and Henry (1988), Fisher *et al.* (1988, 1989) and Fisher (1990). We will discuss some of the main elements and results of this work below.

4.1 Expectations and models

It is perhaps best to begin with a simple general statement of the problems facing modellers upon the introduction of rational expectations. Let the main structural equations for a model consist of the following n equations:

$$y_{it} = f_i(\mathbf{Y}_t, \mathbf{X}, {}_t\mathbf{Y}^e_{t+1}) \quad i = 1 \ldots n \quad t = 1 \ldots T \qquad (7.12)$$

where $\mathbf{Y}$ is the vector of current and lagged values of the n endogenous variables $(y_{it} \ldots y_{it-k}$, where k is the lag length of the model), $\mathbf{X}$ is the vector of exogenous variables over all time periods $(x_0 \ldots x_T)$ where T is the final period of the time horizon under consideration), and ${}_t\mathbf{Y}^e_{t+1}$ is the expectation based upon information available at t of Y in period $t + 1$. This expectation may in general be viewed as being derived from another set of relationships:

$$(_ry^e_{t+1} = g_k(\mathbf{Y_t},\mathbf{X}) \quad k = 1...nl. \tag{7.13}$$

Of course if we were considering extrapolative expectations of one form or another, such as adaptive expectations, this second block of equations would simply represent a further group of essentially standard equations and no special problem arises. Under RE this second block of equations may be thought of in two ways. First, as a structural relationship, we may assume simply that:

$$(_ry^e_{t+1}) = \mathbf{Y}_{t+l}\,|\,t, \tag{7.14}$$

that is, that the expectation is equal to the actual model solution in the future period. Alternatively, we may think of the expectations mechanism as the fully restricted reduced form of both (7.10) and (7.12). It would then be seen as just another extrapolative expectations rule, with the crucial difference that this would be the only rule that would be consistent with the rest of the model and would actually yield a forecast consistent with the final solution from the whole model. It is this second interpretation which lies behind the Blanchard and Kahn solution technique (which was discussed in the last section on linear models), but in general we are not able to solve for the reduced form of a non-linear model and so this approach is not operational for such models. The problem which Fair faced, then, was to develop a solution procedure based on (7.10) and (7.12) which would allow the RE assumption to be incorporated. This involves a range of problems in terms of model solution, the use of terminal conditions, the management of the information sets in policy analysis, the time inconsistency problem and the problem of non-linearities and expectations. We will discuss these problems below, but first it is worth considering the empirical evidence for the importance of expectations effects.

4.2   The importance of expectations

Before considering some of the details of model analysis it is worth mentioning the empirical evidence for the importance and relevance of expectations effects. This paper can not even begin to attempt a survey of the full academic literature on testing and estimating rational expectations models: good introductions to the literature may be found in Pesaran (1987), Lucas and Sargent (1981) and Hoderick (1987). We would, however, stress that one aspect of the work surveyed here is that it deals with non-linear econometric models, that is to say estimated models, in contrast to calibrated models such as those of McKibbin and Sachs (1991). This means that the various model users have had some degree of empirical justification for their use of expectations effects. In practice this varies from cases where the expectations are barely data acceptable to cases where the use of expectations has allowed a major improvement in model specification. Work has also been undertaken on the formal testing of the Lucas critique, for example, Hendry (1988).

Perhaps the most striking example of such an area of positive achievement is the exchange rate. The fact that exchange rates are almost impossible to model in a structural way has almost become a piece of received wisdom within the economics profession, and yet the exchange rate sector is one of the more obvious areas of convergence between the main large models which include rational expectations; the empirical evidence supporting this emerging common relationship is both strong and consistent across data sets. The emerging consensus rests on the use of the uncovered arbitrage relationship to represent the fundamental behaviour of investors and attempts to estimate a model based on an augmented version of it. If we relax the risk neutrality assumption, then a risk premium may be added, Z_t, and stating the relationship in logs with the general possibility of a lag structure provides a simple equation of the following form:

$$e_t = \phi_1(L)e_{t+1} + \phi_2(L)\,(r_t - r_{tf}) + \phi_3(L)z_t. \tag{7.15}$$

A series of papers has investigated structural models of this form with some success. Explicit allowance has generally been made for the expectations terms by using the Wickens (1982) and McCallum (1976) errors in variables approach to rational expectations hypothesis (REH) estimation, and many of the applications have also made allowance for the endogeneity of interest rates and the risk premium variable (often proxied by some form of current account effect). Estimation of this form of relationship may be found in Hall (1987a, 1987b), Currie and Hall (1989), Gurney *et al.* (1989), Fisher *et al.* (1990), Hall (1992) and Hall and Garratt (1992a, 1992b). The presence of lags may be justified in a number of ways: Hall (1987a) proposes a government which follows a 'leaning into the wind' policy of trying to slow down movements in the exchange rate; while Currie and Hall (1989) derive explicit dynamic effects as a result of the interaction of asset stocks and flows. Overall, the results lend considerable support to the risk augmented open arbitrage view of exchange rate determination: the lags have generally been found to be short or in many cases non-existent, the coefficients on the exchange rate terms are generally very close to unity (thus confirming the unit root hypothesis of the open arbitrage model), and the interest rate coefficient is not generally significantly different from unity. The risk premium term is normally found to be significant, suggesting that risk effects are quite important in the determination of the exchange rate. Contrasting the success of this approach relative to that of the reduced form approach normally used, suggests strongly to us that expectations are a crucial factor in exchange rate determination and that the reduced form treatment of expectations does not make adequate allowance for the instability in expectations formation.

So while we might accept that expectations are of only marginal empirical importance in some areas, other areas such as exchange rates cannot be well understood without the explicit treatment of these effects. We would suggest that this is not only true of foreign exchange markets but also true of other financial markets.

4.3   Solution procedures

The first applications of RE to empirical non-linear models was undertaken by Anderson (1979) and Fair (1979) and independently by Minford *et al.* (1979,1980): the most complete statement of the solution technique used in these applications may be found in Fair and Taylor (1983). The basic Fair–Taylor algorithm consists of a two part iteration scheme: first, values for the expectations variables are taken as given and conventional Gauss–Siedel solution methods (see Hall and Henry, 1988) are used to solve the model conditional on these given values for expectations; secondly, the expectations variables are set equal to the solution values from the model derived in the first stage. The whole process is then repeated until the expectations variables used in the first stage are consistent with their updated values at the second stage.

This is an intuitively appealing way to address the problem but Hall (1985) argued that it will not in general be computationally efficient and that the most general approach is to set up the problem without taking account of the time dimension of the model. Conventional model solution procedures exploit the recursive nature through time of non-RE models; thus they solve the first period first and then progress sequentially to the last period. Under RE, the model no longer has this natural recursive structure and the insight of Hall was that we can effectively ignore the time dimension by restating the model from a set of n equations solved for T periods to a general set of Txn equations with no restrictions on the temporal interlinkage. Once this is done then any standard solution method may be applied to the restated general problem. Fisher *et al.* (1985, 1986) developed a family of iteration schemes which are particularly efficient within the overall Hall framework.

While the above class of solution procedures has proved to be the most widely used, in practice there are two other techniques which should be mentioned. The first is the derivative-based procedure of Holly and Zarrop (1979, 1983) which uses an optimal control procedure to solve the model for the expectations variables by minimizing the following objective function:

$$MinC = \sum_{t=1}^{T} \sum_{i=1}^{n} \Lambda_{it} \left({}_t Y_{it+1}^e - Y_{it+1} \right) \tag{7.16}$$

where Λ_{it} is a suitable set of weights.

This will reach an absolute minimum when each expectation is set equal to the actual outcome and thus is equal the RE solution. The other technique is multiple shooting; this originates from the engineering literature and was introduced into economics by Lipton *et al.* (1982). This procedure essentially involves renormalizing an equation with an expectation term, so that the expectation term becomes the dependent variable. The equation may then be solved recursively through time once some unknown starting condition is set. This initial condition is then chosen so that the dynamic path generated by the model hits a given condition in the terminal period, hence the name. Both of these techniques are useful in special circumstances, but in general they are less efficient and general than the iterative schemes outlined above.

4.4   Terminal conditions

The discussion above ignored the problem of how the expectations were handled after the end of the solution period. In the section on linear models above, the analytical solution derived is for an infinite time horizon problem and the conditions on the unstable eigenvalues were sufficient to ensure a unique solution. In non-linear models an infinite horizon solution is impossible to achieve, and the explicit finite solution requires an explicit set of terminal conditions to allow the solution to exist. The problem is to achieve a satisfactory form for these conditions. There have basically been two approaches to the choice of terminal conditions. The first, put forward in Minford *et al.* (1979), suggests that the equilibrium solution to the model should be used as the appropriate terminal condition. The second approach, put forward in Fair and Taylor (1983), suggested that any arbitrary condition could be used as long as it was far enough into the future not to affect the early period of interest. Both approaches are reasonable for models with rapid dynamic adjustment, and it is obviously ideal to combine the two, that is to say, to use equilibrium conditions which do not affect the early part of the solution. However, much recent work has emphasized that many of the large models do not adjust quickly and that they often do not have well-defined equilibrium conditions. A further complication is that some of the most important uses of expectations produce a root in the model which is very close to unity (for example, the open arbitrage condition in the exchange markets), and this means that very long time horizons would be needed to make a solution robust to the terminal condition. (An interesting alternative is that desirable policy rules may have the characteristic of moving roots away from the unit circle, but there may be severe limits on the scope for this.) It appears that terminal conditions may be having a much greater effect on model solutions than is either desirable or than we were formerly aware.

4.5   Information sets

The above two sections deal essentially with technical issues of model solution, but a conceptually more difficult problem is the way information sets are used in policy analysis. For example, large models are often used in tracking exercises and to provide an analysis of historical policy (see Budd *et al.* (1989), for example). However, once RE is incorporated into such a model its use for such exercises becomes much more complex. A model such as (7.10) and (7.12) may be viewed as giving a solution for $\mathbf{Y}_t \dots \mathbf{Y}_T$ conditional on information at t. We can therefore compare the forecast for t with the outturn for t as an indicator of the model's accuracy. We cannot, however, compare $\mathbf{Y}_{t+1}|t$ with $\mathbf{Y}_{t+1}$ in any simple way, as the discrepancy between the two will be a combination of the revision in the information set and the model's errors. As a concrete example, if we solve an RE model over the period 1975–80 using actual historical exogenous variables, we would expect the exchange rate to jump well above its historical values initially because the given information set would include knowledge of the rise in oil prices in 1979. This knowledge was clearly not part of the information set in 1975, and so the model fails drastically to mimic the past simply because we have given it an inappropriate information set. Analysing a historical period, then, entails deriving an appropriate sequence of information sets and a similar sequence of model solutions where only the first period of any solution may be compared with an actual outturn in an unambiguous way. Hall (1987), Mathews and Minford (1987) and Fisher and Wallis (1990) are the only attempts to analyse historical periods with RE models using successive information sets, as far as we are aware. The small number of examples of this type of work illustrates the relative complexity of the problem posed by RE in this context.

4.6   Time inconsistency

A closely related problem to the informational problem outlined above is the problem of time inconsistency. This was first highlighted by Kydland and Prescott (1977) and was discussed at some length in the last section on linear models. Time inconsistency is not related to the question of linearity as such: it is simply the product of the expectations structure of the model and the assumption of consistent expectations. Nonetheless, non-linearity poses some major problems in dealing with time inconsistency, and as most real world policy analysis is carried out with non-linear models it is worth considering these.

The essence of the time inconsistency problem is that if an optimal policy is calculated for a model which has RE terms over a given time horizon, then if we implement that policy in the first period, and even assuming that everything occurs in the first period exactly as expected, that policy will no longer be optimal from the second period onwards. The reason for this is that in the first period we achieve certain results by asserting what will happen in the future purely on the basis of expectations. In the second period we no longer have to stick to the original announcement, as we have already achieved the desired results for the first period. So time inconsistency gives rise to the question of credibility on the part of the policy maker and reputational effects become important.

These issues may be formalized by following the simple illustration of Kydland and Prescott. State a general welfare function for two periods as:

$$S(x_1, x_2, \pi_1, \pi_2) \qquad (7.17)$$

where x_1 and x_2 are economic outcomes in period 1 and 2 and π_1, π_2 are government policies in periods 1 and 2, where:

$$x_1 = X_1(\pi_1, \pi_2) \qquad (7.18)$$

and

$$x_2 = X_2(x_1, \pi_1, \pi_2). \qquad (7.19)$$

Now if we derive the first order condition for policy in period 2 from the standpoint of a policy maker in period 1 we get:

$$\frac{\delta S}{\delta x_2} \cdot \frac{\delta x_2}{\delta \pi_2} + \frac{\delta S}{\delta \pi_2} + \frac{\delta S}{\delta x_1} \cdot \frac{\delta x_1}{\delta \pi_2} = 0. \qquad (7.20)$$

Now if we consider the first order conditions in period 2, assuming everything occurred in period 1 as originally planned, the conditions become:

$$\frac{\delta S}{\delta x_2} \cdot \frac{\delta x_2}{\delta \pi_2} + \frac{\delta S}{\delta \pi_2} = 0. \qquad (7.21)$$

Unless the last term in (7.19) is zero, which it will not generally be, the two sets of first order conditions are different, and the optimal strategy changes as we move through time. This occurs simply because the economic outcome in the first period is affected by the announced policy for the second period.

In the analysis of linear models and time inconsistency it was found to be useful to begin by describing the extremes of 'full reputation', which allows the government to pursue the time-inconsistent policy (which is the best outcome which it can possibly achieve) and 'no reputation', which allows the government only to achieve the optimal time-consistent policy (this will always be inferior to the time-inconsistent policy but it is the best the policy maker can do when agents ignore announced policies). In the non-linear case we need to make exactly the same comparison. Calculating the time-inconsistent policy is straightforward and is the result of standard control algorithms. Calculating the optimal time-consistent problem is, however, more complex: this problem was addressed in Hall (1986, 1987) which proposed an algorithm which solved the optimal control problem for the time-consistent solution, (Fisher (1990) proposed a generalization of this algorithm). Given this algorithm it is then possible to analyse the full range of reputational questions much as in the linear case outlined in the last section.

4.7   Non-linearities and expectations

The usual hypothesis which underlies both the RE assumption and the analysis of linear models is that agents take the mathematical expectation of the relevant model as their measure of expectations. A further complication which arises in non-linear models is that generally the deterministic solution to the model will not be the mathematical expectation of the probability distribution of the stochastic model. This is due to the simple property of non-linear functions that in general:

$$E f(y_t) \neq f(E(y_t)). \tag{7.22}$$

This means that in general the deterministic solution to the model (that is the solution when all the error terms are set to their expected value), will not produce the expected value for the endogenous variables. The deterministic solution will in fact yield a biased forecast of the endogenous variables, and in so far as under the RE solution techniques outlined above we take this value as our measure of expectations, we will be using a less than fully rational expectation.

The general technique for analysing the probability distribution of models is known as stochastic simulations: a survey of this technique may be found in Hall and Henry (1988) and we will not discuss it here. The use of stochastic simulations has, however, shown that the bias involved in using a deterministic forecast as a measure of expectations can be considerable, and as a result Hall and Henry (1988) term these forms of model solution as model consistent rather than rational. It is possible to use stochastic simulations to solve a model for the expectation rather than the deterministic value and thus to derive true rational solutions, but this has only been done rarely. One reason for this is the complexity and computer burden involved, but a less pragmatic reason is also that the non-linear model will give rise to non-normal probability distributions. Once this occurs there is no strong reason to use the expected value as a measure of agents' expectations in preference to one of the other measures of central tendency, such as the median or the mode of the distribution. Hall (1988) argues that many apparent contradictions which arise because of non-linearities may be reconciled by using the median as the relevant measure of expectations along with suitable distributional assumptions. The mean of the distribution is the correct choice if agents have a quadratic loss function in expectations errors, but other loss functions are quite reasonable alternatives: an absolute error loss function, for example, gives the median of the distribution. For a large class of models the deterministic model solution may be associated with the median and so model consistent solutions may be seen as having as much relevance as full rational (in the sense of using the expected value) solutions.

4.8 Rational expectations: an assessment

The 1980s saw the introduction of RE into a number of large forecasting models. It quickly became apparent that this innovation posed a number of technical problems of model solution and use which took some time fully to solve. We have now reached a point where these technical difficulties have been overcome and we may begin to assess the economic relevance of RE and its practical usefulness.

On the positive side, few model proprietors would remain unconvinced as to the importance of expectations effects. Areas such as exchange rate modelling, as well as our understanding of both company and personal sector behaviour, have been improved dramatically through the use of explicit models of expectations. This is so well established that it is even an accepted part of basic economics teaching: 'Most economists accept that beliefs about the future are an important determinant of behaviour today' (Begg *et al.*, 1991, p. 568). However, this does not mean that the full use of model consistent expectations is so completely accepted.

The first point to emphasize is that econometric evidence for the importance of expectations is almost uniformly based on the weak form of RE (that is, that agents do not make systematic mistakes), rather than the strong form (that they use a particular model to form their expectations). It is clearly a significant step to go from the statement that agents are 'on average' correct in their expectations to the much stronger one that they use a particular model which they believe completely. Experience with RE has also been rather mixed in the sense that, while in simulation and policy exercises the presence of RE often provides rich insights, it has not been general practice to use RE in a forecasting context. The reason for this is not merely the pragmatic one of avoiding the increases in solution time during a busy forecasting round, but more fundamentally that the presence of RE tends to cause jumps in the initial period value of a range of variables (most notably the exchange rate) which are considered implausible by the forecasters. A more obvious example of this problem is that it is actually impossible to analyse many policy options under RE. For example, a permanent rise in interest rates would lead to an infinitely large jump in the exchange rate under the open arbitrage condition and the model would not yield a solution. It may be argued that this is in fact correct and that governments cannot maintain interest rates above competitors' rates for ever, but if a government announces that it is going to raise interest rates with no announced intention of lowering them in the future it should be possible to analyse this option with the model. The reconciliation of these two views is, of course, that agents do not believe the government's intention of raising interest rates permanently and hence the exchange rate will only rise by a modest amount. The problem with RE is that it makes no allowance for this lack of credibility. In our view this casts a serious doubt on the models, in that a good model should be suitable both for forecasting and policy analysis across a wide range of policy scenarios. To find that a particular assumption about expectations formation renders the models inoperable for one of their main purposes seriously undermines the usefulness of that assumption.

The dilemma facing model-builders, then, is that expectations are undeniably important in the specification of individual structural relationships of their models, but the assumption of model consistent expectations is too simplistic to be acceptable. If we reject adaptive expectations because it leads to systematic and long-term errors in expectations, we need also to question the model consistent assumption which is implicitly ruling out the possibility of ever making any mistake about the even very distant future. We would argue that adaptive expectations and model consistent expectations are in reality both extreme assumptions and that some alternative needs to be found. One approach is to try and design policies which are robust across expectations formation mechanisms (this is proposed as a minimum requirement for good policy design by Currie (1985)), but ultimately a modeller needs to make a single choice of the best expectations formation mechanism so there is a strong incentive to find an alternative approach to these extremes. This alternative was found in the emerging theoretical literature on learning, briefly surveyed in section 2. We now turn to the newest strand of development in the treatment of expectations, the explicit recognition of learning.

4.9   Learning in non-linear models

Learning requires the specification of an expectations rule such as (7.14) and the assumption that some element of the rule is not known with certainty. This element of uncertainty is usually taken to be the parameters of the rule, and the basic idea is that through time the economic agent will use some method to increase his knowledge about the true value of these parameters. So if we restate (14) explicitly to include parameters:

$$(_{t}\mathbf{Y}^{e}_{t+1}) = g_{k}(\mathbf{Y}_{t}, \mathbf{X}, \mathbf{D}_{t}) \qquad k = 1\ldots nl \qquad (7.23)$$

where $\mathbf{D}_{t}$ is the vector of agents' estimates of the parameters at period t. Then once a mechanism which governs the evolution of these parameters through time is specified, it is possible to make the whole learning apparatus operational.

This approach to the treatment of expectations was first adopted in the exchange rate sector of the London Business School model of the UK economy (Hall and Garratt, 1992a, 1992b) and it has subsequently been applied to wage behaviour in three countries in the GEM (Barrell, *et al.*, 1992). Hall (1992) reported on the econometric specification of the learning rule and proposed using the Kalman Filter as an optimal way of implementing learning. The Kalman Filter is a very general estimation (or filtering) technique which can be interpreted as a minimum squared error estimator; it nests the least squares learning techniques of the theoretical literature, discussed in the first section, as special cases. These applications may then be thought of as direct applications of the techniques proposed in the learning literature to large non-linear econometric models.

To illustrate the way learning has been implemented in these applications it is useful to discuss the issue in a whole model context. We essentially have three blocks of equations, (7.10), (7.23) and:

$$\mathbf{D}_t = \mathbf{D}_{t-1} + e_t \qquad (7.24)$$
$$\text{where } e_t \sim (0, \Gamma).$$

Assuming we know $\mathbf{D}_{t-1}$ we can solve (7.21) for the expected value of $\mathbf{D}_t$, which is simply the Kalman Filter prediction equations for D. Given $\mathbf{D}_t$ we can solve (7.23) for the expected value of $\mathbf{Y}^e_t$, and given this we can solve (7.10) for $\mathbf{Y}_t$. Γ (the covariance matrix of the errors in the equations governing the evolution of the parameters, or in Kalman Filter terms the state equation error terms), is given by the original estimation and we have an estimate for P_{t-1} (the uncertainty of the parameters or state variables). We can therefore use the Kalman Filter prediction equation for P, to derive an estimate of $P_{t|t-1}$. Having solved the complete model (7.10) for $\mathbf{Y}_t$ we can then define $\mathbf{V}_t = \mathbf{Y}^e_t - \mathbf{Y}_t$, that is, the error which occurs between the expectation of the vector $\mathbf{Y}_t$ derived from the learning model and the models' final solution for $\mathbf{Y}_t$. We can therefore use the Kalman Filter updating equations to derive revised estimates of $\mathbf{P}_t$ and $\mathbf{D}_t$. The updating is done on the basis of the observed errors between the whole model solution and the original expectations model forecast.

The process can then be repeated for the next period, starting from the new updated estimates of $\mathbf{D}_t$ to predict $\mathbf{D}_{t+1}$, and so on. In this way the learning model will adjust its own parameters to cope with any change in structure or regime of the whole model.

It is perhaps worth stressing that the underlying assumptions of this process are really still quite strong, and that the spirit of the approach is not strongly divorced from that of the rational expectations approach. Agents are still assumed to process all available information in an optimal fashion and the degree of sophistication on the part of economic agents is still considerable. The only departure from the strong form of RE is that agents are not assumed to have full information and so they are likely to make mistakes in the short run, although they may well not make systematic errors over an extended period, and hence the learning model may fulfil the criteria for weak RE.

As noted in the general section above, the learning model may converge on a rational expectations equilibria and a sufficient condition for this is that the parameters of the learning rule cease changing over time. In the applications cited above for both the London Business School and GEM models, the learning rules did in fact converge on an expectations equilibria and so in the long run both models still reach a rational expectations solution.

Two major advantages of the learning approach are particularly important. First, the assured informational demands are weaker and therefore more acceptable in the learning case than the strong RE assumption. Secondly, many policy debates essentially hinge on the question of credibility and how rapidly economic agents will come to recognize a new regime. The questions raised by the UK's entry into the ERM are a good example of this, if credibility is achieved quickly the cost of ERM membership is small, while if credibility takes a long time to be built up then ERM costs may be very large. RE essentially assumes that credibility appears instantaneously and completely, and so it is inherently either very difficult or impossible to address questions of how credibility may arise and what will happen before it is fully achieved. Learning, on the other hand, goes to the heart of the credibility issue, and the treatment of expectation through learning models allows the satisfactory modelling of the build-up of credibility to be undertaken for the first time.

This is illustrated in the application of learning to UK ERM membership, in the work of Hall and Garratt. On entry, the risk premium on sterling remained large, narrowing only gradually as private agents learnt (perhaps erroneously, in fact) about the commitment to the ERM parity. Only over time did the DM/£ interest differential narrow. The learning approach incorporates these effects with ease, and also facilitates analysis of the risk premium on sterling after withdrawal from the ERM. It also offers insights concerning the effect of the choice of initial parity on subsequent learning and credibility. By contrast, the RE assumption cannot address these questions.

5. Conclusion

We have reviewed the development of the treatment of expectations from three viewpoints: the general theoretical macroeconomic literature, the work dealing with more complex linear models, and the developments in large non-linear econometric models. The three strands of literature have paralleled each other to a remarkable degree, although there are clear differences in emphasis. Early formal models largely ignored expectations effects, although abstract discussions of the general problem often qualified the formal models by pointing to the importance of expectations. Expectations were first treated explicitly through the use of backward extrapolation rules, such as adaptive expectations. It quickly became obvious that these models suffered from the problem of implying long-run predictable errors on the part of agents under certain circumstances and the early 1970s saw the beginning of the move towards the widespread use of rational expectations. This assumption has proved immensely powerful in analytical work which is more concerned with long-run equilibrium effects. More complex linear models have allowed the investigation of questions of credibility and time inconsistency under the RE assumption and have given rise to many important insights. It is perhaps the large empirical models where the weakness of the RE assumption has become most apparent: as a tool for analysing long-run behaviour in abstract, RE is both powerful and useful but it is not a good representation of the short-run dynamic behaviour of many markets, and the large models have really emphasized this weakness. The natural progression of the treatment of expectations effects is to move from the strong *RE* assumption to a weaker model which gives the possibility of making errors in the short run while ruling out the implausible long-run systematic errors. This gives rise to the introduction of learning models; these have remained to a large extent a side issue in the theoretical literature, but it is our view that these models will constitute an increasingly important feature of the empirical models. This represents a move back from the assumption of full rationality in expectations towards the ideas of bounded rationality more consistent with the psychological literature on learning processes.

Bibliography

Anderson, P.A. (1979) 'Rational expectations forecasts from non rational models', *Journal of Monetary Economics*, **5**, 67–80.

Attfield, C.L.F., Demery, D. and Duck N.W. (1985) *Rational Expectations in Macroeconomics*, Oxford: Basil Blackwell.

Ball, R.J. (1964), *Inflation and the Theory of Money*, London: Allen and Unwin.

Ball, R.J. and Drake P.S. (1964), 'Investment intentions and the prediction of private gross capital formation', *Economica*, August, 229–47.

Barrell R., Caporale G.M., Garratt, A. and Hall, S.G. (1992), 'Learning about monetary union: an analysis of boundedly rational learning, in European labour markets'. Paper presented at the ESRC Macromodelling Conference, Warwick.

Barrell, Christodoulakis, Garratt, Ireland, Kemball-Cook, Levine and Westaway (1992), 'Policy analysis and model reduction techniques using GEM', in Bryant, R.C., Hooper, P., Mann, C.L., and Tryon, R.W. (eds), *Evaluating Policy Regimes: New Research in Empirical Macroeconomics*, Brookings Institution.

Barro, R.J. (1976), 'Rational expectations and the role of monetary policy', *Journal of Monetary Economics*, **2**, 1–33.

Barro, R.J. (1977), 'Unanticipated monetary growth and unemployment in the United States', *American Economic Review*, **67**, 101–15.

Barro, R.J. and Gordon, D.A. (1983), 'Rules, discretion and reputation in a model of monetary policy', *Journal of Monetary Economics*, **13**, 101–21.

Begg, D.K.H. (1982), *The Rational Expectations Revolution in Macroeconomics*, Oxford: Phillip Allan.

Begg, D., Fischer, S. and Dornbusch, R. (1991), *Economics*, 3rd Edition, London: McGraw-Hill.

Blanchard, A.J. and Kahn, C.M. (1980), 'Backward and forward solutions for economies with rational expectations', *Econometrica*, **48**, (5), 1305–11.

Bray, M.M. (1983), 'Convergence to rational expectations equilibrium' in Frydman R. and Phelps, E.S. (eds), *Industrial Forecasting and Aggregate Outcomes*, Cambridge: Cambridge University Press.

Bray, M.M. and Kreps, C. (1984), 'Rational learning and rational expectation', mimeo Cambridge University.

Bray, M.M. and Savin, N.E. (1986), 'Rational expectations equilibria, learning and model specification', *Econometrica*, **54**, 1129–60.

Budd, A., Christodoulakis, N., Holly, S. and Levine, P. (1989), 'Stabilisation policy in Britain', in Britton, A. (ed.), *Policy Making with Macroeconomic Models*, Aldershot: Gower.

Cagan, P. (1956), 'The monetary dynamics of hyperinflation', in M. Friedman (ed.), *Studies in the Quantity Theory of Money*, Chicago University Press.

Currie, D.A. (1985), 'Macroeconomic policy design and control theory – a failed partnership?' *Economic Journal*, **95**, 285–306.

Currie, D.A. and Hall, S.G. (1989), 'A stock–flow model of the determination of the UK effective exchange rate', in Macdonald, R. and Taylor, M.P. (eds), *Exchange Rates and Open Economy Macroeconomics*, Oxford: Basil Blackwell.

Currie, D.A. and Levine, P. (1987), 'Credibility and time consistency in a stochastic world', *Journal of Economics*, **47**, 225–52.

Currie, D.A, Levine, P. and Vidalis, N. (1987), 'International cooperation and reputation in an empirical two-bloc model', in Bryant, R. and Portes, R. (eds), *Global Macroeconomics: Policy Conflict and Cooperation*, Macmillan.

Currie, D.A., Levine, P. and Pearlman, J. (1992), 'European monetary union or hard -EMS?', *European Economic Review*, **36**, 1185–1204.

Cuthbertson, K., Hall, S.G. and Taylor, M.P. (1992), *Applied Econometric Techniques*, Michigan University Press.

DeCanio, S.J. (1979), 'Rational expectations and learning from experience', *Quarterly Journal of Economics*, **93**, 47–57.

Driffill, J. and Miller, M. (1992) 'Learning about a shift in exchange rate regime'. Paper presented to the annual conference of the Royal Economic Society, London.

Duesenberry, J.S., Fromm, G., Klein, L.R. and Kuh, E. (eds) (1965), *The Brookings Quarterly Econometric Model of the United States*, Chicago and Amsterdam: Rand McNally and Co. and North Holland.

Eisner, R. (1965), 'Realizations of investment anticipations' in Duesenberry *et al.* (eds) (1965).

Evans, G.W. (1983) 'The stability of rational expectations in macroeconomic models', in Frydman, R. and Phelps, E.S. (eds), *Individual Forecasting and Aggregate Outcomes*, Cambridge: Cambridge University Press.

Evans, G.W. (1985), 'Expectational stability and the multiple equilibria problem in RE models', *Quarterly Journal of Economics*, (100), 1217–33.

Evans, G.W. (1986a), 'Expectational stability and the multiple equilibria problem in linear rational expectations models', *Quarterly Journal of Economics*, 1217–33.

Evans, G.W. (1986b), 'Selection criteria for models with non-uniqueness', *Journal of Monetary Economics*, 147–57

Fair, R.C. (1979), 'An analysis of a macro-econometric model with rational expectations in the bond and stock markets', *American Economic Review*, **69**, 539–52.

Fair, R.C. (1984), *Specification, Estimation and Analysis of Macroeconometric Models*, Harvard: Harvard University Press.

Fair, R.C. and Taylor, J.B. (1983), 'Solution and maximum likelihood estimation of dynamic nonlinear rational expectations models', *Econometrica*, **51**, 1169–86.

Feige, E.L and Pearce, D. (1976), 'Economically rational expectations: are innovations in the rate of inflation independent of innovations in measures of monetary and fiscal policy?', *Journal of Political Economy*, 84, 499–522.

Fisher, P.G. (1990), 'Simulation and control techniques for nonlinear rational expectations', ESRC Macroeconomic Modelling Bureau, mimeo.

Fisher, P.G. and Wallis, K.F. (1990), 'Historical tracking performance of UK macroeconomic models 1978–1985', *Economic Modelling*.

Fisher, P.G., Holly, S. and Hughes Hallett, A.J. (1985), 'Efficient solution techniques for dynamic nonlinear rational expectations models', ESRC Macroeconomic Modelling Bureau, Discussion Paper No. 4.

Fisher, P.G., Holly, S. and Hughes Hallett, A. J. (1986) 'Efficient solution techniques for dynamic nonlinear rational expectations models', *Journal of Economic Dynamics and Control*, **10**, 139–45.

Fisher, P.G., Tanner, S.K. Turner, D.S., Wallis, K.F. and Whitley, J.D. (1988), 'Comparative properties of models of the UK economy', *National Institute Economic Review*, **125**, 69–88.

Fisher, P.G., Tanner, S.K. Turner, D.S., Wallis, K.F. and Whitley, J.D. (1989), 'Comparative properties of models of the UK economy', *National Economic Review*, **129**, 69–88.

Fisher, P.G., Tanner, S.K. Turner, D.S. and Wallis, K.F. (1990), 'Econometric evaluation of the exchange rate in models of the UK economy', *Economic Journal*, **100**, 403, 1230–44.

Flemming, J.S. (1976), *Inflation*, Oxford: Oxford University Press.

Friedman, B.M. (1975), 'Rational expectations are really adaptive after all', Howard Institute of Economic Research, Discussion Paper No. 430.

Friedman, M. (1968), 'The role of monetary policy', *American Economic Review*, **53**, 381–4.

Frydman, R. (1982), 'Towards an understanding of market processes, individual expectations: learning and convergence to rational expectations equilibrium', *American Economic Review*, **72**, 652–8.

Grunberg, E. and Modigliani, F. (1954), 'The predictability of social events', *Journal of Political Economy*, **62**, 465–78.

Gurney, A. (1990), 'Fiscal policy simulations using forward-looking exchange rates in GEM', *National Institute Economic Review*, No. 131, February, 47–50.

Gurney, A., Henry, S.G.B. and Pesaran, B. (1989), 'The exchange rate and external trade', in Britton, A. (ed.) *Policy-making With Macroeconomic Models*, Aldershot: Gower.

Hall, S.G. (1984), 'An investigation of time inconsistency and optimal policy formulation in the presence of rational expectations using the national institutes model 7', NIESR discussion Paper No. 71, NIESR.

Hall, S.G. (1985), 'On the solution of large economic models with rational expectations', *Bulletin of Economic Research*, **37**, 157–61.

Hall, S.G. (1986), 'An investigation of time inconsistency and optimal policy formulation in the presence of rational expectations', *Journal of Economic Dynamics and Control*, **10**, 323–6.

Hall, S.G. (1987), 'Analyzing economic behaviour 1975–1985 with a model incorporating consistent expectations', *National Institute Economic Review*, **114**, 58–68.

Hall, S.G. (1987a), 'A forward looking model of the exchange rate', *Journal of Applied Econometrics*, **2**, 47–60.

Hall, S.G. (1987b), 'An empirical model of the exchange rate incorporating rational expectations', in Chrystal, K.A. and Sedgwick, R. (eds), *Exchange Rates and the Open Economy*, New York: St Martin Press.

Hall, S.G. (1988), 'Rationality and Siegels paradox: The importance of coherency in expectations', *Applied Economics*, **20**, (11), 1533–40.

Hall, S.G. (1992), 'Modelling the sterling effective exchange rate using expectations and learning', Forthcoming.

Hall, S.G. and Garratt, A. (1992a), 'Model consistent learning: the sterling Deutschmark rate in the London Business School Model', LBS-CEF Discussion Paper No. 92-02.

Hall, S.G. and Garratt A. (1992b), 'Expectations and learning in economic models', *Economic Outlook* **16**, (5) 52–3.

Hall, S.G. and Henry, S.G.B. (1985), 'Rational expectations in an econometric model, NIESR Model 8', *National Institute Economic Review*, **114**, 58–68.

Hall, S.G. and Henry, S.G.B. (1986), 'A dynamic econometric model of the UK with rational expectations', *Journal of Economic Dynamics and Control*, **10**, 219–33.

Hall, S.G. and Henry, S.G.B. (1988), *Macroeconomic Modelling*, Amsterdam: North Holland.

Hendry, D.F. (1988), 'The encompassing implications of feedback V. Feed forward mechanisms in econometrics', *Oxford Economic Papers*, **40**, 132–49.

Hoderick, R.J. (1987), *The Empirical Evidence on the Efficiency of Forward and Future Exchange Markets*, London: Harwood Academic Publishers.

Holden, K., Peel, D.A. and Thompson, J.L. (1985), *Expectations Theory and Evidence*, London: Macmillan.

Holly, S. and Corker, R. (1984), 'Optimal feedback and feedforward stabilisation of exchange rates, money, prices and output under rational expectations' in Hughes Hallett, A.J. (ed.), *Applied Decision Analysis and Economic Behaviour*, Dordrecht: Martinus Nijhoff Publishers.

Holly, S. and Zarrop, M.B. (1979), 'Calculating optimal economic policies when expectations are rational' PROPE Discussion Paper No. 30, Imperial College.

Holly, S. and Zarrop, M.B. (1983), 'Calculating optimal economic policies when expectations are rational', *European Economic Review*, **20**, 23–40.

Katona, G. (1951), *Psychological Analysis of Economic Behaviour*, New York: McGraw-Hill.

Katona, G. (1958), 'Business expectations in the framework of psychological economics (towards a theory of expectations)', in Bowman, M.J. (ed.), *Expectations, Uncertainty and Business Behaviour*, Social Science Research Council, New York.

Kemball-Cook, D. (1992), 'Macroeconomic policy design under uncertainty', unpublished PhD thesis, University of London.

Klein, L.R. (1987), 'The ET interview: Prof L.R. Klein interviewed by Roberto S. Mariano', *Econometric Theory*, **3**, 409–60.

Kydland, F.E., and Prescott, E.C. (1977), 'Rules rather than discretion: the inconsistency of optimal plans', *Journal of Political Economy*, **85**, 473–91.

Lahti, A. and Viren, M. (1989), 'The Finnish rational expectations QMED model: estimation, dynamic properties and policy results', Bank of Finland Discussion Paper 23/89.

Levine, P. and Currie, D.A. (1987), 'The design of feedback rules in linear stochastic rational expectations models', *Journal of Economic Dynamics and Control*, 11, 1–28.

Lipton, D., Poterba, J., Sachs, J. and Summers, L. (1982), 'Multiple shooting in rational expectations models', *Econometrica*, **50**, 1329–33.

Lucas, R.E. Jr (1972a), 'Econometric testing of the natural rate hypothesis' in Eckstein, O. (ed.), *Econometrics of Price Determination*, Washington D.C., Federal Reserve System, Board of Governors.

Lucas, R.E. Jr (1972b), 'Expectations and the neutrality of money', *Journal of Economic Theory*, **4**, 103–24

Lucas, R.E. Jr (1973), 'Some international evidence on output inflation trade-offs', *American Economic Review*, **65**, 326–34.

Lucas, R.E. Jr (1975), 'An equilibrium model of the business cycle', *Journal of Political Economy*, **83**, 1113–44.

Lucas, R.E. (1976), 'Econometric policy evaluation: a critique', in K. Brunner and A. H. Meltzer (eds), *The Phillips Curve and Labour Markets*, Carnegie Rochester Conference Series on Public Policy, **1**, 19–46, Supplement to the *Journal of Monetary Economics*.

Lucas, R.E. Jr and Rapping, L. (1969), 'Real wages, employment and inflation', *Journal of Political Economy*, **77**, 721–54.

Lucas, R.E. Jr and Sargent, T.J. (eds),(1981), *Rational Expectations and Econometric Practise*, London: George Allen and Unwin.

Marcet, A. and Sargent, T.J. (1988), 'The fate of systems with adaptive expectations', *American Economic Review*, 168–71.

Marcet, A. and Sargent, T.J. (1989a), 'Convergence of least-squares learning in environment with hidden state variables and private information', *Journal of Political Economy*, **97**, (6), 1306–22.

Marcet, A. and Sargent, T.J. (1989b), 'Least squares learning and the dynamics of hyperinflation' in Barnett, W.A., Geweke, J. and Shell, K. (eds), *Economic Complexity, Chaos, Sunspots Bubbles and Nonlinearity*, Cambridge: Cambridge University Press.

Masson, P.R., Symansky, S., Hass, R. and Dooley, M. (1988), 'MULTIMOD: a multi-region econometric model', IMF Working Paper No. 88/23, Washington, DC.

Mathews, K.G.P. and Minford, A.P.L. (1987), 'Mrs Thatcher's economic policies 1979–1987', *Economic Policy*, **5**, 57–101.

McCallum, B.T. (1976), 'Rational expectations and the national rate hypothesis: some consistent estimates', *Econometrica*, **44**, 43–52.

McKibbin, W.J. and Sachs, J. (1991), *Global Linkages: Macroeconomic Interdependence and cooperation in the world economy*, Washington D.C.: The Brooking Institute.

Minford, A.P.L., Mathews, K.G.P. and Marawaha, S.S. (1979), 'Terminal conditions as a means of ensuring unique solutions for rational expectations models with forward expectations', *Economic Letters*, **4**, 117–20.

Minford, A.P.L. Mathews, K.G.P. and Marawaha, S.S. (1980), 'Terminal conditions, uniqueness and the solution of rational expectations models', mimeo, University of Liverpool.

Minford, A.P.L. Marwaha, S., Mathews, K. Sprague, A., (1984), 'The Liverpool macroeconomic model of the United Kingdom', *Economic Modelling*, **1**, 24–62.

Murphy, C.W. (1989), 'The macroeconomics of a macroeconomic model', mimeo, Australian National University.

Muth, J.F. (1961), 'Rational expectations and the theory of price movements', *Econometrica*, **29**, (6).

Nerlove, M.J. (1958), 'Distributed lags and estimation of long-run supply and demand elasticities, theoretical considerations', *Journal of Farm Economics*, **40**, 301–11.

Pearlman, J., Currie, D.A. and Levine, P. (1986), 'Rational expectations with partial information', *Economic Modelling*, **3**, 90–105.

Pesaran, M.H. (1985), 'Formation of inflation expectations in British manufacturing industries', *Economic Journal*, **95**, (380) December.

Pesaran, M.H. (1987), *The Limits of Rational Expectations*, Oxford: Basil Blackwell.

Radner, R. (1982), 'Equilibrium under uncertainty' in K.J. Arrow and M.D. Intriligator (eds), *Handbook of Mathematical Economics*, vol 2, Amsterdam: North Holland.

Sargent, T.J. (1973), 'Rational expectations, The real rate of interest and the natural rate of unemployment', *Brookings Papers on Economic Activity*, **2**, 429–72.

Sargent, T.J. (1976). 'A classical macroeconomic model of the United States', *Journal of Political Economy*, **84**, 207–37.

Sargent, T.J. and Wallace, N. (1973), 'Rational expectations and the dynamics of hyperinflation', *International Economic Review*, **14**, 328–50.

Sargent, T.J. and Wallace, N. (1975), 'Rational expectations, the optimal monetary instrument and the optimal money supply rule', *Journal of Political Economy* **83**, 241–54.

Sargent, T.J. and Wallace, N. (1976), 'Rational expectations and the theory of economic policy', *Journal of Monetary Economics*, **2**, 169–83.

Shiller, R.J. (1978), 'Rational expectations and the dynamic structure of macroeconomic models', *Journal of Monetary Economics*, **2**, 169–83.

Taylor, J. (1979), 'Estimation and control of a macroeconomic model with rational expectations', *Econometrica*, **47**, 1267–86.

Tobin, J. (1959), 'On the predictive value of consumers intentions', *Review of Economics and Statistics*, Feb.

Townsend, R.M. (1978), 'Market anticipation, rational expectation and Bayesian analysis', *International Economic Review*, **19**, 481–94.

Townsend, R.M. (1983), 'Forecasting the forecast of others', *Journal of Political Economy*, **91**, 546–88.

Vines, D., Maciejowski, J. and Meade, J. (1983), *Demand Management*, London: Allen Unwin.

Walters, A.A. (1971), 'Consistent expectations, distributed lags and the quantity theory', *Economic Journal*, **81**, 273–81.

Westaway, P. (1989a), 'Does time inconsistency really matter?', IFAC symposium on Dynamic Modelling and Control of National Economies, Preprints.

Westaway, P. (1989b), 'Partial credibility: a solution technique for econometric models', IFAC symposium on Dynamic Modelling and Control of National Economies, Preprints.

Westaway, P. and Whittaker, R. (1986), 'Consistent expectations in the treasury model', Government Economic Services Working Paper no. 87.

Wickens, M.R. (1982), 'The efficient estimation of econometric models with rational expectations', *Review of Economic Studies*, **49**, 55-67.

Woodford, M. (1990), 'Learning to believe in Sunspots', *Econometrica*, 277–308.

8 On a theory of intercept corrections in macroeconometric forecasting

David F. Hendry and Michael P. Clements*

1. Introduction

It is widely recognized that published forecasts from large-scale macroeconometric models reflect in varying degree the properties of the model and the skills of the model's proprietors. Forecasts are rarely based on the estimated model alone. Rather, extensive adjustments are usually made to the model-based predictions in arriving at a final forecast. These adjustments are typically to the constant terms or intercepts in the model's equations, and thus are alternatively known as intercept corrections, residual adjustments, add-factors or, somewhat more emotively, *ad hoc* factors, con adjustments, and so on. We shall adopt the first pseudonym in this chapter, which will be taken to refer to the specification of non-zero equation error terms over the forecast period, irrespective of the source of the correction. In general, the evidence provided by the ESRC Macroeconomic Modelling Bureau's annual reviews of the forecasts from the main UK macroeconomic forecasting groups suggests that such adjustments to purely model-based forecasts do result in value-added in terms of improved forecast accuracy (see, for example, Wallis *et al.*, 1986, especially Table 4.8, and Wallis *et al.*, 1987, Figures 4.3 and 4.4).

Intercept corrections are typically divided into two broad categories in the literature:

(a) those which represent the influence of anticipated future events on a model's variables and are not explicitly incorporated in the specification of the model; and

(b) projecting into the future, past errors based on apparent model misspecification or non-constancy of an unknown source which is nevertheless expected to persist (cf. Turner, 1990, Young, 1979).

In this chapter, we seek to furnish a more general theory of intercept corrections. Any theory of intercept corrections must be based on the relationships between the data generating process (DGP), the estimated econometric model, the mechanics of the forecasting technique, the data accuracy, and any infor-

*Financial support for this paper from the UK Economic and Social Research Council (ESRC Grant R000233447) is gratefully acknowledged.

mation about future events held at the beginning of the forecast period. We will use the taxonomy of information suggested by Hendry and Richard (1982, 1983) (see also Gilbert, 1986) in the context of evaluating models within which to couch our theory of intercept corrections. This should help to ensure that our theory is reasonably exhaustive in coverage. The six strata of the information taxonomy are:

(1) The relative past.
(2) The relative present.
(3) The relative future.
(4) Theory information.
(5) Measurement information.
(6) Rival models.

The temporal segregation here is relative to time T, the beginning of the forecast period, although we will also consider the possibility that the split is relative to T^e, the end of the estimation sample period.

The relative past may convey evidence of model misspecification, exactly as in the model evaluation context. The first-best solution would be to improve the model, at least up to the point where its error is a homoscedastic innovation process and the within-sample parameters are constant. In practice, this option may be ruled out by deadlines which do not permit such in-depth analysis. In such a case, there is a *prima facie* argument for adjusting the future values of the equation intercept in an attempt to make some allowance for the perceived problems with the equation. Typically, it is not just the equation intercept term which is thought to be incorrect; for example, Turner (1990) outlines the form of intercept correction implied by a perceived change in the coefficient of an exogenous variable. Intercept corrections motivated by apparent model misspecification over the estimation period (or the period prior to the forecast), as evidenced by the (estimated) residuals, are discussed in sections 5 and 7.

The relative present will include information on how well the equation performs around time T or T^e: the relevance of that in the current context is that the data observations on which the most recent residuals are calculated may be measured subject to substantial error. Section 3 discusses the implications for intercept corrections of near-contemporaneous equation errors resulting from measurement errors.

The relative future may indicate a role for intercept corrections if it is thought that the underlying DGP may change so that a hitherto reasonably congruent econometric model will cease to be so. Of course, model failure may arise when the correlations between variables change but the DGP is unaltered: such epochs can be useful in detecting model misspecification and discriminating between contending models which were hitherto nearly observationally equivalent. Conceptually at least, the situation we have in mind here is distinct from (a): we conjecture a change in the underlying relationships rather than, say, changes in tax rates/allowances in an otherwise unchanged world. This distinction will be blurred in practice, párticularly if changing the value of certain policy variables causes economic agents to behave in a fundamentally different way (the so-called Lucas critique, Lucas, 1976; but see Engle and Hendry, 1993 and Favero and Hendry, 1992 on the likely force of the critique and a theory of testing for its applicability). These considerations are discussed in more detail in section 6.

Theory information in the context of intercept corrections can be interpreted in terms of the properties of different predictors or methods of prediction based on statistical theory. One example (section 4) is the relationship between conditional and unconditional forecasts of stationary processes that may be exploited to reduce forecast error variance in some circumstances: this is a small-sample result due to estimation uncertainty. Another is what we term 'setting the forecast back on track'. Even if the model is not obviously misspecified, with the possible exception of the parameter estimate having an inordinately large variance, forecast accuracy as measured by mean squared forecast error may be improved by adding to the current forecast value the previous period's forecast error (in the case of 1-step ahead forecasts). An illustration is given in section 5.

Measurement information relates to 'data admissibility' and data accuracy, as in the context of model evaluation. However, for forecasting, this source is closely related to the relative present (2) discussed above, and is also discussed in section 3.

Finally, rival model information can formally encapsulate knowledge about the future from other sources, which gives rise to the rationale for intercept corrections described in (a) above. However, we will not discuss forecast encompassing here (see Clements and Hendry, 1993).

The above taxonomy is comprehensive in coverage and nests many of the justifications for intercept corrections that have been advanced in the literature on a more *ad hoc* basis. For example: 'where a model is not well specified or structurally stable' (Turner, 1990, p. 315), is an example of (1) or possibly (3); misspecification in terms of omitted variables (Young, 1979, p. 269), is an example of (1), but again may involve (3) if sample correlations change in the future; and measurement errors (Young, 1979; Wallis, 1989) fall under (5). In particular, Turner (1990) examines a number of key residual adjustments in forecasts produced by the National Institute of Economic and Social Research (NIESR) and the London Business School (LBS) and concludes that the adjustments are made in response to systematic past errors in the equations, suggesting that (1) may be prevalent. However, the failure to account for the recent rise in consumers' expenditure in the second half of the 1980s may in part represent measurement error in terms of the under-recording of income, or could be a structural break due to financial innovation.

We show below that the nature of the required intercept correction depends upon its rationale, so that the theory of intercept corrections furnishes positive prescriptions. Conversely we treat each source in isolation in this chapter.

It is illuminating to contrast our approach to the understanding of intercept corrections with that of Artis *et al.* (1992) who seek to develop an expert system to replace/mimic the judgemental role of the forecaster in generating final forecasts from macroeconometric models. That is, they seek to reduce the judgemental role exercised by the forecaster to a set of computer-implementable rules. In so doing, Artis *et al.* are essentially *describing* and formalizing what it is that expert forecasters actually do, rather than attempting to explain why it is that what forecasters do works (or not!). We have analysed methods of evaluating forecast accuracy for systems in a separate paper (see Clements and Hendry, 1993).

All the above justifications for modifying model-based forecasts via intercept corrections are analysed in a number of simple examples. A scalar first-order autoregressive DGP suffices for the most part to illustrate our arguments. We begin by formally outlining the task of the forecaster.

2. Intercept corrections and macroeconometric forecasting

We shall begin by outlining the commonly used method of forecasting in large-scale models to highlight the role played by intercept corrections, following the account given in Young (1979). Such models can be characterized as a system of non-linear equations of the form:

$$f_i(\mathbf{y}_t, \mathbf{Y}_{t-1}, \mathbf{X}_t ; \mathbf{\Psi}) = \varepsilon_{it} \qquad (8.1)$$

for $i = 1 \ldots N$, where $\mathbf{y}_t$ is a $N \times 1$ vector of current valued endogenous (that is, modelled) variables, $\mathbf{Y}_{t-1}$ contains all lagged values of endogenous variables, $\mathbf{X}_t$ contains current and/or lagged values of non-modelled variables, and $\mathbf{\Psi}$ denotes the parameters. Then the forecast is constructed as follows. Suppose we have a set of estimates of the parameters from the sample period 1 to T, denoted $\hat{\mathbf{\Psi}}$, and projections for the future values of $\mathbf{X}_{T+h}$, given by $\tilde{\mathbf{X}}_{T+h}$. For a forecast at period T + h, then, $\tilde{\mathbf{X}}_{T+h} = [\mathbf{X}_T^1 : \tilde{\mathbf{X}}_{T+h}^{T+1}]$ so that the variables in the first part of the partition refer to variables known at time T, and those in the second part are projections. In practice, there is a 'ragged edge' (see Wallis *et al.*, 1986, for a discussion of the additional complications that this raises). We return to this below in an analysis of the related idea that measurement errors are likely to be larger for more recent data. The forecasts for $\mathbf{y}_{T+h}$, denoted $\hat{\mathbf{y}}_{T+h}$, solve:

$$f_i(\hat{\mathbf{y}}_{T+h}, \hat{\mathbf{Y}}_{T+h-l}, \tilde{\mathbf{X}}_{T+h}; \hat{\mathbf{\Psi}}) = \tilde{\varepsilon}_{iT+h} \text{ for h} > 0, \tag{8.2}$$

where the $^\wedge$ on $\mathbf{Y}_{T+h-l}$ indicates that for forecast values of more than one period ahead the lagged values of the endogenous variables will themselves be forecasts, and the $^\sim$ on the disturbance terms is meant to suggest that these variables are also projections, in much the same way that the exogenous variables are.

The $\{\varepsilon_{it}\}$ in (8.1) for the estimation period 1 to T are denoted by $\hat{\varepsilon}_{it}$ to indicate an estimated residual. However, the intercept corrections that are commonly projected into the future are defined by:

$$r_{it} = y_{it} - \hat{y}_{it} \text{ for t} = 1...T, \tag{8.3}$$

where $\hat{y}_{it}$ is the fitted value for y_{it} implicitly defined in (8.1). Thus, r_{it} will not coincide with the disturbances in (8.1) or (8.2) when f_i is non-linear. Several authors have questioned the deterministic solution of (8.1) as described by (8.2) when the equations are non-linear. See, for example, Mariano and Brown (1983) who also cite the earlier studies that led to the recognition that deterministic solutions to a system of non-linear equations will yield biased predictions. They establish that the asymptotic bias will be of first order [O(1)] when the model parameters are consistently estimated, but that the asymptotic bias can be reduced to being $O(T^{-1})$ for a stochastic predictor based on a Monte Carlo approach. In that case, an estimated (stochastic) prediction is obtained by averaging over predictions calculated by solving the model for different realizations of the disturbance terms drawn from a specified distribution.

Whilst these issues are clearly of interest, we do not pursue them. Mariano and Brown (1983) observed that most forecasts from non-linear systems were deterministic, and this still appears to be true of recent practice. Of interest here would be whether such considerations support intercept corrections in deterministic solutions, although it is not clear whether any general prescriptions as to the required form of correction suggest themselves. Moreover, whether we have a deterministic or a stochastic solution, the issue of intercept corrections would appear to be the same: in the stochastic case the intercept correction would be implemented either by taking realizations from a distribution with a non-zero mean or from a zero-mean distribution and adding on an additional (deterministic) factor.

The importance (at least in principle) of the non-linear model deterministic solution bias has been established for the evaluation of econometric (non-linear) models by comparison to time-series models. Wallis (1984) argues that finding in favour of a time-series model over an econometric model in mean squared forecast error comparisons, in the non-linear case, does not necessarily imply the inadequacy of the latter (as in the linear case). Wallis advocates obtaining the conditional expectation of the non-linear model by simulation and using this as the basis for between-model forecast error comparisons.

Following Young (1979) and Kennedy (1983), we can deduce the relationship between $\{r_{it}\}$ and $\{\varepsilon_{it}\}$ when the equation is in log-linear form (in the sense that the additive error in this form is normal). This may be regarded as the typical case in time series econometrics. The formulations below essentially assume that the variables (y_{it}, and in subsequent sections, w_t) are stationary. In principle this allows for $I(1)$ variables but assumes that a certain number of linear combinations of these variables co-integrate, and that the models in this chapter are expressed in differences and co-integrating combinations (the transformation from the $I(1)$ levels of the variables to the $I(0)$ representation, w_t, is described in Clements and Hendry, 1992).

For the ith equation we can write:

$$\ln y_{it} = \ln \hat{y}_{it} + \hat{\varepsilon}_{it}. \tag{8.4}$$

We assume that $\hat{\varepsilon}_{it} = \varepsilon_{it} + o_p(1)$ (so consistent estimates have been used) and neglect the second term for the remainder of this section. Then:

$$y_{it} = \hat{y}_{it} \cdot exp(\varepsilon_{it}) \tag{8.5}$$

so that from (8.3) and (8.5)

$$r_{it} = \hat{y}_{it}(exp(\varepsilon_{it}) - 1). \tag{8.6}$$

Hence, even assuming that $\varepsilon_{it} \sim \text{IN}(0, \sigma^2)$, r_{it} is the product of a log-normal variate and $\hat{y}_{it}$. However, using the expansion of the exponential, $exp(\varepsilon_{it}) = 1 + \varepsilon_{it} + \frac{1}{2}\varepsilon_{it}^2 \ldots$, then:

$$r_{it} = \hat{y}_{it}\varepsilon_{it} + \frac{1}{2}\hat{y}_{it}\varepsilon_{it}^2 \ldots, \text{ and so } E[r_{it}] \approx \frac{1}{2}\hat{y}_{it}\sigma^2. \tag{8.7}$$

This is a reasonable approximation because $\hat{y}_{it}$ should be independent of ε_{it}, and under the normality of ε_{it}, the next term in the expansion (being the third moment of a normally distributed variate) would disappear. For log-linear equations, practitioners often use multiplicative (rather than add) factors so (8.3) becomes:

$$r_{it}^* = y_{it}/\hat{y}_{it} \tag{8.8}$$

and the relationship between the intercept correction r_{it}^* and the disturbance in (8.4) is given by:

$$r^*_{it} = exp(\varepsilon_{it}) \tag{8.9}$$

which is now independent of the level of the variable, although the mean of r^*_{it} exceeds unity:

$$E[r^*_{it}] = exp(E(\varepsilon_{it}) + \tfrac{1}{2}\sigma^2) = exp(\tfrac{1}{2}\sigma^2) \approx 1 + \tfrac{1}{2}\sigma^2, \tag{8.10}$$

which yields a similar relative error to (8.7) (see Aitchison and Brown, 1957, on the log-normal distribution). Indeed, for most economic time series, σ is less than 0.05, so the expressions for $(y_{it} - \hat{y}_{it})/\hat{y}_{it}$ in (8.7) and (8.10) are close to zero. Consequently, we focus on the linear case without much loss of generality, and with a considerable gain in tractability.

3.   Measurement errors

The effects of measurement errors on the properties of parameter estimates are well known for regressions involving stationary variables and are discussed in standard econometrics textbooks. For the consequences of measurement errors on regression estimators when variables are non-stationary and integrated, see, for example, Stock (1988) and Banerjee *et al.* (1993). Our interest is in the potential role for intercept corrections created by the possibly increasing unreliability of observations at the end of the period for which data are available. The frequency with which preliminary data are subsequently revised suggests that forecasts may often be conditioned on data measured with a substantial degree of error. Wallis (1989, p. 32) attributes an important role to measurement error-related issues in justifying a role for intercept corrections: 'the continuing presence of data discrepancies and delays is one reason why there remains a role for informed judgement in forecasting'.

Below we show that measurement errors lead to autocorrelation in the model's residuals. In analysing measurement errors we abstract from the effects on parameter estimates by using known parameters. This can be justified by assuming that only a few observations at the end of the sample period are badly measured, thus having a negligible effect on full-sample parameter estimates. We expect whole sample tests for autocorrelation to fail to detect this problem. However, careful end-of-sample residual analysis might prove useful. The simple conceptualization we adopt below divides time into three non-overlapping periods: the estimation period $(1...T^e)$, during which the data are observed without error; a period during which the data are observed with error $(T^e+1...T)$, followed by the forecast period $(T + 1...T + h)$. The assumption that the estimation period does not extend right up to the beginning of the forecast period reflects the fact that the size of models currently in use probably makes it prohibitively expensive to re-estimate the models' equations each time a new data point becomes available (and possibly undesirable if the latest data are unreliable).

We mainly consider uncertainty concerning the initial conditions, characterized in our simple example by only the period T observation being observed with error.

The DGP we consider is deliberately very simple to highlight the logic of the analysis, namely:

$$w_t = \Psi w_{t-1} + v_t, \ t = 1 \dots T + h \text{ where } v_t \sim IN(0, \sigma_v^2) \text{ and } |\Psi| < 1. \qquad (8.11)$$

In the absence of measurement errors and assuming a correctly specified model with known parameters, the estimated model coincides with (8.11) for t = 1...T^e, and then becomes:

$$w_s = \Psi w_{s-1} + e_s, \quad s = T^e + 1 \dots T, \qquad (8.12)$$

where the disturbance e_s denotes that (8.12) is not a regression residual since the parameter 'estimation period' ends at T^e. Since the model is not misspecified and the DGP remains unaltered, here e_s in fact equals v_s. However, when the parameters are estimated, e_s and v_s differ by $(\hat{\Psi} - \Psi) w_{s-1}$.

Suppose now that the observed series is the actual series w_s measured with error, θ_s:

$$w_s^* = w_s + \theta_s, s = T^e + 1 \dots T \text{ where } \theta_s \sim IN(0, \sigma_s^2) \text{ and } E[w_s \theta_t] = 0 \ \forall t, s. \qquad (8.13)$$

By construction, $\sigma_s^2 = 0$ for s = 1...T^e and $\sigma_s^2 > 0$ for s > T^e. Substituting w_s^* into (8.12):

$$w_s^* - \theta_s = \Psi(w_{s-1}^* - \theta_{s-1}) + e_s, s = T^e + 1 \dots T, \qquad (8.14)$$

so that when using $w_s^* = \Psi w_{s-1}^* + e_s^*$:

$$e_s^* = e_s + \theta_s - \Psi \theta_{s-1}. \qquad (8.15)$$

Thus, the observed residual series will exhibit the following properties over the period immediately prior to the forecast period:

$$E[e_s^*] = 0, \qquad (8.16)$$

if the measurement errors have zero mean; and

$$V[e_s^*] = \sigma_e^2 + \sigma_s^2 + \Psi^2 \sigma_{s-1}^2 \qquad (8.17)$$

Here $\sigma_e^2 \equiv V[e_s]$ is equal to the error variance, σ_v^2. Also:

$$E[e_s^* e_{s-1}^*] = -\Psi \sigma_{s-1}^2 \qquad (8.18)$$

leading to error autocorrelation ρ_s^* of the form:

$$\rho_s^* = \frac{E\left[e_s^* e_{s-1}^*\right]}{\sqrt{V\left[e_s^*\right]} \sqrt{V\left[e_{s-1}^*\right]}}. \qquad (8.19)$$

Although heteroscedastic measurement errors seem likely (with σ_s^2 increasing as time T approaches), we will assume a constant $\sigma_s^2 = \sigma^2$ where this permits more useful analytical formulae. With that homoscedasticity assumption, we have:

$$\rho_s^* = \frac{-\Psi \sigma^2}{\sigma_e^2 + \left(\Psi^2 + 1\right)\sigma^2}. \qquad (8.20)$$

Further, if we assume that $\sigma_e^2 = \sigma^2$, so that the error variance and the variance of the measurement error are equal, then $\rho_s^* = -\Psi/(2 + \Psi^2)$ so $|\rho_s^*| < 1/3$. For $\Psi > 0$, $\rho_s^* < 0$, so measurement errors imply that the adjacent residuals observed by the forecaster will be negatively correlated in such dynamic models. Heteroscedasticity would lead to changing autocorrelation, and smaller measurement errors to less (absolute) autocorrelation. However, the importance of recent measurement errors for forecast accuracy does not depend only on this end-of-sample autocorrelation.

To derive the implications of measurement errors for intercept corrections, we make use of the literature on 'signal-extraction' popularized in the macroeconomics literature by Lucas (1973) in his islands model. The problem is to derive the optimal predictor of w_{T+h} given information available at period T. To highlight the main issue, we assume that only the last observation, w_T^*, is error ridden, which is essentially the case of initial condition uncertainty. Thus, the information set (denoted by I_T^*) contains the values of w_s for $s < T$; knowledge of the model given by (8.11); and w_T^*. Then, the optimal predictor is given by $E[w_{T+h} | I_T^*]$, which must be inferior relative to the predictor in the absence of measurement error, namely $E[w_{T+h} | I_T]$, where I_T replaces w_T^* by w_T. From (8.11):

$$w_{T+h} = \Psi^h w_T + \sum_{i=0}^{h-1} \Psi^i v_{T+h-i}, \qquad (8.21)$$

where the expectation of the last term is zero for all forecast horizons. Consequently, we can view the forecasting task as a 'two-stage' procedure: first, obtain the best estimate of w_T, which we denote $\hat{w}_T$, and then forecast w_{T+h} from $\Psi^h \hat{w}_T$. Hence it is the first stage that is of interest when there are measurement errors (and the true parameters of the model are assumed known) since then the problem boils down to estimating $E[w_T|I_T^*]$. Conceptually, the information set at our disposal consists of: (1) the model given by (8.11), and (2) an information set I_T^0, which comprises the past values of observed data, and the relationship between w_s^* and w_s given by (8.13). We consider the optimal predictor of w_T given each of these information sets in turn, and then combine the two predictors in an optimal fashion by choosing weights that minimize the squared prediction error (cf. Nelson, 1972, for example).[1] Appendix 1 records the details, where we show that the composite predictor has the form:

$$E[w_T|I_T^*] = (1 - \mu)\hat{w}_T + \mu\Psi w_{T-1}, \tag{8.22}$$

where μ weights the two component predictors, and $\hat{w}_T = k_T w_T^*$ where k_T depends on the relative variability of the measurement error component to the underlying uncertainty in the DGP. Minimizing the squared prediction error from (8.22) yields a value of μ, say μ^*, so that the optimal predictor becomes:

$$\hat{w}_T = \hat{w}_T - \mu^*(\hat{w}_T - \Psi w_{T-1}) = w_T^* - (1 - \mu^*)(1 - k_T)w_T^* - \mu^* e_T^*. \tag{8.23}$$

When measurement error is confined to period T, so that $\hat{w}_{T-1} = w_{T-1}$, this formula has a straightforward interpretation since μ^* varies positively with the variability of the measurement error (see Appendix 1). Thus, the noisier the measurement error, the greater the reliance on the model-based predictor. In the limit, as $\sigma_T^2 \to \infty$, $\mu^* \to 1$, and hence $\hat{w}_T = \Psi w_{T-1}$ so the model-based predictor of the initial condition is the 1-step ahead conditional expectation, based on the model (8.11) at $T-1$, completely ignoring the period T observation. The converse holds if $\sigma_T^2 = 0$.

The second stage forecast of w_{T+h} using the first-stage estimate $\hat{w}_T$ yields:

$$\hat{w}_{T+h} = \Psi^h \hat{w}_T = \Psi^h w_T^* - \Psi^h[(1 - \mu^*)(1 - k_T)w_T^* + \mu^* e_T^*]. \tag{8.24}$$

When predicting using $\Psi^h w_T^*$ rather than $\Psi^h w_T$, the required intercept correction is given by the second term in (8.24). For example, when $k_T \approx 1$, the last term is approximately $-\mu^* \Psi^h e_T^*$, which diminishes in h under the assumption that w_t is stationary.

---

[1] Survey-based information could be incorporated in a similar way.

4.   Conditional and unconditional predictors

Forecasts from macroeconomic models are conditional forecasts given the
initial values of the variables as well as the projected future time paths of any
non-modelled variables. One rationale for intercept corrections is, somewhat
paradoxically, to exploit the potential information in unconditional forecasts.
The asymptotic formulae for multi-step mean squared forecast errors are derived
by Baillie (1979a, 1979b). Analysis of these indicates that conditional forecast
error variances for a stationary process can exceed the unconditional variance
of the process. Chong and Hendry (1986) interpret such results as providing a
potential justification for intercept corrections, since a weighted average of the
conditional and unconditional predictions may have a smaller variance than either
alone. They suggest the 'long-run growth rate' of the variable as a plausible
unconditional predictor for the difference. In this section we illustrate these ideas
with our simple first-order scalar autoregressive process where the coefficient
value is no longer assumed known, and outline the form of intercept correction
that would be entailed. The process remains as in (8.11) and we continue to assume
stationarity, but no measurement errors. The h-step ahead conditional forecast
for period $T + h$ based on period T information is:

$$\hat{w}_{T+h} = \hat{\Psi}^h w_T, \tag{8.25}$$

where $^\wedge$ is used to denote both forecasts and estimated coefficients. The true
value of w_{T+h} is given by (8.21) so that the h-step ahead conditional forecast
error is:

$$e_{T+h} = w_{T+h} - \hat{w}_{T+h} = \left(\Psi^h - \hat{\Psi}^h\right)w_T + \sum_{i=0}^{h-1}\Psi^i v_{T+h-1}. \tag{8.26}$$

Then the h-step ahead conditional mean squared forecast error (MSFE$_h$) is:

$$E_T\left[e_{T+h}^2\right] = \text{MSFE}_h = E_T\left[\left(\sum_{i=0}^{h-1}\Psi^i v_{T+h-i}\right)^2\right] + E_T\left[\left\{\left(\Psi^h - \hat{\Psi}^h\right)w_T\right\}^2\right],$$

$$\tag{8.27}$$

where E_T denotes an expectation conditional on period T information. The form
of (8.27) results from the product of the two terms in (8.26) having a zero expectation by the assumption of independence of $\{v_t\}$: the first term in (8.27) is the
contribution of future disturbances, and the second is parameter uncertainty,
based on past disturbances. The second term in (8.27) is evaluated using the
asymptotic formula in Baillie (1979a, equation 1.6, p. 676), so the whole
expression is:

$$\text{MSFE}_h = [(1 - \Psi^{2h})/(1 - \Psi^2)]\sigma_v^2 + T^{-1}w_T^2 h^2 \Psi^{2(h-1)}(1 - \Psi^2). \tag{8.28}$$

In deriving (8.28) from (8.27), use is made of $(\Psi - \hat{\Psi})$ and w_T being asymptotically independent to $o(T^{-1})$ (see Schmidt, 1977, p. 998), so that (8.28) is valid to $o(T^{-1})$. Ericsson and Marquez (1989, p. 5) provide details of the derivation of (8.28).

The first term in (8.28) is monotonically increasing in h, approaching the unconditional variance of w_T asymptotically:

$$E[w_T^2] = \sigma_v^2/(1 - \Psi^2). \tag{8.29}$$

Chong and Hendry (1986) note that $h^2\Psi^{2(h-1)}$ in (8.28) has a maximum at $h = -1/log\Psi$, and so is not monotonic. Hence for certain values of the parameters the value of the expression in (8.28) may exceed the unconditional variance in (8.29). To illustrate numerically, assume the following set of parameter values $\{\sigma_v^2 = 1, T = 40, \Psi = 0.8\}$. Then the unconditional variance of w_t is 2.78, which will be less than the MSFE_h when w_T^2 exceeds the values shown in Table 8.1.

Table 8.1   The unconditional variance of w_t

h	1	4	5	10
w_T^2	198	13	8	2

Now, consider the behaviour of a composite predictor formed by combining linearly the conditional predictor $\hat{w}_{T+h}$ and $\bar{w}$, where the latter does not depend on time and is a function of the information set at time T; for example, $\bar{w}$ could be the mean of a very long sample of historical data. Intuitively, w_t can be thought of as a growth rate so that $\bar{w}$ is a sample estimate of the average growth rate of the series, but we treat it as having zero variance. There is a large literature on the combination of forecasts and the related notion of forecast encompassing (see Diebold (1989) and Clements and Hendry (1993) for a discussion and some references). In the above example, the w_t process has a zero mean, so that we set $\bar{w} = 0$. The composite predictor is then given by:

$$\tilde{w}_{T+h} = \alpha\bar{w} + (1 - \alpha)\hat{w}_{T+h} = (1 - \alpha)\hat{w}_{T+h}, \tag{8.30}$$

where $0 \le \alpha \le 1$, and the associated h-step ahead composite forecast error is:

$$\tilde{e}_{T+h} \equiv w_{T+h} - \tilde{w}_{T+h} = \alpha\tilde{e}_{T+h} + (1 - \alpha)e_{T+h}, \tag{8.31}$$

where e_{T+h} is defined in (8.26) and $\bar{e}_{T+h} \equiv w_{T+h} - \bar{w} = w_{T+h}$. As (8.30) reveals, the benefit (if any) is due to 'shrinkage' and we are presently investigating more general shrinkage methods (such as Stein–James) applied to multi-period forecasts (see, for example, Judge and Bock, 1978).

Consider the conditional MSFE for the composite predictor:

$$
\begin{aligned}
E_T[\tilde{e}^{\,2}_{T+h}] &= \alpha^2 E_T[\bar{e}^2_{T+h}] + (1-\alpha)^2 E_T[e^2_{T+h}] + 2\alpha(1-\alpha)E_T[\bar{e}_{T+h}e_{T+h}] \\
&= \alpha^2 E_T[w^2_{T+h}] + (1-\alpha)^2 E_T[e^2_{T+h}] + 2\alpha(1-\alpha)E_T[w_{T+h}e_{T+h}].
\end{aligned}
\tag{8.32}
$$

Expanding the third term in (8.32) using (8.21) and (8.26), we obtain:

$$
\begin{aligned}
E_T[w_{T+h}e_{T+h}] &= E\{\Psi^h(\Psi^h - \hat{\Psi}^h)w^2_T + (\Psi^h w_T \\
&\quad + (\Psi^h - \hat{\Psi}^h)w_T)\sum_{i=0}^{h-1}\Psi^i v_{T+h-1} + [\sum_{i=0}^{h-1}\Psi^i v_{T+h-i}]^2\} \\
&= [(1-\Psi^{2h})/(1-\Psi^2)]\sigma^2_v,
\end{aligned}
\tag{8.33}
$$

since the first two terms are zero. Hence, using (8.28), (8.32) becomes:

$$
\begin{aligned}
E_T[\tilde{e}^{\,2}_{T+h}] &= \alpha^2 E_T[w^2_{T+h}] + (1-\alpha^2)[(1-\Psi^{2h})/(1-\Psi^2)]\sigma^2_v + \\
&\quad (1-\alpha)^2 T^{-1}w^2_T h^2 \Psi^{2(h-1)}(1-\Psi^2) \\
&= \alpha^2 \Psi^{2h}w^2_T + [(1-\Psi^{2h})/(1-\Psi^2)]\sigma^2_v + \\
&\quad (1-\alpha)^2 T^{-1}w^2_T h^2 \Psi^{2(h-1)}(1-\Psi^2)
\end{aligned}
\tag{8.34}
$$

since $E_T[w^2_{T+h}] = [(1-\Psi^{2h})/(1-\Psi^2)]\sigma^2_v + \Psi^{2h}w^2_T$. Minimizing (8.34) with respect to α yields:

$$
\alpha^* = [1 + T\Psi^2/h^2(1-\Psi^2)]^{-1}
\tag{8.35}
$$

which does not depend on w^2_T. From (8.35), the overall MSFE may be reduced by using the composite predictor defined in (8.30). However, α will be close to zero unless h is large and T is small, so the gains may not be large and may be lost by estimating the long-run mean. Typically, the conditional variance will be less than the unconditional initially, and then rise above it as h increases, suggesting increasing α from 0 to 1 as h increases (or from zero rising to a maximum and then back to zero, since the conditional and unconditional forecast error variances converge). From (8.30) this implies an intercept correction that adjusts the model prediction towards zero by an increasing amount as the number of steps ahead increases, and then tails off after some point to leave the 'pure' model forecasts.

5. Setting the forecast back on track

Forecasters often set models 'back on track', so that under- (over-) prediction of an equation in the past leads to a commensurate adjustment in the future. In this section we assume that the model is not misspecified. We can make the analysis of this behaviour operational by assuming that the forecaster adds in the residual of the current period to the next period's forecast value for 1-step ahead forecasts. Hence the adjustment to the forecast is based only on the error in the forecast of the current period. This formulation lets us establish conditions under which such behaviour will improve forecast accuracy, as well as relate the potential gains to the properties of the DGP and the econometric model being used for forecasting.

We continue to consider only scalar processes, with the DGP given by (8.11) so the forecast for period $T + 1$ based on period T information is:

$$\hat{w}_{T+1} = \hat{\Psi} w_T, \tag{8.36}$$

with a forecast error given by:

$$e_{T+1} = w_{T+1} - \hat{w}_{T+1} = (\Psi - \hat{\Psi}) w_T + v_{T+1}. \tag{8.37}$$

The forecast from setting the model 'back on track' is:

$$\hat{w}^*_{T+1} = \hat{\Psi} w_T + e_T, \tag{8.38}$$

with a forecast error $\hat{e}_{T+1}$ given by:

$$\hat{e}_{T+1} = w_{T+1} - \hat{w}^*_{T+1} = (\Psi - \hat{\Psi}) w_T + v_{T+1} - e_T. \tag{8.39}$$

From (8.39):

$$\hat{e}_{T+1} = (\Psi - \hat{\Psi}) w_T + (v_{T+1} - v_T) + (v_T - e_T), \tag{8.40}$$

and since from (8.37) lagged one period:

$$(v_T - e_T) = -(\Psi - \hat{\Psi}) w_{T-1}, \tag{8.41}$$

then:

$$\hat{e}_{T+1} = (\Psi - \hat{\Psi}) \Delta w_T + \Delta v_{T+1} = \Delta e_{T+1} \tag{8.42}$$

where the second equality follows from differencing (8.37).

Thus, (8.42) gives the relationship between the two forecast errors defined in (8.37) and (8.39). Resetting forecasts has the interesting property of inducing the difference in the original forecast error, such that:

$$V[\hat{e}_{T+1}] = V[\Delta e_{T+1}] = V[e_{T+1}] + V[e_T] - 2\,C[e_{T+1}e_T], \qquad (8.43)$$

where C[.] denotes a covariance. Assuming stationarity, so that $V[e_j] = V[e_t]$ $\forall$ j:

$$V[\hat{e}_{T+1}] = 2V[e_t] - 2\rho_e V[e_t] = 2(1 - \rho_e)V[e_t], \qquad (8.44)$$

where ρ_e is the correlation coefficient between adjacent (ordinary) forecast errors, $\{e_t\}$. Hence, setting the forecast on track reduces the expected squared forecast error if $\rho_e > \frac{1}{2}$. This condition is in terms of the estimated residuals. To see the implications in terms of the parameters of the DGP and the estimator of the econometric model, from (8.37):

$$V[e_{T+1}] = E[\{(\Psi - \hat{\Psi})w_T + v_{T+1} - E[(\Psi - \hat{\Psi})w_T + v_{T+1}]\}^2] = V(\hat{\Psi})V[w_t] + V[v_t], \qquad (8.45)$$

where we assume that the estimator is unbiased, and ignore the (small) correlation between $(\Psi - \hat{\Psi})$ and w_T. The final equality again requires stationarity. Now:

$$E[e_{T+1}e_T] = E[(\Psi - \hat{\Psi})^2(\Psi w_{T-1} + v_T)w_{T-1}] + E[(\Psi - \hat{\Psi})(\Psi w_{T-1} + v_T)v_T]$$
$$+ E[(\Psi - \hat{\Psi})w_{T-1}v_{T+1}] + E[v_{T+1}v_T]. \qquad (8.46)$$

Absence of serial correlation in $\{v_t\}$, due to its being an innovation process with respect to the information available to the forecaster, implies that the last two terms are zero. The second term is also negligible as $E[\Psi - \hat{\Psi}] \approx 0$, so that (8.46) becomes:

$$E[e_{T+1}e_T] = E[(\Psi - \hat{\Psi})^2]\Psi E[w_{T-1}^2] = V(\hat{\Psi})\Psi V(w_t), \qquad (8.47)$$

again assuming stationarity. From (8.43), and substituting from (8.45) and (8.47):

$$\rho_e = V(\hat{\Psi})\Psi V(w_t)/[V(\hat{\Psi})V[w_t] + V[v_t]]. \qquad (8.48)$$

From (8.11), $V(w_t) = V[v_t]/(1 - \Psi^2)$, so that:

$$\rho_e = \Psi/[1 + (1 - \Psi^2)/V(\hat{\Psi})]. \qquad (8.49)$$

For a given value of $\Psi > \frac{1}{2}$, $\rho_e > \frac{1}{2}$ will hold for a sufficiently imprecise estimator of Ψ. Notice that a necessary condition for this form of residual adjustment to work is that Ψ is positive. This parallels the requirement that the estimated residuals are at least positively correlated.

By itself, this rationale for an intercept correction is not overly interesting. However, particular forms of structural breaks may generate positive autocorrelation in post-estimation sample residuals, and the present form of correction may well be effective in those circumstances. This issue is discussed in the following section.

6. Structural change during the forecast period

Before outlining a simple analytical model that features some of the key points, we refer to an example documented by Turner (1990).

Turner (1990) quotes Haache and Townend (1981) who state that for forecasting the exchange rate: 'we are left without any stable empirical relationship which might be used'. In terms of our taxonomy of information, the exchange rate equation is misspecified, but to such an extent that past errors are not believed to provide any useful indication as to how the equation might perform in the future. As documented by Turner (1990), the NIESR forecasters impose a time path for the exchange rate in their forecast, based upon their view of the rate of depreciation of sterling that the Government would be prepared to countenance. Thus, the intercept correction here is due to information based on the relative future, albeit that overriding an equation completely is a polar extreme of intercept correction.

The NIESR forecasters' view about the Treasury's reaction to likely downward pressure on sterling during the forecast period was probably formed on the basis of information from a variety of sources. An important strand would presumably be the way in which the Government had reacted in the past to similar circumstances, although this clearly had not proved amenable to formal modelling.

In general, if anticipated future changes in policy are reasonably well correlated with past episodes, then previous ex-post errors may suggest a pattern for future intercept corrections. Periods over which forecasts perform badly highlight areas of model weakness and provide an impetus to model development. Wallis (1989) documents the new avenues of research opened up by a poor track record during the 1974–5 and 1979–81 recessions.

Consider a structural break in Ψ from the sample period value to a new value, Ψ^*, at $t = T + 1 \ldots T + h$, where for simplicity we abstract from estimation uncertainty. Thus, for $i = 1 \ldots h$:

$$w_{T+i} = \Psi^* w_{T+i-1} + v_{T+i} = \Psi^{*i} w_T + \sum_{j=0}^{i-1} \Psi^{*j} v_{T+i-j}. \qquad (8.50)$$

The forecaster, however, uses:

$$\hat{w}_{T+i} = \Psi^i w_T, \qquad (8.51)$$

which results in a sequence of forecast errors given by:

$$w_{T+i} - \hat{w}_{T+i} = (\Psi^{*i} - \Psi^i)w_T + \sum_{j=0}^{i-1} \Psi^{*j}v_{T+i-j}. \qquad (8.52)$$

Assuming that the underlying error distribution is unaltered, the average sequence of conditional forecast errors is given by:

$$E[w_{T+i} - \hat{w}_{T+i} | w_T] = (\Psi^{*i} - \Psi^i)w_T. \qquad (8.53)$$

Then the sequence of forecast errors will, on average: (1) all have the same sign, positive if $\Psi^* > \Psi$ and negative if the strict inequality holds the other way; (2) diminish to zero as $h \to \infty$, since the conditional forecasts approach the unconditional forecasts (of zero, given that it is a zero mean stationary process, marking the limit to forecastability); but (3) typically will increase initially. The most useful implication is (1), which implies that on average the forecast errors will be positively autocorrelated. This is distinct from the usual autocorrelation due to multi-step forecasting and will be observable ex-post in the one-step forecasts over the break period.

Suppose now that a structural break has taken place prior to the forecast period, between periods $T - 1$ and T, say, but that this is unbeknown to the forecaster. Abstracting from considerations of parameter uncertainty, but allowing for a non-zero intercept:

$$w_{T+i} = \gamma^* + \Psi^* w_{T+i-1} + v_{T+i}, \quad i = 0...h, \qquad (8.54)$$

also noting the difference from (8.50) in the timing of the break relative to the agents' information sets. This is important, because agents now observe the period T residual given by:

$$e_T = w_T - \hat{w}_T = \gamma^* - \gamma + (\Psi^* - \Psi)w_{T-1} + v_T, \qquad (8.55)$$

since $\hat{w}_T = \gamma + \Psi w_{T-1}$. To forecast period $T + 1$, there are two options: (1) the period T error can be ignored, so that $\hat{w}_{T+1} = \gamma + \Psi w_T$, with an associated forecast error of:

$$e_{T+1} = \gamma^* - \gamma + (\Psi^* - \Psi)w_T + v_{T+1}, \qquad (8.56)$$

or, (2) set the forecast back on track using $\tilde{w}_{T+1} = \hat{w}_{T+1} + e_T$, which produces the forecast error:

$$\tilde{e}_{T+1} = \gamma^* - \gamma + (\Psi^* - \Psi)w_T + v_{T+1} - e_T = (\Psi^* - \Psi)\Delta w_T + \Delta v_{T+1} = \Delta e_{T+1} \qquad (8.57)$$

where the second equality follows from substituting for e_T from (8.55).

Thus, as in section 5, the strategy of adding back in the previous period's residual will prove successful if the correlation between the errors exceeds $\frac{1}{2}$, or $(\gamma^* - \gamma)$ is large. Here, the relevant correlation is between e_{T+1} and e_T, whereas before the $\{e_t\}$ were assumed stationary in the absence of model misspecification or changes in the data generation mechanism, and thus had a constant correlation. If no break has occurred, the cost of using (8.57) may be an increase in the forecast error variance subject to the considerations in section 5.

Consider now the problem of forecasting period T + 2. We compare two alternatives to the conditional expectation from the (now misspecified) model which is:

$$\hat{w}_{T+2} = \gamma + \Psi\gamma + \Psi^2 w_T. \tag{8.58}$$

The first method uses $\tilde{w}_{T+2}$, defined by:

$$\tilde{w}_{T+2} = \gamma + \Psi\tilde{w}_{T+1} = \gamma + \Psi\hat{w}_{T+1} + \Psi e_T = \hat{w}_{T+2} + \Psi e_T, \tag{8.59}$$

whereas the second uses $\overset{\leftrightarrow}{w}_{T+2}$:

$$\overset{\leftrightarrow}{w}_{T+2} = \hat{w}_{T+2} + e_T. \tag{8.60}$$

In the first case, the (false) model is used to generate a two-step ahead forecast using the adjusted 1-step ahead forecast. As can be seen from (8.59), this amounts to adjusting the (false) conditional expectation by a fraction of e_T, given by Ψe_T. The second strategy adjusts the conditional expectation by the full extent of the error. For these two predictors, the forecast errors are:

$$\tilde{e}_{T+2} = e_{T+2} - \Psi e_T = \Delta e_{T+2} + (e_{T+1} - \Psi e_T); \text{ and:} \tag{8.61}$$

$$\overset{\leftrightarrow}{e}_{T+2} = e_{T+2} - e_T = \Delta_2 e_{T+2}. \tag{8.62}$$

From (8.53) we deduced that the structural break would induce positive autocorrelation in the sequence $\{e_t\}$, which has a non-zero mean: this holds *a fortiori* if an intercept change is also allowed. For sufficient positive autocorrelation, (8.61) and (8.62) will, on average, be smaller than the forecast error from the conditional expectation based on the false assumption of no break.

7. Model misspecification

Suspected model misspecification is perhaps the most obvious and best understood rationale for extrapolating non-zero residuals into the future, and for this reason we spend little time on it here. Notice that the examples in the previous sections can either be adapted to allow for model misspecification or directly indicate the implications for intercept corrections of certain forms of model misspecification. In section 6, for example, we analysed the consequences of a changed DGP and an unchanged model. Alternatively we could view this as a form of model misspecification. In the analysis of 'setting the forecast back on track' in section 5, model misspecification could be incorporated by amending the assumption of an innovation disturbance term, allowing for serial correlation, and so on. For example, suppose that the econometric model is such that v_t in (8.11) is not a serially uncorrelated innovation relative to w_{t-1}, then (8.46) becomes:

$$E[e_{T+1}e_T] = V(\hat{\Psi})\Psi V(w_t) + V(\hat{\Psi})E[v_T w_{T-1}] + E[v_{T+1}v_T], \qquad (8.63)$$

so that setting the forecast back on track is more likely to be successful if $E[v_T w_{T-1}] > 0$ and $E[v_{T+1}v_T] > 0$.

8. Conclusions

We have suggested a variety of situations under which intercept corrections will enhance forecast accuracy. The resulting forms of intercept correction differ and in any practical setting would have to be combined. However, we have not considered interactions between the situations and only investigated the simplest case of a scalar first-order autoregression. Nevertheless, we have shown that intercept corrections are amenable to analysis and in some cases appear to have the potential to improve forecast accuracy (as we know they do in practice).

Conversely, if modellers use intercept corrections with any of the properties of those analysed above and models are misspecified or structural changes occur, then improved forecast accuracy is a possibility, in line with present empirical evidence.

Although the results presented here are only a first step, we consider that it is possible to develop a more general approach to the theory of economic forecasting which explicitly recognizes both that the model is not the mechanism, and that the mechanism is subject to change. Some results are recorded in Hendry (1991) and we report our more general analysis in Clements and Hendry (1994a,b).

References

Aitchison, J. and Brown, J.A.C. (1957), *The Lognormal Distribution*. London: Cambridge University Press.
Artis, M., Moss, S. and Ormerod, P. (1992), 'A smart automated macroeconometric forecasting system', mimeo, University of Manchester.
Baillie, R.T. (1979a), 'Asymptotic prediction mean squared error for vector autoregressive models', *Biometrika*, **66**, (3), 675–8.
Baillie, R.T. (1979b), 'The asymptotic mean squared error of multistep prediction from the regression model with autoregressive errors', *Journal of the American Statistical Association*, **74**, 175–84.

Banerjee, A., Dolado, J.J., Galbraith, J.W. and Hendry, D.F. (1993), *Cointegration, Error Correction and the Econometric Analysis of Non-Stationary Data.* Oxford: Oxford University Press.

Chong, Y.Y. and Hendry, D.F. (1986), 'Econometric evaluation of linear macro-economic models', *Review of Economic Studies, LIII,* 671–90.

Clements, M.P. and Hendry, D.F. (1992), 'Forecasting in cointegrated systems', Institute of Economics and Statistics Discussion Paper No. 139, Oxford.

Clements, M.P. and Hendry, D.F. (1993), 'On the limitations of comparing mean square forecast errors', *Journal of Forecasting,* **12,** 617–37.

Clements, M.P. and Hendry, D.F. (1994a), 'Towards a theory of economic forecasting', in C. Hargreaves (ed.), *Non-stationary Time-Series Analyses and Cointegration,* Oxford: Oxford University Press, forthcoming.

Clements, M.P. and Hendry, D.F. (1994b), *Economic Forecasting,* Cambridge: Cambridge University Press, forthcoming.

Diebold, F.X. (1989), 'Forecast combination and encompassing: reconciling two divergent literatures', *International Journal of Forecasting,* **5,** 589–92.

Engle, R.F. and Hendry, D.F. (1993), 'Testing super exogeneity and invariance in regression models', *Journal of Econometrics,* **56,** 119–39.

Ericsson, N.R. and Marquez, J. R. (1989), 'Exact and approximate multi-period mean-square forecast errors for dynamic econometric models', Federal Reserve International Finance Discussion Paper No. 348.

Favero, C. and Hendry, D.F. (1992), 'Testing the Lucas critique: a review', *Econometric Reviews,* **11,** 265–306.

Gilbert, C.L. (1986), 'Professor Hendry's methodology', *Oxford Bulletin of Economics and Statistics,* **48,** 283–307.

Haache, G. and Townend, J. (1981), 'Exchange rates and monetary policy: modelling sterling's effective exchange rate, 1972–80', in W.A. Eltis (ed.), *The Money Supply and the Exchange Rate,* 201–47, Oxford: Oxford University Press.

Hendry, D.F. (1991), 'On a theory of intercept corrections in macroeconometric forecasting', paper presented to the 35th Anniversary Conference of the Econometrics Institute, Erasmus University, Rotterdam.

Hendry, D.F. (1992), *Dynamic Econometrics.* Forthcoming, Oxford University Press.

Hendry, D.F. and Richard, J.F. (1982), 'On the formulation of empirical models in dynamic econometrics', *Journal of Econometrics,* **20,** 3–33.

Hendry, D.F. and Richard, J.F. (1983), 'The econometric analysis of economic time series', *International Statistical Review,* **51,** 111–63.

Judge, G.G. and Bock, M.E. (1978), *The Statistical Implications of Pre-Test and Stein-Rule Estimators in Econometrics,* Amsterdam: North-Holland.

Kennedy, P. (1983), 'Logarithmic dependent variables and prediction bias', *Oxford Bulletin of Economics and Statistics,* **45,** 389–92.

Lucas, R.E. (1973), 'Some international evidence on output-inflation tradeoffs', *American Economic Review,* **63,** 326–34.

Lucas, R.E. (1976), 'Econometric policy evaluation: a critique', in Brunner, K. and Meltzer, A.H. (eds), *The Phillips Curve and Labor Markets,* 19–46, Amsterdam: North-Holland.

Mariano, R.S . and Brown, B.W. (1983), 'Asymptotic behaviour of predictors in a nonlinear simultaneous system', *International Economic Review,* **24,** (3), 523–36.

Nelson, C. (1972), 'The prediction performance of the FRB–MIT–PENN model of the US economy', *American Economic Review,* **62,** 902–17.

Schmidt, P. (1977), 'Some small sample evidence on the distribution of dynamic simulation forecasts', *Econometrica,* **45,** 97–1005.

Stock, J.H. (1988), 'A re-examination of Friedman's consumption puzzle', *Journal of Business and Economic Statistics,* **6,** (4), 401–7.

Turner, D.S. (1990), 'The role of judgement in macroeconomic forecasting', *Journal of Forecasting,* **9,** 315–45.

Wallis, K.F. (1984), 'Comparing time-series and nonlinear model-based forecasts', *Oxford Bulletin of Economics and Statistics,* **46,** (4), 383–89.

Wallis, K.F. (1989), 'Macroeconomic forecasting: a survey', *Economic Journal,* **99,** 28–61.

Wallis, K.F., Andrews, M.J., Fisher, P.G., Longbottom, J.A., and Whitley, J.D. (1986), *Models of the UK Economy: A Third Review by the ESRC Macroeconomic Modelling Bureau,* Oxford: Oxford University Press.

Wallis, K.F., Fisher, P.G., Longbottom, J.A., Turner, D.S. and Whitley, J.D. (1987), *Models of the UK Economy: A Fourth Review by the ESRC Macroeconomic Modelling Bureau,* Oxford: Oxford University Press.

Young, R.M. (1979), 'Forecasting the US economy with an econometric model', in Ormerod, P.A. (ed.), *Economic Modelling,* London: Heinemann.

Appendix 1: estimating the initial condition

First, consider estimating w_T from w_T^*. From (8.13):

$$\mathrm{E}[w_T|w_T^*] = \mathrm{E}[w_T^*|w_T^*] - \mathrm{E}[\theta_T|w_T^*] \qquad (A1)$$

Define λ_T by:

$$\theta_T = \lambda_T w_T^* + u_T \qquad (A2)$$

where u_T is orthogonal to w_T^* by construction, then $\lambda_T = \mathrm{E}[\theta_T w_T^*]/\mathrm{E}[w_T^{*2}] = \sigma_T^2/\mathrm{E}[w_T^{*2}]$. Note that $0 \le \lambda_T \le 1$. Then (A1) becomes:

$$\mathrm{E}[w_T|w_T^*] = w_T^* - \lambda_T w_T^* = (1 - \lambda_T)w_T^* \equiv k_T w_T^*. \qquad (A3)$$

Next, from I_T^0:

$$\begin{aligned}
\mathrm{E}[w_T|I_T^0] &= \Psi \mathrm{E}[w_{T-1}|I_T^0] + \mathrm{E}[v_T|I_T^0] \\
&= \Psi \mathrm{E}[w_{T-1}^*|I_T^0] - \Psi \mathrm{E}[\theta_{T-1}|I_T^0] \\
&= \Psi w_{T-1}^* - \Psi \lambda_{T-1} w_{T-1}^* = \Psi k_{T-1} w_{T-1}^*.
\end{aligned} \qquad (A4)$$

Underlying (A4) is the relation $w_T = \Psi w_{T-1}^* - \Psi \theta_{T-1} + v_T$, and underlying (A1) is $w_T = w_T^* - \theta_T$, so that taking a convex combination of these:

$$w_T = \mu \Psi w_{T-1}^* - \mu \Psi \theta_{T-1} + \mu v_T + (1 - \mu)w_T^* - (1 - \mu)\theta_T. \qquad (A5)$$

Thus, the composite predictor formed from that combination is $\mathrm{E}[w_T|I_T^*]$ with:

$$\begin{aligned}
\tilde{w}_T &= \mu \Psi k_{T-1} w_{T-1}^* + (1 - \mu)k_T w_T^* \\
&= \hat{w}_T - \mu(\hat{w}_T - \Psi \hat{w}_{T-1}),
\end{aligned} \qquad (A6)$$

where $\hat{w}_T = k_T w_T^*$. This leads to (8.22) in section 3 when $w_{T-1}^* = w_{T-1}$.

In order to calculate the optimal value of μ, form the prediction error:

$$\begin{aligned}
&= -\mu \Psi \theta_{T-1} + \mu v_T + (1 - \mu)w_T^* - (1 - \mu)\theta_T + \mu \Psi \lambda_{T-1} w_{T-1}^* - (1 - \mu)k_T w_T^* \\
&= \mu v_T - \mu \Psi \theta_{T-1} - (1 - \mu)\theta_T + \mu \Psi \lambda_{T-1} w_{T-1}^* + (1 - \mu)\lambda_T w_T^* \\
&= \mu v_T - \mu \Psi u_{T-1} - (1 - \mu)u_T
\end{aligned} \qquad (A7)$$

and then minimize $\mathrm{E}[(w_T - \tilde{w}_T)^2]$ with respect to μ, to give μ^*, say. Then from (A6):

$$\hat{w}_T = \hat{w}_T - \mu^*(\hat{w}_T - \Psi\hat{w}_{T-1}) \tag{A8}$$

where μ^* is given by:

$$\mu^* = [k_T\sigma_T^2 - \Psi^2\lambda_T\sigma_{T-1}^2]/[\sigma_v^2 + \Psi^2(k_{T-1} - \lambda_T)\sigma_{T-1}^2 + (k_T\sigma_T^2 - \Psi^2\lambda_T\sigma_{T-1}^2)] \tag{A9}$$

or in the special case considered in the text when $\sigma_{T-1}^2 = 0$:

$$\mu^* = k_T\sigma_T^2/[\sigma_v^2 + k_T\sigma_T^2], \tag{A10}$$

which approaches unity from below as σ_T^2 gets large, and falls to zero as σ_T^2 goes to zero.

9 Economic forecasting and decision-making under uncertainty

Laurence R. Klein

Introduction – errors and their sources

Decision-makers in private firms or households and in public office must realize that a great deal of uncertainty accompanies many of their future commitments. All too often people act as though present or recently discernible conditions will prevail endlessly, and that is hardly ever the case. Often businessmen blame failed strategies on some stage or other of the trade cycle, but they should know that cycle phases have come and gone for at least two centuries. In the energy field, people acted in the 1950s as though oil would remain plentiful and cheap for ever; then in the 1970s and 1980s many people were trapped by their assumptions that prices would rise for ever.

Birth rates, spending patterns, investment needs, and many other aspects of modern economic life, are always undergoing change. When important decisions are being made, it is unavoidable to try to take future change into account if intelligent decisions are to be made. Sometimes, the decision-maker is lucky enough to have some flexibility or room to manoeuvre and correct mistakes in mid-course, but even then account must be taken of possibilities that can occur in the next stage.

Like it or not, decision-makers must forecast, and attempts to look into the future are error prone. In this opening section, an attempt will be made to lay out the sources of error in order to gain enough understanding to guide decision making under uncertainty.

In order to point out the sources of error, it is useful to show the model that is being used:

$$F (y'_t \cdots y'_{t-p}, x'_t \cdots x'_{t-q}, \theta') = e_t, \qquad (9.1)$$

or, in explicit reduced form:

$$y_t = G (y'_{t-1} \cdots y'_{t-p}, x'_t \cdots x'_{t-q}, \theta', e_t) \qquad (9.2)$$

where:

y_t is an n-element column vector of dependent variables
x_t is an m-element column vector of independent variables

θ is an r-element column vector of parameters

$\mathbf{e}_t$ is an n-element column vector of errors.

$$
F = \begin{pmatrix} f_1 \\ f_2 \\ \cdot \\ \cdot \\ \cdot \\ f_n \end{pmatrix} \qquad G = \begin{pmatrix} g_1 \\ g_2 \\ \cdot \\ \cdot \\ \cdot \\ g_n \end{pmatrix}
$$

If all $f_i (i = 1, 2, ..., n)$ are linear, then the g_i functions will be linear with additive errors that are linear combinations of the elements of $\mathbf{e}_t$ ($e_{1t}, e_{2t}, ..., e_{nt}$).

Forecasts from this system are error-prone for four reasons:

1. Random errors, $\mathbf{e}_t$, are always disturbing the system; they are not observed, but properties of their probability distribution are estimated, and their mean value (zero) is customarily used for forecasts. If the zero-mean is not used, some other value is assigned, and may not be correct. (It *will not, in general, be correct.*)
2. The parameters are not observed and estimates are used. These estimates are based on a sample and are subject to sampling error.
3. In order to compute elements of $\mathbf{y}_t$ from eqn (9.2), input values must be used. These are initial conditions for $\mathbf{y}_{t-1}, \mathbf{y}_{t-2}, \cdots \mathbf{y}_{t-p}$ and values for the independent variables $\mathbf{x}_t, ..., \mathbf{x}_{t-q}$. Economic data are always imperfectly observed; so there are errors of observation for both historical values of $\mathbf{y}_t$ and $\mathbf{x}_t$ and values for $\mathbf{x}_t$ in the projection period.
4. The model may be misspecified.

Not knowing the population distribution from which the $\mathbf{e}_t$ were drawn (by 'NATURE'), econometricians usually assume that they are distributed according to a multivariate normal distribution. This is not a bad assumption, but it need not be correct. The problem can be dealt with if the $\mathbf{e}_t$ are generated by another distribution, provided it is known – up to particular parameter values. The latter can be estimated. In the case of the normal distribution, with zero mean, the investigator must estimate the variance–covariance error of the joint distribution of $\mathbf{e}_t$, over the sample. In practice, these are the statistics that are needed. If (9.1) is linear and $\mathbf{e}_t$ is normal, then the error term for (9.2) will be an additive linear combination of $\mathbf{e}_t$. Its variance–covariance matrix will be made up of terms that are linear combinations of terms in the variance–covariance matrix of $\mathbf{e}_t$.

In large samples, the normality assumptions ought to provide good approximations, but in small samples the estimation of contributions to forecast error from the e_t must be tailored to the particular distribution that is relevant.

In a linear system, the estimates of θ, denoted as $\hat{\theta}$, will be linear functions of the errors e_t. The normal distribution has reproductive properties; so the sampling distribution of $\hat{\theta}$ will also be normal. Again, in large samples, the assumption of normality for $\hat{\theta}$ will be plausible. For small samples, the distribution of $\hat{\theta}$ will be functions of the distribution of e_t. There are formulae that can be used for the evaluation of functions of random variables.

The econometrician never knows the true values for initial conditions or for independent variables in the projection period. Economic data get revised for years and years, decades and decades. Presumably, after a few rounds of revisions, estimated values for these variables should improve, but they are never completely correct. This is especially true for the macroeconomy or aggregated markets. Occasionally revisions may be as large as 10 or 20 per cent, but usually, in the industrial world, they are no more than about 5 per cent. For developing countries and for world totals, the revisions are often large. The degree of revision tells us something about departures from true values, but they rarely tell us the exact amount of the discrepancy. We therefore do not know the exact amounts of this type of error to allow for. Some approximations will be discussed below.

Finally, we may be using the wrong model and thus committing specification error. Within the universe of linear models, the principal form of misspecification will be the deletion or inclusion of elements of x_t or y_t. If elements of y_t are missing, we must enlarge the model in order to keep the system complete. Since the error term, e_t, is additive, as are x_t or y_t (with coefficients), the concept of misspecification in a linear model means the separation of a random variable from terms involving x_t and y_t. The latter are observable; the e_t are not. If we can isolate an estimate of the distribution of e_t, and if these estimates satisfy the properties of a probability distribution of errors, we have some confidence that we have made the correct specification. This concept is testable, but we cannot be sure that the test result is not accidental. We can measure (imperfectly) elements of y_t and x_t, including additional elements that were not used in the original specification, to see if they are correlated with $\hat{e}_t$, the sample residuals of the estimated system in (1). If the correlations are negligible, we have some degree of reason to feel that the specification is satisfactory, but if there are large correlations, we must consider respecification of the system.[1] In the non-linear case, there is no general procedure to test for misspecifica-

[1] In systems that are estimated by single-equation methods, the residuals in a given equation are exactly uncorrelated with 'right-hand side' variables of that same equation, but this property does not necessarily hold with respect to right-hand side variables in other equations.

tion, except through forecasting with repeated checking of accuracy. Although there are four sources of error generally, we shall focus attention on the first three.

It should also be remarked that the economy functions in a changing environment. Political systems, institutional systems, technology and other aspects of the economic environment, are always undergoing some degree of change. We would detect this in a change of θ. Again, there is no fixed rule for detecting change of this type when it occurs, except to keep repeating model usage and to keep looking for evidence of discrepancies that could signal a change of regime. There are well-known tests for parameter change, and these can be implemented when we uncover signals that such changes are contributing to discrepancies.

The linear form of (9.2) is:

$$y_{it} = \sum_{j=1}^{N} \pi_{ij} z_{jt} + v_{it} \tag{9.2}'$$

where z_{jt} is an element of the vector of all predetermined variables of the system, combining the vectors:

$$y_{t-1}, y_{t-2}, \ldots, y_{t-p}, x_t, x_{t-1}, x_{t-2}, \ldots, x_{t-q}$$

and v_{it} is a linear combination of $e_{1t}, \ldots, e_{nt}$. From (9.2)' it is possible to derive:

$$estvar(y_{it}) = \sum_{j=1}^{N}\sum_{k=1}^{N} s_{jk}^{\pi}\left(z_{jt} - \bar{z}_j\right)\left(z_{kt} - \bar{z}_k\right) + \sum_{j=1}^{N}\sum_{k=1}^{N} s_{jk}^{z}\pi_j\pi_k + s_{it}^2 \tag{9.3}$$

In (9.3): s_{jk}^{π} is the jk term of the covariance matrix of the estimates of π_{ij} and π_{ik}; s_{jk}^{z} is the jk term of the covariance matrix of estimates of the (observation) errors of z_{jt} and z_{kt} (observation errors and errors of choice of independent variables in the projection period);

s_{vt}^2 is the estimated variance of the random error v_{it}.

Goldberger *et al.* (1961) showed how to estimate (9.3) directly from sample data, but assumed that all elements of z_{jt} were known accurately. Feldstein (1971) showed how to allow for error in choice of z_{jt}.

The first term on the right-hand side of (9.3) accounts for error in parameter estimation, the second term for input error in initial conditions or independent variables, and the third term for disturbance error in the structural equations of the model.

The formula in (9.3) is instructive and helps us to understand error sources, but it is only an asymptotic approximation for linear systems. By using simulation techniques it will be shown how it is possible to deal with error in non-linear models estimated from finite samples.

Of course, many decision-makers do not use formal models. They make subjective estimates of future magnitudes of y_t, for use in making policy or strategy decisions. Whether or not they have formal models in mind they are subject to the same errors; the only difference is that they lack the general means of identifying the sources of their errors and individual quantifications of the various kinds of error. They lack an error framework.

The reduction of error in decision-making under uncertainty
Error will be present, and in economic decision-making it will be present in large degree. It is generally true that the noise-to-signal ratio is large in economics, but it can be reduced through careful work. In order to improve decision-making, it is extremely important to keep error as low as possible.

For the model-builder, who will be making forecasts (subject to error) in order to advise decision-makers, the obvious suggestion is to improve the model. This is easily said but not easy to execute. It is like telling a country that desires to become more competitive in international markets that it should improve economic efficiency, or become more cost-effective, or raise productivity. These are all worthy goals, but the suggestions are somewhat (not entirely) empty unless they are accompanied by additional suggestions about how to do so.

The implication, however, is not to work in the direction of using existing models more effectively; it is definitely to build a better model. This means different things to different people. To me, it means adding more detail, treating individual economic sectors more carefully, improving the database, and staying in close touch with developments in the economy. These are very different directions for model improvement than:

1. Using methods of optimal control.
2. Generating model consistent expectations.
3. Using more efficient or more sophisticated methods of statistical inference.

Many of the points implied by (1)–(3) have been pursued intensively and extensively in recent years, yet I can detect no sustained improvement from any of them in reducing forecast error or in reducing the noise-to-signal ratio significantly. There are many claims and expressions of (false) hopes, but no systematic documentation that establishes the gains.

As far as work in the United States is concerned, with the elaboration of the *mainstream* model, with more data, better data, more sectors, more non-linearities, close attention to structural change, and more attention paid to changing institutions, there has been a trend improvement in prediction error from the beginning of the 1950s to the beginning of the 1990s. This improvement has been cited by Stephen McNees (1988), the unofficial judge of predictive accuracy.

The US record is cited because it is carefully documented and has been studied over time by Stephen McNees. In a general way, it can be said that all over the world there has been an improvement in the accuracy of economic forecasts. For the UK, Sir Terence Burns (1986) shows how medium-term forecasts have improved.

At the end of the Second World War, some serious attempts at systematic economic forecasting were initiated and fared worse than subsequent efforts. The latter showed definite improvement, with gains in experience as well as facilities.

The trends in economic model building that lay stress on points (1) – (3) above are very popular with the present generation of forecasters and general econometricians. It is not that they are wrong; it is simply that they have not led to discernible improvement by way of error reduction or gains in credibility.

There are, however, avenues of research that do look promising. They are:

1. Forecasting at higher frequencies, using better techniques for estimating the time-shape of economic reactions.
2. Forecasting with improved databases at high frequency on a rolling, repetitive basis.
3. Combining forecasts from different approaches to reduce the variance of error.

The degree of uncertainty, measured by the variance of forecast error, can be improved. While Sir Terence Burns focuses attention on the medium term – say, three to five years – the short term, or high frequency interval, is meant to be one to six months. There are definite possibilities for improvement at this end of the forecasting spectrum, and these improvements can be used to recalibrate models at the quarterly frequency, with cumulative predictive power of one to two years.

First, let us consider high-frequency forecasting under point (1) above. Significant improvements have been made over the last four decades in estimating the time-shape of economic reactions. In general, we are much better prepared to estimate lag distributions with monthly and higher frequency data either by spectral techniques or in the time domain. The data samples are much more plentiful and up to date, with no more than one or two months' delay at the most. There is much serial correlation in economics statistics, and this is fundamental. Time-series methods are well designed to capture that serial correlation.

The existence of serial correlation can be shown in the linear version of equation (9.1):

$$\mathbf{A}(L)\mathbf{y_t} + \mathbf{B}(L)\mathbf{x_t} = \mathbf{e_t} \qquad (9.1)$$

L is a displacement operator, $L^i \mathbf{y_t} = y_{t-i}$; $L^j \mathbf{x_t} = x_{t-j}$
$\mathbf{A}(L)$ and $\mathbf{B}(L)$ are matrix polynomials in powers of L.
The general solution to this system of linear dynamic equations is:

$$\mathbf{y_t} = \mathbf{K}_{\lambda t} - [\mathbf{A}(L)]^{-1} \mathbf{B}(L)\mathbf{x_t} + [\mathbf{A}(L)]^{-1}\mathbf{e_t}$$

where:

$\mathbf{K}$ is a matrix depending on initial conditions
λ is the vector of eigenvalues of (9.1)
$[\mathbf{A}(L)]^{-1} (-\mathbf{B}(L) \mathbf{x_t} + \mathbf{e_t})$ is a particular solution of the system of finite difference equations.

Even if the elements of $\mathbf{e_t}$ are serially uncorrelated, those of $[\mathbf{A}(L)]^{-1} \mathbf{e_t}$ will be serially correlated. They are likely to be highly serially correlated.

In practice, we find a great deal of serial correlation among economic magnitudes. The structure of (9.1) shows why this is likely to be so, and in fact the real world, which can be better approximated by the general non-linear system in (9.1) is likely to retain the same correlated error properties that are evident in (9.1).

Equations of the sort:

$$a_i(L)\mathbf{y_{it}} + b_j(L)\mathbf{x_{jt}} = c_i(L)e_{it} \qquad (9.4)$$

can be estimated by Box–Jenkins and related techniques to get at the serial properties of $\mathbf{y_{it}}$ and also at the effects of some independent variables. Of course, equation (9.4) can be generalized to be vector autoregressions, but there are definite practical limits to the number of cross-serial effects that can usefully and significantly (in the statistical sense) be taken into account.

Under point (1), therefore, it is possible to use time-series methods, with readily available software, to capture the serial correlation that is present in high-frequency data. These data are becoming ever more available in this information age with less and less time delay; therefore it is possible to re-estimate forecasts at frequent intervals within a quarterly period to get improved forecasts by recalibrating models for the next few quarters.

Words from the wise to forecasters are to 'forecast often'. It is possible to make high-frequency forecasts of economic data every day, every week, every fortnight, every month, and so on. For my own tastes, I prefer forecasts at the end of every week, making use of the information stream that has been published that week. These high-frequency data are then related in bridge-equations to the lower frequency series, showing similar economic phenomena, on a quarterly or other basis, that make up a longer range model. The recalibrated longer range model is then used for one and two year forecasts. The high-frequency data are thus filtered regularly into rolling forecasts of quarterly, semestral or annual models (see, for example, Klein and Sojo, 1989; Klein and Park, forthcoming). By making use of new information as it becomes available, it is possible to improve forecast accuracy.

The third approach towards reduced variance of forecast error is to combine forecasts. Every forecast, whether model based or subjective, carries the risk of error. A way of spreading risk is to diversify among forecasts and to base decision making on a combined forecast that is an average over the possible alternatives. There are many ways of doing this, but one particular approach for aggregate economy forecasting, say for the GDP, is to forecast the magnitude from different models.

Klein and Sojo (1989) and Klein and Park (1993) describe techniques for projecting GDP and its price index by forecasting from the expenditure side of the national accounts, from the income side of the national accounts, and from regressions on principal components of many key indicators. These three methods for projecting the same magnitude often give quite different results; so an average – possibly weighted, possibly unweighted – avoids extreme forecasts and reduces variance. There are many ways of reducing risk through averaging within a 'portfolio' of forecasts, but the particular averaging described here appears to be attractive and has been working well. It is all under the control of one investigator.

Construction of regions of uncertainty
The averaging of forecasts across models, described above, was done with point forecasts, but there is another way to allow for risk and uncertainty, namely to present forecasts in a range (single dimension) or a region (multi dimensional). The purpose of averaging across models in connection with the use of adjustments (or recalibrations) from models based on high-frequency information is to try to bring point forecasts from a lower frequency model into closer alignment with the realistic movement of the economy, as detected from the latest information available.

As the economic analyst moves out to a longer horizon of a full year and more, it is safer to present results in a range or region. This will require educating and convincing the decision maker who is using forecast information, that one cannot, in a scientific sense, be certain about the accuracy of point forecasts. The proper way to present forecasts is:

$$P_t(y_F^L \leq y_F \leq y_F^u) = P_0$$

which reads: the probability is P_0 that a future value for y, y_F, will lie between y_F^u (upper boundary for y_F) and y_F^L (lower boundary for y_F).

The technique will be to make many replications of a forecast for y and tabulate the fraction of cases that lie between y_F^u and y_F^L.

If we make assumptions about the probability distribution of e_t in (9.1) and compute the variance of forecast by the formula in (9.3), we can construct a region:

$$\hat{y}_F \pm k\, S\hat{y}_F$$

where k is a constant depending on the probability of making a 'correct' forecast (within the region), and $S\hat{y}_F$ is the square root of the estimated variance of $\hat{y}_F$, the point forecast magnitude.

Linear approximations can be avoided and the power of the computer used to good advantage if the interval is computed by stochastic simulation.

There will have to be an assumption about the law of distribution of e_t. The usual assumption is that e_t is a normal variate, but drawings from other distributions can readily be introduced. To capture the effects of all the sources of error shown in (9.3), the procedure will have to be structured as follows:

1. Over the sample period, choose random drawings of (normally distributed) random variables having the same variance–covariance matrix as that estimated from the residuals for (9.1).
2. Simulate the model dynamically (from observed initial conditions) over the sample period using the point estimates (based on an observed sample) for parameters of the model for each drawing of random errors. The independent variables may remain fixed in these replicated simulations, or they can be computed according to some fixed stochastic model, say an autoregressive model.
3. The simulations generate values, for each sample period, of the dependent variables, y_t. These generated values, together with initial conditions and values for the independent variables constitute a sample – albeit a 'pseudo' sample. With these replicated pseudo samples, we can re-estimate values

for the parameters of the model. Each set of parameter values defines a new estimate of the model.

4.   Given the replicated model estimates, for each case it is possible to draw fresh random disturbances, and fresh errors in a generating process for the independent variables. The set of models can then be projected over the forecast period with stochastic error inputs, initial conditions, and stochastic or fixed inputs for the independent variables. This set of projected solution paths provides a joint distribution of values for y_t that contain allowance for all the error sources.

5.   A variance–covariance matrix of projections can be estimated. The point forecast for the system, plus or minus multipliers of each variable's standard deviation in the forecast period constitutes an interval that reflects the uncertainties of the situation.

For any magnitude y_{iF}, the values presented to decision-makers should not simply be $\hat{y}_{iF}$, the point projection for period F, but:

$$\hat{y}_{iF}, \pm k S \hat{y}_{iF}.$$

A probability value will be attached, depending on the size of k.

Such intervals can be constructed, but they rarely are. This simulation approach was first developed by George Schink (1971), refined by Bianchi and Calzolari (1980), and repeated, with elaborations, by Ray Fair (1980).

The steps in stochastic simulation can be automated. They are a chore and require a great deal of attention. They are not yet standard practice. There are other, simpler, ways to allow for uncertainty. These are not in place of stochastic simulation; they are additional ways of dealing with the issues.

Some large enterprises, in deciding upon business strategies, begin the process by asking the question: what are the ingredients of the worst outcome, namely, one that would drive the firm into bankruptcy? If we denote x^w_F and x^b_F as inputs for the worst case and the best case, respectively, we then solve equations (9.l), given these inputs together with the initial conditions. In this way, scenario analysis provides limits. The extreme scenarios need not be uniquely structured; other inputs can define best and worst cases besides changes in the independent variables. Entire equations can be autonomously modified; new equations can be added to the system, possibly to represent official action. Random events can still occur to disturb scenarios; therefore a combination of stochastic simulation and worst/best case scenarios would be appropriate. It is also worth while examining other scenarios that are not as extreme as the worst/best cases; these are almost always more plausible. Some investigators attach personal probabilities to the different scenarios, but that is distinctly unappealing to me.

It is not possible to anticipate all major external changes – strikes, embargoes, new legislation, military conflict, natural disasters – therefore it is important to have a model on line, in computer storage, ready to be used for scenario analysis as soon as a large unexpected event occurs. If one is forecasting very frequently and always taking account of the very latest data, it is possible to react quickly (often within 24 hours), and thus reduce the amount of uncertainty for the decision-maker.

This process is expensive and not simple. It can, however, usually be directed towards improving the situation, not necessarily towards approximating the optimum but more often than not towards making improvements in the situation confronting the user of econometric information.

References

Bianchi, C. and Calzolari G. (1980), 'The one-period forecast errors in nonlinear econometric models', *International Economic Review*, **21**, 201–8.

Burns, Sir Terence (1986), 'The interpretation and use of economic predictions', *Proceedings of the Royal Society*, London, A 407, 103–25.

Fair, R. (1980), 'Estimating the predictive accuracy of econometric models', *International Economic Review*, **21**, 355–78.

Feldstein, M. (1971), 'The error of forecast in econometric models when the forecast-period exogenous variables are stochastic', *Econometrica*, **39**, January, 55–60.

Goldberger, A.S., Nagar, A.L., and Odeh, H.S. (1961), 'The covariance matrices of reduced form coefficients and of forecasts for a structural econometric model', *Econometrica*, **29**, 556–73.

Klein, L.R. and Sojo, E. (1989), 'Combinations of high and low frequency data in macroeconometric models', in Marquez, J. and Klein, L. R. (eds), *Economics in Theory and Practice: an Eclectic Approach*, Dordrecht: Kluwer, 3–16.

Klein, L.R. and Park, J.Y. (1993), 'Economic forecasting at high frequency intervals', *Journal of Forecasting*, **12**, 501–19.

McNees, S.K. (1988), 'The accuracy keeps improving', *The New York Times*, January 10, Sec. 3, p. 2.

Schink, G. (1971), 'Small sample estimates of the variance–covariance matrix of forecast errors for large econometric models: the stochastic simulation technique', PhD Thesis, University of Pennsylvania.

10 Aggregation and homogeneity of prices in models of the UK Economy

Keith B. Church and Kenneth F. Wallis

1. Introduction

Recent acceptance of the importance of long-run homogeneity in the price and wage equations of UK macromodels is associated with the expansion of their supply side, as Ball and Holly (1991, p. 218) note. Increased attention to the supply side of the economy, particularly in the European context of high unemployment, includes the question of what determines the non-accelerating inflation rate of unemployment (NAIRU). Particularly influential is the small supply-side model of Layard and Nickell (1986), in which goods and labour markets are assumed to be imperfectly competitive. Prices are set by imperfectly competitive firms, given demand; they also set employment, given the wage, which is determined in a bargaining process. In the context of a large-scale model of an open economy, attention to the determination of the exchange rate is also required. Joyce and Wren-Lewis (1991) show how this framework then allows an analytical derivation of the NAIRU in the National Institute of Economic and Social Research (NIESR) model, as a function of the long-run properties of its price and wage equations, in conjunction with the response of the exchange rate. The key property of these equations, on which the existence of the NAIRU rests, is their static homogeneity; their dynamic homogeneity or inflation neutrality in addition ensures that the NAIRU is independent of the steady-state inflation rate and so is, more fundamentally, a 'natural' rate of unemployment.

A similar core supply-side framework is used by Turner (1991) as a benchmark against which to assess the properties of the Treasury model. He highlights two particular price equations whose specification implies that changes in inflation have potentially large effects on the NAIRU, and reiterates Nickell's (1988) argument that such non-neutrality 'is a dangerous characteristic because it will become apparent – in simulations, for example – that any unemployment problem can be solved simply by having a different stable level of inflation. Neither the facts nor the beliefs of policy-makers, one suspects, would be in accord with this feature'. Fisher *et al.* (1990) likewise use the price–wage–exchange rate interaction as a core supply-side framework in which to interpret the simulation responses of six leading UK models. With respect to prices, they note that the extent of disaggregation of the price system differs significantly across the models, as does the speed of adjustment, and that there is a lack of homogeneity in certain equations of certain models. While their paper focuses on the overall properties of the large-scale models, being one of a series of annual reviews published by the ESRC Macroeconomic Modelling Bureau, the present paper undertakes a more detailed exploration of the treatment of prices in the models. Particular questions are whether non-homogeneities can be removed by data-admissible respecification, and what are the relative advantages and disadvantages of a disaggregated approach.

Motivating this paper by reference to recent work should not be allowed to obscure the fact that homogeneity questions have arisen throughout the development of econometric models of the post-war UK economy, to which Jim Ball has made such a distinguished contribution. Two episodes are worth recalling. The price and wage equations of the KBHV model – Klein, Ball, Hazlewood and Vandome (1961), using Nerlove's (1965) abbreviation – were presented in a separate paper by Klein and Ball (1959), and used as a starting point by Sargan (1964) in his classic Colston paper. The equations were linear, given that the model had to be solved by hand with a desk calculator, although Sargan's preferred specification was log-linear. Moreover, the equations were not homogeneous, and Sargan showed how they could be made homogeneous by introducing into an equation expressed in differences a term in the levels of the variables, now popularly known as an 'error-correction' term. This was the first error-correction model, and it led Sargan 'to policy conclusions which differ fundamentally from those implied by previous investigators. In particular they suggest that the effect of devaluation is only temporary ...'.

This connection reappeared in the mid-1970s, with Ball now directing the development of the London Business School (LBS) model and moving away from the Keynesian paradigm. Ball *et al.* (1977) retained the basic income– expenditure framework but adopted the monetary approach to the balance of payments, which led to the LBS model being described as an 'international monetarist' model. In a fixed exchange rate regime, they showed that changes in the nominal exchange rate have little impact on the long-run activity level or inflation rate. Their full-model simulations provided a more general setting for the result that Sargan had obtained in his two-equation model, and provided other results as well. Again, homogeneity of the price–wage system was essential to the long-run neutrality result.

This paper presents a comparative analysis of the treatment of prices in five current large-scale models of the UK economy, namely the models of the LBS, the NIESR, Her Majesty's Treasury (HMT), the Bank of England (BE) and Oxford Economic Forecasting (OEF). The analysis proceeds by means of two standard model exercises. First, in section 2, we present the results of a simulation experiment designed to explore the homogeneity properties of the price–wage system. As noted above, Turner (1991) analyses the simulation properties of the HMT model in some detail, and we concentrate on the remaining four models. The specification of one of these is such as to deliver long-run homogeneity, and the other three models can be appropriately modified: in two cases improved econometric specifications are presented. The dynamic interactions in the disaggregated price–wage systems have a substantial impact on overall model properties, and these are explored through a range of variant simulations. Next, in section 3, we turn to the statistical performance of the price equations. This provides a precise, albeit limited, criterion for assessing the advantages and disadvantages of aggregation, although the large-scale models differ from the standard theoretical set-up in several ways. Our historical tracking exercise assesses the most important of these departures. Section 4 contains concluding discussion.

2.   Homogeneity and the behaviour of prices

2.1   Comparative simulation responses

The comparative properties of the price–wage systems in the five models are illustrated by a partial simulation of their response to an external shock. The simulation is partial in the sense that variables outside the price–wage system are held at their base-run values. Cross-model differences in such feedbacks as the influence of changes in capacity utilization on domestic wholesale prices or changes in unemployment on wages are thereby eliminated from consideration, enabling us to focus on cross-model differences in the price–wage systems themselves.

Following Ball *et al.* (1977), we consider the response of prices to an exchange rate shock. This should be fully transmitted to domestic prices, if the price–wage systems display long-run homogeneity. Since all the wage equations have this property, attention is focused on differences arising from different approaches to the modelling of prices. The transmission of exchange rate shocks into domestic wages and prices is initially through import prices, which generally depend on the ratio of a world price to the effective exchange rate. This functional form implies that a 10 per cent depreciation in the exchange rate gives an 11 per cent increase in import prices, and eventually the same increase in domestic prices under long-run homogeneity. Thus an 11 per cent increase in domestic prices provides the benchmark against which the models can be assessed.

The results of a 10 per cent cut in the exchange rate are shown in Figure 10.1. The key domestic price variable in the LBS and NIESR models is the consumer price index (consumers' expenditure deflator), whereas in the HMT, BE and OEF models it is the retail price index (RPI). The simulation is run for as long a period as is possible on each model, that is, the length of their forecast database. Clearly the one example where the model conforms to the benchmark case is that of the NIESR. The most recent major change to the NIESR model introduced the supply-side framework referred to in the Introduction, and we expect this result to be a feature of the model by design. The remaining models do not show a full pass-through of prices in the simulation period.

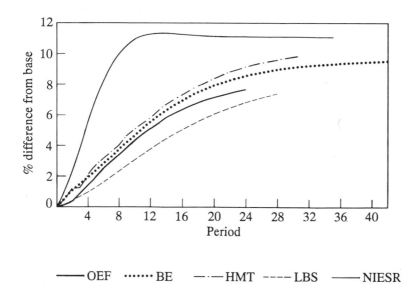

Figure 10.1   Price–wage sector; price response to a 10 per cent cut in the exchange rate

A prerequisite for the benchmark 11 per cent response to be achieved is static homogeneity in all wage and price equations. The list of model equations displaying non-homogeneity is as follows:

1. LBS   –   *PMFL* (Price of fuel imports)
2. HMT   –   *PMS* (Price of imports of services)
           –   *PRMIP* (Price of mortgage interest payments)
           –   *PRNI* (Price charged to industrial consumers by nationalized industries)
           –   *PETR* (Price of petrol)
           –   *PCOAL* (Price of coal)
3. BE   –   *PMS* (Price of imports of services)
4. OEF   –   *PFOOD* (Price of food)

These departures from static homogeneity prevent the LBS, HMT, BE and OEF models from reaching a long-run situation in which a devaluation is fully reflected in an increase in domestic prices. Figure 10.1 shows, however, that none of these four models actually settles at a long-run position in the available simulation horizon, rather, prices are still gradually increasing. The speed of the NIESR model response is in part attributable to the forward-looking behaviour of wages and prices in the model. In explaining the less rapid response in the other models, the dynamics and interactions of certain single equations are important, and we now examine three models in detail.

2.2   The London Business School model

Of the three models whose simulation responses are studied in detail, the LBS model is alone in modelling its key price variable through an aggregate estimated relation. The variable modelled is the consumers' expenditure deflator, and Figure

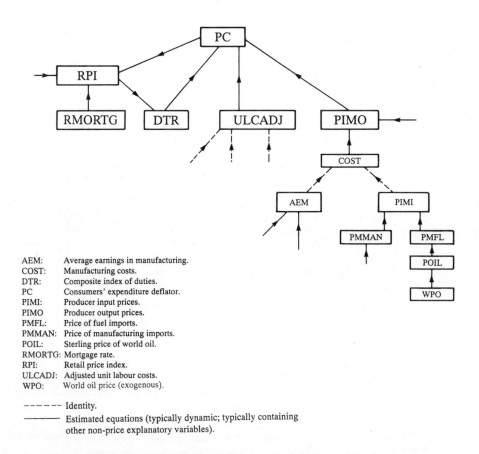

AEM:	Average earnings in manufacturing.
COST:	Manufacturing costs.
DTR:	Composite index of duties.
PC	Consumers' expenditure deflator.
PIMI:	Producer input prices.
PIMO	Producer output prices.
PMFL:	Price of fuel imports.
PMMAN:	Price of manufacturing imports.
POIL:	Sterling price of world oil.
RMORTG:	Mortgage rate.
RPI:	Retail price index.
ULCADJ:	Adjusted unit labour costs.
WPO:	World oil price (exogenous).

------ Identity.

———— Estimated equations (typically dynamic; typically containing other non-price explanatory variables).

Figure 10.2   Consumer prices in the LBS model

10.2 shows the mechanisms by which shocks pass through the price system into the final index. Total costs faced by manufacturers comprise wages and import prices, with weights of 0.7 and 0.3 respectively, the latter representing the only route by which the exchange rate shock feeds into prices.

The one equation that prevents the LBS model from conforming to the benchmark case occurs in the recursively prior import price block, and determines the price of fuel imports. The long-run coefficient of the sterling price of oil of 0.874 is the cause of this non-neutrality. If, alternatively, we ensure that changes in oil prices are fully reflected in import prices, then the simulation response should reach 11 per cent in the long run. The plots of the variant simulations in Figure 10.3 indicate that the imposition of static homogeneity (variant LBS1) is not sufficient to deliver the equilibrium result within the available simulation period. A further small increase in the speed with which the exchange rate shock is transmitted through the model is achieved by imposing the full import price increase instantaneously (LBS2), as opposed to the long distributed lag seen in the LBS1 variant.

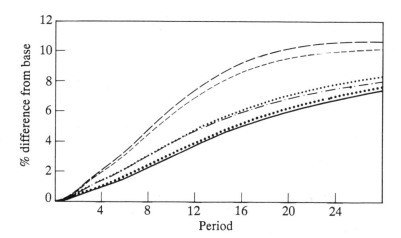

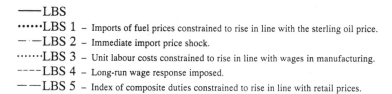

——LBS

······LBS 1 – Imports of fuel prices constrained to rise in line with the sterling oil price.

— ·—LBS 2 – Immediate import price shock.

······LBS 3 – Unit labour costs constrained to rise in line with wages in manufacturing.

----LBS 4 – Long-run wage response imposed.

——LBS 5 – Index of composite duties constrained to rise in line with retail prices.

Figure 10.3   LBS price–wage sector; variant simulations

While unit labour costs move broadly in line with earnings in manufacturing there are two employment tax components of this variable that do not. By targeting unit labour costs to rise in line with wages (LBS3) an increase in prices of one-third of one percentage point over the previous simulation is achieved by the final period. In all of the models of the UK economy, the long-run impact of a unit increase in the key price variable is a similar rise in wages, although these increases take several quarters to feed through. Eliminating these lags in the wage equation (variant LBS4) gives a final-period increase in prices of about one and three-quarter percentage points more than the previous variant. This large increase is a result of the strong influence of wages on consumer prices, working through wholesale prices and unit labour costs. In the final variant (LBS5) we also ensure that the composite index of duties, which accounts for 8 per cent of consumer prices, reaches equilibrium without the delay that is present in the model equation. The cumulative effect of all these changes is that the end-period simulation response is still short of the equilibrium position, with prices being 10.5 per cent above base after 28 quarters and continuing to rise slowly.

2.3   The Bank of England model

The BE model has the most aggregated price system among those models which treat the RPI as the central price variable. This is seen in Figure 10.4. The aggregating identity combines the price of mortgage interest payments and the community charge with 'other' prices which account for about 90 per cent of the total. This price structure ensures a large direct effect on retail prices from an exchange rate shock because import prices feed directly into other retail prices without passing through domestic producer prices. In our simulation experiment the import price response to a 10 per cent exchange rate cut is not the full 11 per cent, due to the departure from static homogeneity in the equation for the price of service imports. This departure feeds into other retail prices through non-oil import prices. The importance of this non-neutrality can be judged by estimating an equation that does possess static homogeneity and substituting it into the BE model. The model equation and our respecified equation are presented in Table 10.1.

The respecified equation uses world producer prices rather than world consumer prices as an explanatory variable, and omits the feedback from the price of service exports. In the model equation, the long-run response of the price of service imports to a unit shock to costs is only 90 per cent. The introduction of a homogeneous equation ensures that import prices rise by the full 11 per cent after devaluation. Given the presence of static homogeneity in the remainder of the price system, this ensures that the increase is fully passed to retail prices in the long run. The effect on the RPI of making this equation homogeneous is shown in the first variant simulation (BE1) in Figure 10.5. The small

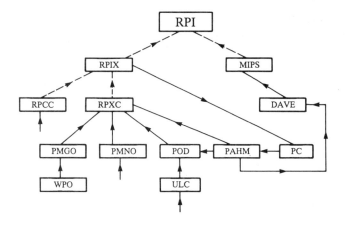

DAVE:	Mortgage debt: average of RPI index households.
MIPS:	Mortgage interest payment component of the RPI.
PAHM:	Price of houses.
PC:	Consumers' expenditure deflator.
PMGO:	AVI imports of crude oil and oil products.
PMNO:	AVI imports of non-oil goods and services.
PQD:	Price of domestic output supplied to the domestic market.
RPCC:	Community charge component of the RPI.
RPIX:	Retail prices index (all items excluding mortgage interest).
RPXC:	Retail prices excluding MIPS and RPCC.
ULC:	Unit labour costs for the whole economy,
WPO:	World dollar price of oil (exogenous).

– – – – – Identity.
———— Estimated equations (typically dynamic; typically containing other non-price explanatory variables).

Figure 10.4   Retail prices in the BE model

size of the increase reflects the low weight of service imports in total imports and hence in total retail prices. And even when the simulation is run for ten years the adjustment to equilibrium is not complete.

The sluggish nature of the adjustment is attributable to the dynamic response of certain price and wage equations, as also illustrated in Figure 10.5. After the exchange rate cut, import prices do not immediately rise by the full amount of the depreciation but instead take several periods to reach the long run. If the long-run response is imposed from the start of the simulation (BE2), the initial reaction of retail prices is speeded up and the model is slightly nearer equilibrium by the final period. A further cause of the sluggishness is the response of

Table 10.1   BE model: price of imports of services

Dependent variable ln (*PMS*) Sample period Estimation method	Model equation 1975:1–1986:4 OLS	Respecified equation 1975:1–1991:2 OLS
Constant	−0.004	0.010
	(0.005)	(0.003)
ln (*PMS*)$_{-1}$	0.49	0.773
	(0.14)	(0.081)
ln (*WPP/EER*)		0.541
		(0.077)
ln (*WPP/EER*)$_{-1}$		−0.314
		(—)
ln (*WPC/EER*)	0.39	
	(0.07)	
ln (*WPC/EER*)$_{-1}$	−0.19	
	(0.10)	
ln (*PXS*)	0.42	
	(0.12)	
ln (*PXS*)$_{-1}$	−0.16	
	(0.10)	
Equation diagnostics		
R^2	0.99	0.76
se	0.018	0.023
Autocorrelation LM(4)	6.5	5.55
Reset (1)		0.25
Normality χ^2_2		0.21
Heteroskedasticity χ^2_1		0.30
t-test on static homogeneity restriction		−1.82

(Standard errors in parentheses.)
EER : Effective UK exchange rate index.
PMS : Price of imports of services.
PXS : Price of exports of services.
WPC: World consumer price.
WPP : World producer price.

wages to changes in retail prices. By targeting wages to rise in line with prices rather than following the lagged response that exists in the model equation, the transmission of the exchange rate shock is much faster (BE3), with half the adjustment to equilibrium occurring in the first year instead of taking three years as in the initial simulation.

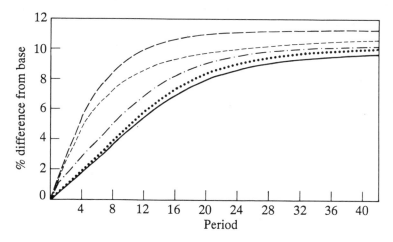

- ——— BE
- ••••••BE 1 – PMS equation with static homogeneity.
- —·—BE 2 – Immediate import price shock.
- ----BE 3 – Long-run wage response imposed.
- — —BE 4 – Long-run mortgage interest repayments response imposed.

Figure 10.5   BE price–wage sector; variant simulations

One feature of the BE and OEF models which distinguishes them from that of HMT is the treatment of the price of mortgage interest payments. Each of these models includes mortgage interest in the RPI; BE and OEF directly and HMT through the price of housing component. In the BE and OEF models this part of the RPI rises in line with other prices, while in the HMT model it is dependent on taxes and interest rates and so does not change following an exchange rate shock. However, mortgage interest payments in the BE model follow other prices with a long lag. This is largely due to the interaction of several dynamic relationships that intervene between consumer prices and mortgages, as shown in Figure 10.5. In the initial simulation, although retail prices are 9.5 per cent above the base by the final period, the response of house prices is only 8 per cent and that of average mortgage debt and mortgage interest payments slightly less than 7 per cent. The final variant shown in Figure 10.5 (BE4) in addition removes the dynamic relationship between mortgage interest payments and consumer prices, and imposes the long-run response instantaneously. This speeds up the response of prices sufficiently for the model to reach the equilibrium increase of 11 per cent within 24 quarters.

2.4 The Oxford Economic Forecasting model

The structure of prices in the OEF model is shown in Figure 10.6. Retail prices are split into four categories: rates/community charge, mortgage interest payments, food prices, and 'others'. Other retail prices account for about 72

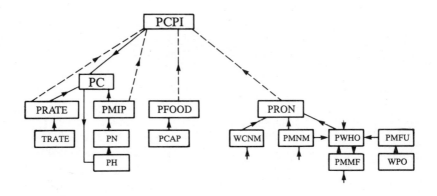

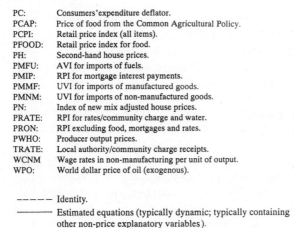

PC:	Consumers' expenditure deflator.
PCAP:	Price of food from the Common Agricultural Policy.
PCPI:	Retail price index (all items).
PFOOD:	Retail price index for food.
PH:	Second-hand house prices.
PMFU:	AVI for imports of fuels.
PMIP:	RPI for mortgage interest payments.
PMMF:	UVI for imports of manufactured goods.
PMNM:	UVI for imports of non-manufactured goods.
PN:	Index of new mix adjusted house prices.
PRATE:	RPI for rates/community charge and water.
PRON:	RPI excluding food, mortgages and rates.
PWHO:	Producer output prices.
TRATE:	Local authority/community charge receipts.
WCNM	Wage rates in non-manufacturing per unit of output.
WPO:	World dollar price of oil (exogenous).

– – – – – Identity.

───── Estimated equations (typically dynamic; typically containing other non-price explanatory variables).

Figure 10.6   Retail prices in the OEF model

per cent of the total, and food prices nearly 16 per cent. In contrast to the BE model there is a direct effect from import prices into producer wholesale prices following an exchange rate shock. Food prices are related to the ratio of the price of food from the Common Agricultural Policy to the green exchange rate. While the green exchange rate moves in line with the effective exchange rate index in the simulation, this change is not fully reflected in food prices because the relevant coefficient is 0.9, not 1. Following the procedure of the previous section, the sensitivity of the simulations to a homogeneous equation is studied by replacing the model equation with the alternative specification given in Table 10.2.

Static homogeneity is obtained by augmenting the OEF relationship with world food prices and wage costs. With fully homogeneous wages and prices the model should now conform to the benchmark case. However, in the simulation experiment no discernible difference occurs from imposing homogeneity. There are two reasons for this outcome. The first is the importance of the exchange rate variables in each of the long-run relationships. Although it lacks homogeneity, the model equation has an elasticity of 0.9 whereas the respecified equation has a combined value of 0.795. The direct effect is larger in the model equation, whereas the remaining 20.5 per cent of the response in the homogeneous equation comes via wage costs and does not feed through quickly. The second reason concerns the dynamics of the green exchange rate and food price equations. Food prices overshoot the long-run solution in simulation and actually rise by more than the 11 per cent response expected from a homogeneous equation. The conclusion is that there are more important explanations for the failure of prices to rise by the full amount of the devaluation.

Figure 10.7 presents the results of variant simulations from the OEF model. Again, an immediate long-run response of import prices to the exchange rate cut (OEF1) does speed up the simulation by a small amount. The treatment of mortgage interest payments can be compared to that in the BE model. Again, mortgage interest payments depend ultimately on consumer prices, but the transmission is through new house prices and then second-hand house prices as seen in Figure 10.6. By constraining payments to rise in line with consumer prices, the retail price index is a further 1.75 per cent higher by the end of the simulation (OEF2). Yet further increases are achieved by ensuring that the indirect tax content of retail prices moves in line with other prices (OEF3) and by imposing the long-run wage equation response instantaneously (OEF4). The combined effect of these changes still does not see the model reach equilibrium in our experiment. Retail prices are about 10 per cent above base after six years and still rising slowly.

Table 10.2   OEF model: food price equation

Dependent variable	Model equation		Respecified equation	
	ln(*PFOOD*)	Δln(*PFOOD*)	ln(*PFOOD*)	Δln(*PFOOD*)
Sample period	1973:1–1987:3	1973:2–1987:3	1975:1–1991:2	1975:2–1991:2
Estimation method	OLS	OLS	OLS	OLS
Constant	0.569	0.0158	0.145	0.006
	(0.049)	(0.003)	(0.020)	(0.003)
ln (*PCAP/RXG*)	0.904		0.730	
	(0.012)		(0.068)	
ln (*WPFF/RXD*)			0.065	
			(0.023)	
ln (*WC*)			0.205	
			(—)	
Δln(*PFOOD*)$_{-1}$		0.510		0.235
		(0.100)		(0.105)
Δln(*PFOOD*)$_{-4}$				0.343
				(0.095)
Δln(*PCAP/RXG*)		0.097		
		(0.070)		
Q3		–0.027		
		(0.005)		
RES$_{-1}$		–0.154		–0.160
		(0.047)		(0.054)
Equation diagnostics				
R^2	0.990	0.60	0.67	0.386
se	0.044	0.015	0.038	0.014
DW	0.52	2.01	0.50	1.64
Autocorrelation LM(4)		0.48		5.90
Reset (1)				0.60
Normality χ^2_2		2.48		13.53*
Heteroskedasticity χ^2_1				4.33*
DF	–2.97‡		–3.17‡	
ADF(1)	–4.08		–4.41	
ADF(2)	–2.52‡		–2.06‡	
ADF(3)	–3.59		–2.67‡	
ADF(4)	–3.75		–2.67‡	
t-test on static	7.89*		1.49	
homogeneity restriction				

(Standard errors in parentheses.)
* Significant at 5% level.
‡ Unit root test not rejected at 5% level.
RES: Residual on first-stage levels equation.
RXD: Dollar exchange rate.
RXG: Green exchange rate.
WC: Index of unit labour costs in manufacturing.

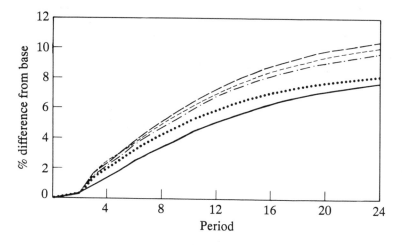

—— OEF
•••••• OEF 1 – Immediate import price shock.
—·—OEF 2 – Long-run mortgage interest repayments response imposed.
-----OEF 3 – Tax rate on 'other' goods constrained to rise in line with prices.
— — OEF 4 – Long-run wage response imposed.

Figure 10.7   OEF price–wage sector; variant simulations

2.5   Concluding comments

The simulation experiment is designed so that the individual model responses can be compared against the benchmark of an 11 per cent increase in the price level in the long run. The most striking result for three of the models is that, even when they are modified so that the theoretical preconditions for achieving the benchmark response are satisfied, the actual response has not reached this level by the end of the available simulation period, typically some seven years after the initial shock. Our modifications to the dynamics of the relevant equations alter this conclusion in only one of the three cases. The simulation is a partial simulation of the price–wage system alone, however, focusing on important supply-side considerations, and the reintroduction of the demand side of the economy would speed up the simulation responses. A devaluation results in a temporary increase in competitiveness, which leads to higher levels of utilization of the factors of production. This introduces inflationary pressures on wages and prices which augment those working through the price–wage system itself. However, the nature of the new steady state and its policy implications depend on the behaviour of utilization, and there are substantial differences across the models in this respect (Fisher *et al.,* 1990) which our partial simulations set on one side.

There are two main distinctions between the one model that does conform to the benchmark case, that of the NIESR, and the four that do not. The first is the presence of model-consistent forward expectations in key wage and price equations of the NIESR model, which has an important influence on its speed of response. The second is the absence of non-neutralities in its price–wage sector. Our variant simulations on other models indicate that the removal of these non-neutralities has a smaller impact on the results than changes to the price dynamics. The level of aggregation cannot by itself be directly related to the models' speed of response. The LBS and NIESR models have the more aggregated description of prices, yet bracket the other three models in Figure 10.1; the HMT model is the most disaggregate and yet has the largest price response of those four models that do not have forward expectations in this sector. Nevertheless, there is some evidence that in a disaggregated system the linking together of several dynamically specified equations slows down the response. This occurs in both the OEF and BE models with respect to the price of mortgage interest payments. Although this eventually moves in line with consumer prices, in both models there are two dynamic relationships concerning the housing sector that intervene, resulting in a sluggish response of the price of mortgage interest payments. On the other hand, it might be argued that the link between general consumer prices, house prices and hence mortgages is not a strong one, indeed in the HMT model the interest payment component of the RPI is unaffected by movements in other prices.

Important differences arise from the magnitude of the impact of import price changes in certain model equations, and their different speeds of response. The slowest mechanism by which import prices feed into the final price index is through wholesale prices, of which they comprise approximately one-third, and this is the only route that exists in the LBS model. In the HMT model, however, immediate direct effects of the shock on the RPI occur through the prices of food, petrol and the output of nationalized industries, each of which is separately identified. On the other hand, the BE model is relatively aggregated, and there is no direct effect from an exchange rate shock on the price of domestic output. An increase in import prices travels directly, with an elasticity of 0.29, into the 'others' component of the RPI, which accounts for about 90 per cent of the total RPI in this model.

We now turn to more general consideration of such aggregation issues.

3. The level of aggregation

3.1 Theoretical and practical considerations

The extent of disaggregation of macro relationships is the main factor determining the size of a macroeconometric model. Although a model may increase in size by treating as endogenous a variable which a smaller model treats as exogenous, in practice the same broad groups of variables are treated as exogenous by the present models, and they differ in size by virtue of the amount of detail they provide. In the first instance the purposes for which the model is to be used determine this choice. For forecasting a small number of aggregate macro variables a relatively small model may suffice, whereas in forecasting

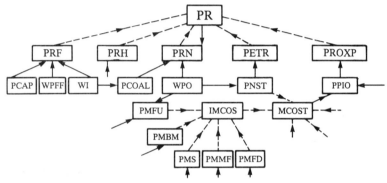

IMCOS:	Index of manufacturers' import costs.
MCOST:	Index of manufacturers' costs.
PCAP:	Price of food from the Common Agricultural Policy.
PCOAL:	Producer price index of coal.
PETR:	Petrol RPI.
PMBM:	AVI for imports of basic materials.
PMFD:	AVI for imports of food, drink and tobacco.
PMFU:	AVI for total imports of fuel.
PMMF:	AVI for imports of manufactures.
PMS:	AVI for imports of services.
PNST:	Producer price of North Sea oil.
PPIO:	Producer output price index.
PR:	Retail prices index (all items).
PRF:	Food RPI.
PRH:	Housing component of the RPI.
PRN	Nationalized industry component of the RPI.
PROXP:	Other retail prices excluding petrol.
WI:	Trend unit labour costs in the private sector.
WPFF:	World food prices.
WPO:	World dollar price of oil (exogenous).

– – – – – Identity.

———— Estimated equations (typically dynamic; typically containing other non-price explanatory variables).

Figure 10.8   Retail prices in the HMT model

and policy analysis exercises where the channels of influence of particular policy instruments need to be elaborated, an increase in size becomes inevitable. In the context of the price system, additional components need to be identified and additional linkages specified if, for example, relatively more attention is given to the housing market or, as another example, it is desired to be able to assess the impact of a change in the Common Agricultural Policy. Comparison of the organization charts in Figures 10.2, 10.4, 10.6 and 10.8 indicates that the present models do indeed reflect different choices in this respect, with the Treasury model, perhaps not surprisingly, offering the greatest amount of detail.

The practical costs of an increase in size are those associated with the building and maintenance of a larger model and its associated database, including the increased opportunity for specification error. Greater attention to the theoretical foundations of the models, and the desire that their theoretical structure should be transparent, has recently led several groups to a more aggregated approach. Rather than requiring carefully designed simulation experiments to elucidate the key properties of a model, these can be perused directly in a simpler, more parsimonious system. In general, however, there is little formal analysis of the costs and benefits of these trade-offs – greater information versus greater ease of communication, for example. The questions posed by Barker and Pesaran (1990) – 'what are the benefits of disaggregation and how can they be established at reasonable cost?' or, from the opposite point of view, 'what are the costs of aggregating in the sense of loss of information, and is aggregation necessarily bad?' – have typically been answered only in a narrow, statistical sense.

Starting with Theil (1954), the empirical literature has considered such questions as the conditions for 'perfect' aggregation and tests thereof, and statistical discrimination between aggregate and disaggregate models. A recent contribution by Pesaran *et al.* (1989) provides a useful generalization, and we briefly present one of their results, before discussing the limitations of this framework. The aggregate variable y_a is the sum of *m* components:

$$y_{at} = \sum_{i=1}^{m} y_{it}.$$

Each component is modelled separately in the disaggregate model, H_d:

$$y_i = X_i \beta_i + u_i, \, i = 1, \ldots, m,$$

and this model has a residual vector e_d in the aggregate variable given as:

$$\mathbf{e_d} = \sum_{i=1}^{m} (\mathbf{y_i} - \hat{\mathbf{y}}_i),$$

where a 'hat' denotes a fitted value. The aggregate model is:

$$\mathbf{y_a} = \mathbf{X_a b} + \mathbf{v_a},$$

with residual $\mathbf{e_a} = \mathbf{y_a} - \hat{\mathbf{y}}_a$. Pesaran *et al.* allow different specifications across the equations of the disaggregate model, and make no assumption about the aggregate regressor matrix $\mathbf{X_a}$, for example, that it is an aggregate of the $\mathbf{X_i}$s. As they note, this generalization is particularly important if the primary purpose of disaggregation is to achieve a better explanation of the macro variable, the potential gains being greater the more divergent is the behaviour of the components, and it is particularly relevant to the present context. The sums of squares of least squares residuals, $\mathbf{e'_d e_d}$ and $\mathbf{e'_a e_a}$, are scaled so as to produce unbiased estimates of the error variance of y_a, s_d^2 and s_a^2, and Pesaran *et al.* show that under H_d:

$$E(s_d^2) \le E(s_a^2)$$

Thus, finding that $s_d^2 > s_a^2$ suggests that H_d is misspecified.

Several departures from this framework nevertheless occur in the present context. First, the aggregate price indexes are weighted sums of the component indices, with weights that vary over time, thus:

$$y_{at} = \sum_{i=1}^{m} \alpha_{it} y_{it}, \qquad \sum_{i=1}^{m} \alpha_{it} = 1.$$

Second, the regression models at both aggregate and disaggregate level are typically log-linear, ensuring positivity of prices and facilitating the imposition of homogeneity restrictions, whereas aggregation is linear as above. Thus the inverse transformation represents an additional source of bias in predictions of the variable of interest, namely the price level. Thirdly, a relationship among the regressors often exists in that the aggregate model includes in $\mathbf{X_a}$ important explanatory variables from the disaggregate model. That is, a modeller taking an aggregate approach may nevertheless select regressors that help to explain the behaviour of the components. Of course, if $\mathbf{X_a}$ is simply the union of the $\mathbf{X_i}$s and these are all distinct, then in the absence of the first two problems Pesaran *et al.*'s weak inequality becomes an equality. But in practice $\mathbf{X_a}$ includes rather fewer variables than this. Finally, we note that the formal results are typically obtained under the assumption that the disaggregated model is correctly specified, whereas specification uncertainty is endemic, and little is known about its impact. In a time-series context, Lutkepohl (1984) considers the requirement of forecasting an aggregate variable obtained as a sum of components generated by a multivariate ARMA process: it can be shown that, if the process is known, then it is better to aggregate forecasts of the components than to forecast the aggregate from its own past. However, this result fails to hold if the models on which forecasts are based have to be specified empirically, and in these circumstances the univariate forecast of the aggregate variable may prove superior; in particular (Lutkepohl, 1985), univariate forecasts may be preferable for longer horizons. In what follows we do not resolve these issues, but simply present standard goodness-of-fit measures for comparative purposes, and illustrate the impact on model-based analysis of time-varying compositional weights.

3.2   Modelling the consumer price index
In the absence of formal tests appropriate to the present aggregation procedures, we compare the results of different approaches through simple goodness-of-fit statistics. Of course, such criteria may conflict with the model-builder's wish to incorporate features which guarantee sensible long-run properties for the model as a whole. The residual sum of squares is minimized if an equation is freely estimated, with no imposed restrictions. Estimating the same equation and imposing the static homogeneity restriction increases the residual sum of squares.

The central price variable in the LBS model is the consumer price index, as noted above, which is modelled through a single aggregate relationship, estimated over 1966:2–1989:2. It is a dynamic relationship, displaying static homogeneity, and in the long run the consumer price index depends on unit labour costs, producer wholesale output prices and a composite index of duties. For comparative purposes we consider the OEF model, in which the consumer price index also features, although the model's main aggregate price variable is the RPI. As indicated in Figure 10.6, the consumers' expenditure deflator is modelled in terms of the two most relevant components of the RPI, namely the 'food' and 'other' components, each of which is separately modelled. In the estimation period (1970:1–1987:3) these two components are combined according to their time-varying RPI weights, and the fitted equation can be regarded as an approximation to the definition of the consumers' expenditure deflator that allows the model to capture its principal determinants. In forecasting and policy analysis with the current version of the model, however, the RPI weights are kept constant at their current (1991) values, and so the variation in these weights, as illustrated for 1975–91 in Table 10.3, influences the accuracy of model-based analysis whenever the component prices do not move together.

Table 10.3   Retail price index: component weights

	Food	Mortgages	Rates/ community charge	Petrol and oil	Others
1975	0.227	0.025	0.028	0.047	0.673
1980	0.209	0.038	0.031	0.043	0.679
1985	0.184	0.046	0.045	0.050	0.675
1990	0.158	0.075	0.045	0.033	0.689
1991	0.151	0.076	0.055	0.033	0.685

The two different approaches to describing consumer prices are compared by calculating the difference between the actual values and those predicted by the model equations. For the LBS model these errors come from the single equation, whereas for the OEF model there are errors from modelling other retail prices and food prices in addition to the errors in the equation that combines these into estimates of consumer prices. Figure 10.9 shows the errors from the two models over the largest common sample period, together with those from the OEF model when static homogeneity is imposed in the food price equation. The root mean square percentage errors reported in Table 10.4 indicate that the aggregate approach of the LBS gives the smallest errors in all periods, while changing the specification of the OEF model to ensure static homogeneity (denoted OEF*) results in a relatively small deterioration in its goodness of fit. The results also illustrate, however, the difficulty caused by the use of fixed weights over a long period. A relative improvement in the goodness of fit of the OEF model occurs as we move towards the present time, that is, as the underlying time-varying weights converge to the fixed weights used throughout the exercise. The relatively poor performance of the OEF model in the first sub-period reflects not only an apparent disadvantage of the disaggregated approach, but also the use of inappropriate weights, to which we return below. Finally we note a small positive average error in the LBS single-equation estimates, as expected when predicting the price level from a log-linear equation without transformation bias correction.

Table 10.4   Consumers' expenditure deflator: root mean square percentage errors

Period	LBS	OEF	OEF*
1976:2–1979:4	0.578	0.921	1.00
1980:1–1984:4	0.513	0.590	0.685
1985:1–1989:2	0.346	0.447	0.472
Overall	0.484	0.663	0.718
Average error	0.080	—	—

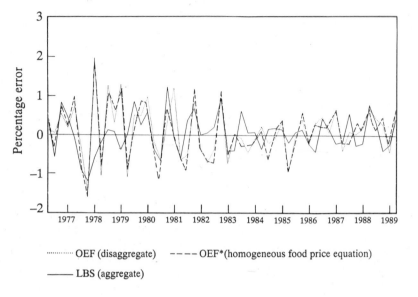

Figure 10.9   Errors in modelling consumer prices

3.3   Modelling retail prices

A similar comparison can be undertaken with respect to the treatment of retail prices in the HMT, BE and OEF models. Although none of these models possesses an aggregate retail price equation, the extent of disaggregation varies, with the BE model identifying three components of the RPI, the OEF model four and the HMT model five.

The errors from the three models are shown in Figure 10.10. Whereas the theoretical literature suggests that if the individual price equations are correctly specified then the model with minimum error is expected to be the most disaggregate one, the conclusions from this exercise are not so clear cut. The residuals in the HMT model are mostly negative, indicating persistent over-prediction of the RPI. Errors from the BE model show no consistent sign, nor any tendency to increase or decrease over time. The OEF model stands out thanks to the magnitude of the errors over the early part of the sample and the under-prediction that occurs until the final five quarters. The goodness-of-fit measures presented in Table 10.5 confirm the improvement in performance of the OEF model over time. Over the largest common sample period, the measures of fit suggest that there is little to choose between the models, OEF having marginally smaller errors than the other two.

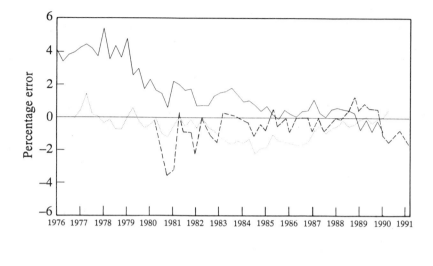

.... HMT   ----- BE   ——— OEF

Figure 10.10   Errors in modelling retail prices

Table 10.5   Retail price index: root mean square percentage errors

Period	HMT	OEF	BE	OEF‡
1975:1–1979:4	0.634	3.911	—	0.691
1980:1–1984:4	1.28	1.444	1.420	0.441
1985:1–1989:4	1.011	0.502	0.597	0.508
1980:2–1990:1[*]	1.088	1.026	1.080	0.489

[*]Largest common sample

These aggregate results can be further analysed by decomposing the residuals so that the relative importance of the error in each of the component price equations can be assessed. The identity that combines the different components of the RPI is also a potential source of error, as noted above. Whereas it has time-varying weights, the corresponding HMT and OEF model equations have fixed weights, appropriate only for the current year. Thus even if the correct values of the component prices are substituted into the identity, the resulting estimate of the RPI cannot be correct in all periods. The models' fixed-weight counterpart to the immediately preceding equation is:

$$\hat{y}_{at} = \sum_{i=1}^{m} \alpha_i \hat{y}_{it},$$

hence the residual can be expressed as:

$$y_{at} - \hat{y}_{at} = \sum \alpha_i (y_{it} - \hat{y}_{it}) + \sum (\alpha_{it} - \alpha_i) y_{it}.$$

As in the first term on the right-hand side, in our illustrations we scale the component residuals by the (fixed) RPI weights. Their sum would then be equal to the overall residual in the absence of time-varying weights, whose contribution is given by the second term on the right-hand side, obtained as the remainder in this equation and referred to as the error in the identity. Finally, all terms are expressed as percentages of the actual RPI value, y_{at}.

The resulting decomposition for the HMT model is shown in Figure 10.11. The importance of the error in the identity decreases over time as the current weights used in the model become more appropriate. The largest contributions to the total error are from the two most important components of the RPI, namely food and 'other' prices. The 'other' prices' equation under-predicts, with the scaled error being approximately 2 per cent of the total RPI. The food price equation has an error of similar magnitude but opposite sign, which helps the HMT model in the overall comparison.

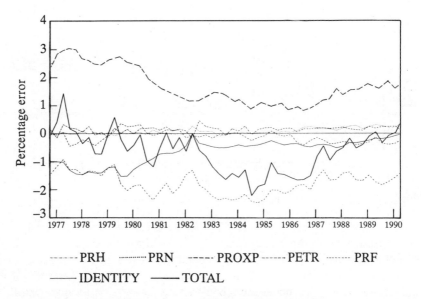

Figure 10.11   HMT model; decomposition of RPI residuals

For the OEF model, the results of the decomposition shown in Figure 10.12 indicate that the individual price equations fit well over the entire sample period. The most important source of error is therefore the identity linking these components, and these results provide a dramatic illustration of the effect of using fixed weights to construct the model's estimate of the RPI, in the face of the variation described in Table 10.3. The first three columns of the table relate to three of the OEF disaggregate components, and summing the last two gives the weight on the OEF definition of 'other' retail prices. Clearly the proportion of expenditure devoted to food has dropped since 1975, with a reduction in the weight of about seven percentage points, while the trend towards owner occupation is partly reflected in a five percentage point increase in the weight on mortgage interest payments. Associated with these changes is a fall in the relative price of food and an increase in those of the mortgage interest and rates/community charge components, resulting in the error of approximately four percentage points in the early part of the period. The contribution to the total error from using inappropriate weights decreases over the period, as the actual weights used in constructing the RPI converge to the current values used in the OEF model.

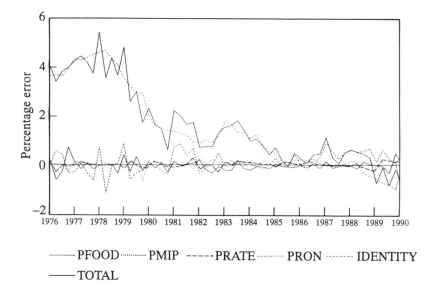

Figure 10.12 OEF model; decomposition of RPI residuals

In contrast, the BE model uses time-varying weights in the aggregating identity. As shown in Figure 10.13, which uses the historical weights, the total

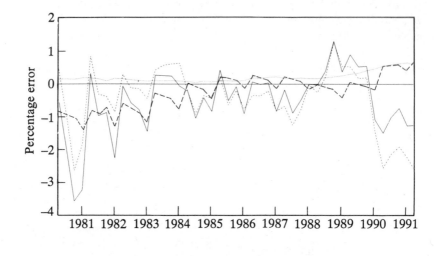

Figure 10.13   BE model; decomposition of RPI residuals

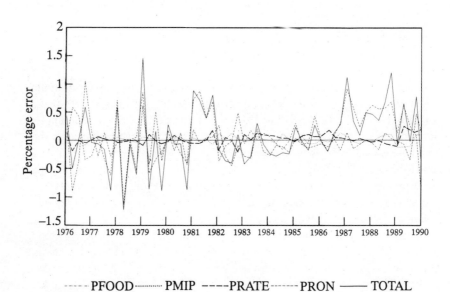

Figure 10.14   OEF model; decomposition of RPI residuals using actual values of the weights

error closely follows that in the 'others' category, which in this model accounts for approximately 90 per cent of the total. The most striking errors in this component occur at the start of each decade, when the overestimation is about three per cent of the total retail price index. In simulation, the time-varying weights are modelled to reflect, with a lag, changes in relative prices. If a component does not change in line with the overall RPI, then the weight of that component in the RPI changes in the following year.

As a final comparison, we present in Figure 10.14 an equivalent calculation applying historical weights to the components used in the OEF model. This removes the dominant error in the early part of the period, noting the change of scale from Figure 10.12. The final column of Table 10.5 gives corresponding goodness-of-fit measures for this case. Over the largest common sample period, this modified version of the OEF price system, denoted OEF†, achieves a considerable improvement over the BE model, indicating that its four-component approach is preferable to the BE model's three-component approach, once these are made directly comparable.

3.4   Concluding comments

The results in this section identify time variation in the weights used in aggregation not only as an important departure from the standard textbook treatment but also as an important source of error. A completely aggregate model avoids this problem. Hence we find that the LBS equation for consumer prices has smaller errors than the disaggregated OEF approach, whose relative performance nevertheless improves through time as the use of the current weights becomes more appropriate.

The role of time-varying weights emerges more clearly in our analysis of the RPI residuals. The OEF model fits relatively poorly over the last half of the 1970s but gives the smallest errors over the most recent section of the sample. Rather surprisingly, the overall pattern of the BE model's behaviour over the two halves of the 1980s is somewhat similar, this model performing slightly less well in the latter period yet only slightly better in the earlier period. This is surprising because this model allows for time variation in the weights. On the other hand, it has the most aggregated treatment of the RPI, with only two relatively small-weighted components treated separately and the 'others' category representing some 90 per cent of the total. This category includes food prices, which are modelled separately in the OEF and HMT models. Separating food prices is preferable, since these have behaved differently from the remainder, and combining these disparate components causes difficulties for the BE model. The HMT model has component equations for the price of output from nationalized industries and the price of petrol, which are not modelled by OEF and BE. These two variables are of policy interest to the Treasury but tend to follow the general level of prices and so can be included in the 'others' category without serious difficulty.

In its aggregate behaviour, the HMT model performs relatively less well in the most recent period, and some of the component equations have relatively large errors throughout the period. Although the theoretical results favour the disaggregated model, these do not allow for specification uncertainty, and it appears that the greater amount of detail desired in the HMT model results in increased opportunities for specification error.

The three models in the present comparison differ to only a small extent in the degree of disaggregation of the RPI, separating three, four or five components, yet there are striking differences in their historical tracking ability. These results suggest that the treatment that would be preferred on statistical grounds is the four-component approach of the OEF model combined with a method of modelling time variation in the weights. The impact of such variation in the historical analysis also suggests that it should not be neglected in simulation analysis whenever the policy experiment has a different impact on different components of aggregate price indexes.

4. Discussion

The ways in which the large-scale models have evolved reflect the requirements and objectives of the different model proprietors. Some wish to describe the movements of several different components of aggregate prices so that various policy alternatives can be evaluated in detail, whereas others are more concerned with the overall picture. If the decision problem which is required to be solved by model-based analysis is fully specified, then it is clear what information is required and hence, in particular, what level of aggregation is appropriate. The consequences of an inappropriate choice or of missing information can also be evaluated through the appropriate loss function. In practice, however, models have multiple purposes, none of which is subject to decision analysis of this kind. Thus discussion of the advantages and disadvantages of more or less aggregation remains rather general, except when it focuses on quantified criteria of a different kind, namely statistical ones, and the theoretical literature has largely concentrated on these. Statistical criteria play an important part in the specification of the large-scale models, and whereas they can on occasion conflict with requirements derived from economic theory, the requirement of homogeneity considered in the present exercise is not an example of such conflict.

A major strand of the statistical literature focuses on whether the aggregate variable is better modelled, in some statistical sense, by an aggregate or a disaggregate model. The value of the additional information provided by the disaggregate model does not enter the calculation, as noted above, but this information is typically available if the usual prescription of this literature is adopted, namely to take a disaggregated approach. In practice this is a matter of degree, however, and the more disaggregated approaches considered here nevertheless contain considerable aggregation. Statistical performance is improved whenever different components of the aggregate behave differently and these different behaviours can be successfully modelled. Whether this requires direct modelling of the components or an aggregate model that simply captures their different determinants directly is an open question, and in one of our comparisons the latter route seems preferable. If the components are to be modelled separately, then the increased risk of specification error clouds the theoretical picture, although the fact that the compositional weights vary over time represents a more important departure from the textbook case. Modelling this variation is a burden to be borne by disaggregated models, one that requires much more attention than it has received hitherto.

References

Ball, R.J. and Holly, S. (1991), 'Macroeconometric model-building in the United Kingdom', in Bodkin, R.G., Klein, L.R. and Marwah, K. (eds), *A History of Macroeconometric Model-Building*, 195–230, Aldershot: Edward Elgar.

Ball, R.J., Burns, T. and Laury, J.S.E. (1977), 'The role of exchange rate changes in balance of payments adjustment – the United Kingdom case', *Economic Journal, 87*, 1–29.

Barker, T.S. and Pesaran, M.H. (1990), 'Disaggregation in econometric modelling – an introduction', in Barker, T.S. and Pesaran, M.H. (eds), *Disaggregation in Econometric Modelling*, 1–14, London: Routledge.

Fisher, P.G., Turner, D.S., Wallis, K.F. and Whitley, J.D. (1990), 'Comparative properties of models of the UK economy', *National Institute Economic Review*, No. 133, 91–104.

Joyce, M. and Wren-Lewis, S. (1991), 'The role of the real exchange rate and capacity utilisation in convergence to the NAIRU', *Economic Journal, 101*, 497–507.

Klein, L.R. and Ball, R.J. (1959), 'Some econometrics of the determination of absolute prices and wages', *Economic Journal, 69*, 465–82.

Klein, L.R., Ball, R.J., Hazlewood, A. and Vandome, P. (1961), *An Econometric Model of the United Kingdom*, Oxford: Basil Blackwell.

Layard, P.R.G. and Nickell, S.J. (1986), 'Unemployment in Britain,' *Economica, 53* (supplement), S121–69.

Lutkepohl, H. (1984), 'Forecasting contemporaneously aggregated vector ARMA processes,' *Journal of Business and Economic Statistics, 2*, 201–14.

Lutkepohl, H. (1985), 'Comparison of three predictors for contemporaneously aggregated time series,' *Methods of Operations Research, 50*, 317–33.

Nerlove, M. (1965), 'Two models of the British economy: a fragment of a critical survey,' *International Economic Review, 6*, 127–81.

Nickell, S.J. (1988), 'The supply side and macroeconomic modeling,' in Bryant, R.C. *et al.* (eds), *Empirical Macroeconomics for Interdependent Economies*, 202–21, Washington, D.C.: Brookings Institution.

Pesaran, M.H., Pierse, R.G. and Kumar, M.S. (1989), 'Econometric analysis of aggregation in the context of linear prediction models', *Econometrica, 57*, 861–88.

Sargan, J.D. (1964), 'Wages and prices in the United Kingdom: a study in econometric methodology', in Hart, P.E., Mills, G. and Whitaker, J.K. (eds), *Econometric Analysis for National Economic Planning*, 22–54, London: Butterworth. Reprinted in Hendry, D.F. and Wallis, K.F. (eds), *Econometrics and Quantitative Economics*, 275–314, Oxford: Basil Blackwell, 1984.

Theil, H. (1954), *Linear Aggregation of Economic Relations*, Amsterdam: North-Holland.

Turner, D.S. (1991), 'The determinants of the NAIRU response in simulations on the Treasury model', *Oxford Bulletin of Economics and Statistics, 53*, 225–42.

Index